The Dissenters
★

LIBRARY OF FREEDOM

The Dissenters

AMERICA'S VOICES
OF OPPOSITION

———★———

EDITED, WITH INTRODUCTIONS, BY

John Gabriel Hunt

GRAMERCY BOOKS
NEW YORK • AVENEL

ACKNOWLEDGMENTS

The following sources are gratefully acknowledged for their permission to reprint texts: Frances T. Gates, for the selections by Norman Thomas from his books *The Conscientious Objector in America* and *The Test of Freedom*; Alexander Sanger, literary executor, estate of Margaret Sanger, for "The War Against Birth Control" by Margaret Sanger; Beacon Press, for the interviews with Malcom X and Martin Luther King, Jr., from *The Negro Protest* by Kenneth B. Clark, copyright © 1963 by Beacon Press; Sierra Club Books, for the introduction by Ralph Nader to *Ecotactics: The Sierra Club Handbook for Environment Activists,* copyright © 1970; and *McCall*'s magazine, for the selection by Betty Friedan from "Betty Friedan's Notebook," copyright © 1971 by the New York Times Company.

This 1993 edition is published by Gramercy Books,
distributed by Outlet Book Company, Inc.,
a Random House Company,
40 Engelhard Avenue, Avenel, New Jersey 07001.

Random House
New York • Toronto • London • Sydney • Auckland

Printed and bound in the United States of America

Library of Congress Cataloging-in-Publication-Data
The Dissenters : America's voices of opposition / edited, with
introductions, by John Gabriel Hunt.
p.   cm. — (Library of Freedom)
ISBN 0-517-09346-4
1. Dissenters—United States—History—Sources.
2. Social reformers—United States—History—Sources.
3. United States—Politics and government—Sources.
4. United States—Social conditions—Sources.
I. Hunt, John Gabriel, 1952–   .   II. Series.
E183.D57   1993   93-15527
323'.092'273—dc20   CIP
8   7   6   5   4   3   2   1

CONTENTS

INTRODUCTION

THE AMERICAN PATRIOT wears many hats and changes clothes often. The extraordinary leaders and great thinkers who helped mold the Republic are not only the figures traditionally highlighted in history textbooks. Equally patriotic were those Americans who fought against the status quo, who agitated for economic and social reform, who championed the rights of those whose rights had not yet been acknowledged, and whose ideas were new and revolutionary in their own times. It is the words of these men and women, the creative opposition, that appear in *The Dissenters*.

The foremost dissenters, of course, were the courageous leaders of the American Revolution—men like Samuel Adams, Thomas Paine, and Thomas Jefferson—who opposed the tyranny of England's rule over the colonies, and who, in fomenting revolution, created the American nation. After the establishment of the United States, dissent often exploded into insurrection—for example, in the western Pennsylvania farmers' revolt known as the Whiskey Rebellion; in the struggle of Native American tribes against the white settlers' usurpation of their lands; and in the greatest revolt of all, the Southern states' secession from the Union.

During the 1800s, opposition movements supporting abolitionism, temperance, women's rights, and new laws to protect the poor and the mentally ill were led by such notable men and women as William Lloyd Garrison, John Brown, Sojourner Truth, Elizabeth Cady Stanton, Dorothea Dix, and Jane Addams. Opposing voices in the early 1900s furthered revolutionary economic and political aims, particularly in the area of workers' rights—as exemplified by the anarchism of Emma Goldman, the labor agitation of Mother Jones, and the socialism of Eugene Debs and, by the 1920s, Norman Thomas.

Dissent throughout the twentieth century has been considerably more varied: opposition to the death penalty for criminals (Clarence Darrow); forest preservation and the creation of national parks (Theodore Roosevelt); the dissemination of birth control information (Margaret Sanger); black civil rights (Malcolm X and Martin Luther King, Jr.); and the protest against the Vietnam War (Daniel Ellsberg). The effects of the feminist movement of the 1970s reverberated in the landmark U.S. Supreme Court decision of 1973, *Roe v. Wade.* In *The Dissenters,* both the opinion of the Court, which overturned the nation's established abortion laws, and the dissenting opinion are included, since each reveals an outstanding voice of opposition to a still divisive issue.

In other Supreme Court cases presented in this book, the true dissenters are the justices who wrote opinions against the status-quo-supporting decisions of the Court. The subjects of these cases range from the rights of slaves as citizens *(Dred Scott v. Sandford)* to the religious rights of schoolchildren *(Minersville School District v. Gobitis).* In assembling these lengthy judicial decisions—as well as the passages from government testimony—certain technical references and esoteric digressions have been omitted. And while many of the other selections are presented in their entirety, some have been condensed because of excessive length.

The men and women whose words fill *The Dissenters* may all be considered great Americans. In their own times, their cries were revolutionary and often violently opposed. In the annals of history, however, their names are written on the roster of outstanding and truly patriotic Americans.

JOHN GABRIEL HUNT

New York
1993

SAMUEL ADAMS

——— ★ ———

The Rights of the American Colonists

From the Boston *Gazette*, December 23, 1771

Samuel Adams (1722–1803) was an outspoken opponent of re-
pressive British tax measures such as the Sugar Act of 1764 and the
Stamp Act of 1765. As clerk of the lower house of the Massachu-
setts legislature from 1865 until 1874, he became a leader of the
American independence movement in the state. Adams was active
in political as well as literary arenas during the colonial struggle
with Great Britain and took leading roles in the Boston chapter of
the Sons of Liberty, the protest against the Boston Massacre, the
Boston Tea Party, and the Committee of Correspondence of
Boston. He wrote the influential tracts True Sentiments of America *(1768),* Appeal to the World *(1769), and* The Rights of the
Colonists as Men, as Christians, and as Subjects *(1772). Using a*
number of pseudonyms, Adams reached a wide audience with his
rousing articles, which called for separation from England and
appeared in the Gazette, *a Boston newspaper. Samuel Adams*
served as a delegate to the Continental Congress from 1774 to 1881
and as governor of Massachusetts from 1794 to 1797.

The writer in the Massachusetts *Gazette*, who signs "Chronus," in his address to the public, recommended petitioning and humbly representing the hardship of certain measures;
and yet before he finished his first paper, he pointed out to us
the unhappy effects in former times of the very method he had
prescribed. Those "intemperate patriots" it seems, the majority
of both houses of the general assembly, not hearkening to the

cool advice of the few wise men within and without doors, must needs make their humble representations to the king and Council upon the claims of New Hampshire and Rhode Island. And what was the consequence? Why, he says the province lost ten times the value of the land in dispute. Did Chronus mean by this, and such like instances, to enforce the measure which he had recommended? They certainly afford a poor encouragement for us to persevere in the way of petitioning and humble representation. But perhaps he will say the General Assembly had at that time no reason to complain of the encroachment of these sister colonies; their claims were just; and the discerning few who were in that mind were in the right. Just so he says is the case now. For he tells us that "no one has attempted to infringe the people's rights." Upon what principle then would he have us petition? It is possible, for I would fain understand him, that what Candidus and others call an *invasion of our rights,* he may choose to denominate a *grievance;* for if we suffer no grievance, he can certainly have no reason to advise us to represent the hardship of certain measures. And I am the rather inclined to think that this is his particular humor, because I find that the Stamp Act, which almost everyone looked upon as a most *violent infraction* of our natural and constitutional rights, is called by this writer a *grievance.* And he is so singular as to inquire what *liberties* we are now deprived of, although an act of Parliament is still in being, and daily executed, very similar to the Stamp Act, and formed for the very same purpose, viz., the raising and establishing a revenue in the colonies by virtue of a supposed inherent right in the British Parliament, where the colonies cannot be represented, and therefore without their consent. The exercise of such a power Chronus would have us consider as a *grievance* indeed, but not by any means a deprivation of our rights and liberties, or even so much as the least *infringement* of them.

Mr. Locke has often been quoted in the present dispute between Britain and her colonies, and very much to our purpose. His reasoning is so forcible that no one has even attempted to confute it. He holds that "the preservation of property is the end of government, and that for which men enter into society." It therefore necessarily supposes and requires that the people should have property, without which they must be supposed to lose that by entering into society, which was the *end* for which they entered into it; too gross an absurdity for any man to own. Men therefore *in society having property,* they have such a right to the goods, which by the law of the community are theirs, that nobody hath the right to take *any part* of their subsistence from them without their consent; without this, they could have no property at all. For I truly can have no property in that which another can by right take from me when he pleases, against my consent. Hence, says he, it is a mistake to think that the supreme power of any commonwealth can dispose of the estates of the subjects arbitrarily, or *take any part of them* at pleasure. The prince or senate can never have a power to take to themselves the whole or any part of the subjects' property without *their own* consent; for this would be in effect to have *no property* at all. This is the reasoning of that great and good man.

And is not our own case exactly described by him? Hath not the British Parliament made an act to take *a part* of our property against our *consent?* Against our repeated submissive petitions and humble representations of the hardship of it? Is not the act daily executed in every colony? If therefore the preservation of property is the very *end* of government, we are deprived of that for which government itself is instituted. 'Tis true, says Mr. Locke, that "government cannot be supported without great charge; and 'tis fit that everyone who enjoys a share in the protection should pay his proportion for the maintenance of it. But still it must be with their own *consent,* given by themselves or their representatives." Chronus will not say that the monies that are every day paid at the customhouses in America for the express purpose of maintaining all or any of the governors therein, were raised with the *consent* of those who pay them, given by themselves or their representatives. "If anyone," adds Mr. Locke, "shall *claim* a power to lay and levy taxes on the people by his own authority and without such *consent* of the people, he thereby *subverts the end of government.*" Will Chronus tell us that the British Parliament doth not *claim* authority to lay and levy such taxes, and doth not actually lay and levy them on the colonies without their *consent?* This is the case particularly in this province. If therefore it is a *subversion of the end of government,* it must be a subversion of our civil liberty, which is supported by civil government only.

And this I think a sufficient answer to a strange question which Chronus thinks it "not improper for our zealous patriots to answer," viz., what those liberties and rights are of which we have been deprived. If Chronus is really as ignorant as he pretends to be, of the present state of the colonies, their universal and just complaints of the most violent infractions of their liberties, and their repeated petitions to the throne upon that account, I hope I shall be excused in taking up any room in your valuable paper, with a view of answering a question which to him must be of the utmost importance. But if he is not, I think his question not only impertinent, but a gross affront to the understanding of the public. We have lost the *constitutional right* which the Commons of America in their several Assemblies have ever before possessed, of giving and granting *their own money,* as much of it as *they please,* and *no more;* and appropriating it for the support of their *own government,* for their *own defense,* and such other purposes as *they please.*

The great Mr. Pitt, in his speech in Parliament in favor of the repeal of the Stamp Act, declared that "we should have been *slaves* if we had not enjoyed this right." This is the sentiment of that patriotic member, and it is obvious to the common sense of every man. If the Parliament have a right to take as much of our money as *they please,* they may take *all.* And what liberty can that man have, the produce of whose daily labor *another* has the right to take from him if he pleases and, which is similar to our case, take a part of it to convince him that he has the power as well as the pretense of right?

That sage of the law Lord Camden declared, in his speech

upon the declaratory bill, that his searches had more and more convinced him that the British Parliament have no right to tax the Americans. Nor, said he, "is the doctrine new. It is as old as the Constitution. Indeed, it is its *support.*" The taking away this right must then be in the opinion of that great lawyer, the removal of the very *support* of the Constitution, upon which all our civil liberties depend. He speaks in still stronger terms: "Taxation and representation are inseparably united. This position is founded on the laws of nature. It is more: it is itself an eternal law of nature. Whatever is a man's own is absolutely his own; and no man has a right to take it from him without his consent, either expressed by himself or his representative. Whoever attempts to do it attempts an injury. Whoever does it commits a robbery. He throws down the distinction between liberty and slavery."

Can Chronus say that the Americans ever consented, either by themselves or their representatives, that the British Parliament should tax them? That they have taxed us we all know; we all feel it. I wish we felt it more sensibly. They have therefore, according to the sentiments of the last mentioned nobleman, which are built on nature and common reason, thrown down the very distinction between liberty and slavery in America. And yet this writer, like one just awoke from a long dream, or, as I cannot help thinking there are good grounds to suspect, with a design to "mislead his unwary readers (and unwary they must needs be, if they are thus misled) to believe that all our liberties are perfectly secure, he calls upon us to show "which of our liberties we are deprived of"; and in the face of a whole continent, as well as of the best men in Europe, he has the effrontery to assert, without the least shadow of argument, that "no one has attempted to infringe them." One cannot, after all this, be at a loss to conceive what judgment to form of his modesty, his understanding or sincerity.

It might be easy to show that there are other instances in which we are deprived of our liberties. I should think a people would hardly be persuaded to believe that they were in the full enjoyment of their liberties while their capital fortress is garrisoned by troops over which they have no control, and under the direction of an administration in whom, to say the least, they have no reason to place the smallest confidence that they shall be employed for their protection, and not, as they have been, for their destruction—while they have a governor absolutely independent of them for his support, which support as well as his political being depends upon that same administration, though at the expense of their own money taken from them against their consent—while their governor acts not according to the dictates of his own judgment, assisted by the constitutional advice of his council, if he thinks it necessary to call for it, but according to the edicts of such an administration. Will it mend the matter that this governor, thus *dependent upon the crown,* is to be the judge of the *legality* of instructions and their consistency with the Charter, which is the Constitution? Or if their present governor should be possessed of as many angelic properties as we have heard of in the late addresses, can they enjoy that tranquillity of mind arising from their sense of safety, which Montesquieu defines to be civil liberty, when they consider how precarious a person a provincial governor is, especially a good one? And how likely a thing it is, if he is a good one, that another may soon be placed in his stead, possessed of the principles of the Devil, who for the sake of holding his commission which is even now pleaded as a weighty motive, will execute to the full the orders of an abandoned minister, to the ruin of those liberties which we are told are now so secure.

Will a people be persuaded that their liberties are safe, while their representatives in general assembly, if they are ever to meet again, will be deprived of the most essential privilege of giving and granting what part of their own money they are yet allowed to give and grant, unless, in conformity to a ministerial instruction to the governor, solemnly read to them for their direction, they exempt the commissioners of the customs, or any other favorites or tools of the ministry, from their equitable share in the tax?

All these and many others that might be mentioned, are the natural effects of that capital cause of complaint of all North America, which, to use the language of those "intemperate patriots," the majority of the present assembly, is "a subjugation to as arbitrary a tribute as ever the Romans laid upon the Jews, or their other colonies."

What now is the advice of Chronus? Why, much may be done, says he, "by humble petitions and representations of the *hardship* of certain measures." Ask him whether the colonies have not already done it—whether the assembly of this province, the convention, the town of Boston, have not petitioned and humbly represented the hardship of certain measures, and all to no purpose—and he tells you either that he is "a stranger to those petitions," or that "they were not duly timed, or properly urged," or that "the true reason why all our petitions and representations met with no better success was because they were accompanied with a conduct quite the reverse of that submission and duty which they seemed to express"—that "to present a petition with one hand, while the other is held up in a threatening posture to enforce it, is not the way to succeed." Search for his meaning, and inquire when the threatening hand was held up, and you'll find him encountering the resolves of the town of Boston to maintain their rights, (in which they copied after the patriotic assemblies of the several colonies) and their instructions to their representatives.

Here is the sad source of all our difficulties. Chronus would have us petition, and humbly represent the hardships of certain measures, but we must by no means *assert our liberties*. We must acknowledge, at least tacitly, that the Parliament of Great Britain has a constitutional authority "to throw down the distinction between liberty and slavery" in America. We may indeed, humbly represent it as a hardship, but if they are resolved to execute the purpose, we must submit to it, without the least intimation to posterity that we looked upon it as unconstitutional or unjust. Such advice was sagely given to the colonists a few years ago, at second hand, by one who had taken a trip to the great city, and grew wonderfully acquainted, as he said, with Lord Hillsborough; but his foibles are now "buried under the mantle of charity." Very different was his advice from that of another of infinitely greater abilities, as well as experience in the public affairs of the nation, and the colonies: I mean Dr. Benjamin Franklin, the present agent of the House of Representatives. His last letter to his constituents, as I am well informed, strongly recommends the holding up our constitutional rights, by *frequent resolves*, etc. This we know will be obnoxious to those who are in the plan to enslave us. But remember, my countrymen, it will be better to have your liberties wrested from you by *force*, than to have it said that you even implicitly *surrendered* them.

I have something more to say to Chronus when leisure will admit of it.

CANDIDUS

Thomas Paine

—— ★ ——

Reconciliation or Independence?

From *Common Sense*, 1776

Born in England, Thomas Paine (1737–1809), the great political philosopher and revolutionary agitator, was encouraged by Benjamin Franklin to emigrate to America. In Philadelphia, Paine became the editor of the Pennsylvania Magazine *and wrote "radical" articles on such issues as women's rights, slavery, copyrights, and humanitarianism. Paine's pamphlet* Common Sense, *published in January 1776, called for a free and independent America that would usher in a new age of enlightened republican government. Widely circulated, it energized the American colonists in their struggle against the British monarchy and encouraged adoption of the Declaration of Independence. Paine added to his fame—and his notoriety—with his revolutionary and rationalist books* The Rights of Man *(1791–1792) and* The Age of Reason *(1794, 1796) as well as by his participation in French Revolution politics.*

The present state of America is truly alarming to every man who is capable of reflection. Without law, without government, without any other mode of power than what is founded on and granted by courtesy. Held together by an unexampled concurrence of sentiment, which is nevertheless subject to change, and which every secret enemy is endeavoring to dissolve. Our present condition is legislation without law; wisdom without a plan; a constitution without a name; and, what is strangely astonishing, perfect independence contending for dependance. The instance is without a precedent; the case never existed before; and who can tell what may be the event? The property of no man is secure in the present unbraced system of things. The mind of the multitude is left at random, and feeling

9

no fixed object before them, they pursue such as fancy or opinion starts. Nothing is criminal; there is no such thing as treason;
wherefore, everyone thinks himself at liberty to act as he
pleases. The Tories dared not to have assembled offensively,
had they known that their lives by that act were forfeited to the
laws of the state. A line of distinction should be drawn between
English soldiers taken in battle and inhabitants of America
taken in arms. The first are prisoners, but the latter traitors. The
one forfeits his liberty the other his head.

Notwithstanding our wisdom, there is a visible feebleness in
some of our proceedings which gives encouragement to dissen-
tions. The continental belt is too loosely buckled. And if something is not done in time, it will be too late to do anything, and
we shall fall into a state in which neither *reconciliation* nor
independance will be practicable. The ——— and his worthless
adherents are got at their old game of dividing the continent,
and there are not wanting among us printers who will be busy
spreading specious falsehoods. The artful and hypocritical letter
which appeared a few months ago in two of the New York
papers, and likewise in two others, is an evidence that there are
men who want either judgment or honesty.

It is easy getting into holes and corners and talking of reconciliation. But do such men seriously consider how difficult the
task is and how dangerous it may prove, should the continent
divide thereon? Do they take within their view all the various
orders of men whose situation and circumstances, as well as
their own, are to be considered therein? Do they put themselves
in the place of the sufferer whose *all* is *already* gone, and of the
soldier, who hath quitted *all* for the defense of his country? If
their ill-judged moderation be suited to their own private situations *only,* regardless of others, the event will convince them
that "they are reckoning without their Host."

Put us, says some, on the footing we were on in '63—to
which I answer, The request is not *now* in the power of Britain
to comply with; neither will she propose it. But if it were, and
even should be granted, I ask, as a reasonable question, By what

means is such a corrupt and faithless court to be kept to its engagements? Another Parliament, nay, even the present, may hereafter repeal the obligation, on the pretense of its being violently obtained, or unwisely granted; and in that case, where is our redress? No going to law with nations; cannon are the barristers of crowns; and the sword, not of justice, but of war, decides the suit. To be on the footing of '63, it is not sufficient that the laws only be put on the same state, but that our circumstances likewise be put on the same state; our burnt and destroyed towns repaired or built up, our private losses made good, our public debts (contracted for defense) discharged; otherwise, we shall be millions worse than we were at that enviable period. Such a request, had it been complied with a year ago, would have won the heart and soul of the continent; but now it is too late—"The Rubicon is passed."

Besides, the taking up arms, merely to enforce the repeal of a pecuniary law, seems as unwarrantable by the divine law, and as repugnant to human feelings, as the taking up arms to enforce obedience thereto. The object, on either side, doth not justify the ways and means; for the lives of men are too valuable to be cast away on such trifles. It is the violence which is done and threatened to our persons; the destruction of our property by an armed force; the invasion of our country by fire and sword, which conscientiously qualifies the use of arms. And the instant in which such a mode of defense became necessary all subjection to Britain ought to have ceased; and the independancy of America should have been considered, as dating its era from, and published by, *the first musket that was fired against her*. This line is a line of consistency; neither drawn by caprice nor extended by ambition, but produced by a chain of events of which the colonies were not the authors.

I shall conclude these remarks with the following timely and well-intended hints. We ought to reflect that there are three different ways by which an independancy may hereafter be effected; and that one of those three will one day or other be the fate of America, vis., by the legal voice of the people in Congress; by a military power; or by a mob. It may not always happen that our soldiers are citizens, and the multitude a body of reasonable men; virtue, as I have already remarked, is not hereditary; neither is it perpetual.

Should an independancy be brought about by the first of those means, we have every opportunity and every encouragement before us to form the noblest, purest constitution on the face of the earth. We have it in our power to begin the world over again. A situation, similar to the present, hath not happened since the days of Noah until now. The birthday of a new world is at hand, and a race of men perhaps as numerous as all Europe contains, are to receive their portion of freedom from the event of a few months. The reflection is awful—and in this point of view, how trifling, how ridiculous, do the little, paltry cavelings of a few weak or interested men appear, when weighed against the business of a world.

Should we neglect the present favorable and inviting period, and an independance be hereafter effected by any other means, we must charge the consequence to ourselves, or to those rather whose narrow and prejudiced souls are habitually opposing the measure, without either inquiring or reflecting. There are reasons to be given in support of independance, which men should rather privately think of than be publicly told of. We ought not now to be debating whether we shall be independant or not but anxious to accomplish it on a firm, secure, and honorable basis, and uneasy rather that it is not yet began upon. Every day convinces us of its necessity. Even the Tories (if such beings yet remain among us) should, of all men, be the most solicitous to promote it; for, as the appointment of committees at first protected them from popular rage, so a wise and well-established form of government will be the only certain means of continuing it securely to them. Wherefore, if they have not virtue enough to be Whigs, they ought to have prudence enough to wish for independance.

In short, *independance* is the only bond that can tie and keep us together. We shall then see our object, and our ears will be legally shut against the schemes of an intriguing as well as a cruel enemy. We shall then too be on a proper footing to treat with Britain; for there is reason to conclude that the pride of that court will be less hurt by treating with the American states for terms of peace than with those whom she denominates "rebellious subjects," for terms of accommodation. It is our delaying it that encourages her to hope for conquest, and our backwardness tends only to prolong the war. As we have, without any good effect therefrom, withheld our trade to obtain a redress of our grievances, let us *now* try the alternative, by *independantly* redressing them ourselves and then offering to open the trade. The mercantile and reasonable part of England will be still with us; because, peace *with* trade is preferable to war *without* it. And if this offer be not accepted, other courts may be applied to.

On these grounds I rest the matter. And as no offer hath yet been made to refute the doctrine contained in the former editions of this pamphlet, it is a negative proof, that either the doctrine cannot be refuted, or that the parties in favor of it are too numerous to be opposed. Wherefore, instead of gazing at each other with suspicious or doubtful curiosity, let each of us, hold out to his neighbor the hearty hand of friendship, and unite in drawing a line, which, like an act of oblivion, shall bury in forgetfulness every former dissention. Let the names of Whig and Tory be extinct; and let none other be heard among us, than those of a good citizen, an open and resolute friend, and a virtuous supporter of *the* RIGHTS *of* MANKIND *and of the* FREE AND INDEPENDANT STATES OF AMERICA.

THOMAS JEFFERSON

———— ★ ————

The Declaration of Independence

Original Version, June 20, 1776

Thomas Jefferson (1743–1826), philosopher, architect, political theorist, diplomat, educator, and one of the Founding Fathers, became the third president of the United States. His service to the American colonies and nation began with his election to the Virginia House of Burgesses in 1769 and the issuing of his 1774 revolutionary pamphlet A Summary View of the Rights of British America. *A member of the Continental Congress in 1775 and 1776, Jefferson was requested to create a document declaring the colonies independent of England. His draft, with some minor changes, was adopted on July 4, 1776, as the Declaration of Independence.*

When, in the course of human events, it becomes necessary for one people to dissolve the political bands which have connected them with another, and to assume among the powers of the earth the separate and equal station to which the laws of nature and of nature's God entitle them, a decent respect to the opinions of mankind requires that they should declare the causes which impel them to the separation.

We hold these truths to be self-evident: that all men are created equal; that they are endowed by their Creator with inherent and inalienable rights; that among these are life, liberty, and the pursuit of happiness; that to secure these rights, governments are instituted among men, deriving their just powers from the consent of the governed; that whenever any form of government becomes destructive of these ends, it is the right of the people to alter or to abolish it, and to institute new government, laying its foundation on such principles, and organizing its powers in such form, as to them shall seem most likely to effect their safety and happiness. Prudence, indeed, will dictate that governments long established should not be changed for light and transient causes; and accordingly all experience hath shown that mankind are more disposed to suffer while evils are sufferable, than to right themselves by abolishing the forms to which they are accustomed. But when a long train of abuses and usurpations, begun at a distinguished period and pursuing invariably the same object, evinces a design to reduce them under absolute despotism, it is their right, it is their duty to throw off such government, and to provide new guards for their future security. Such has been the patient sufferance of these colonies; and such is now the necessity which constrains them to expunge their former systems of government. The history of the present king of Great Britain is a history of unremitting injuries and usurpations, among which appears no solitary fact to contradict the uniform tenor of the rest, but all have in direct object the establishment of an absolute tyranny over these states. To prove this, let facts be submitted to a candid world for the truth of which we pledge a faith yet unsullied by falsehood.

He has refused his assent to laws the most wholesome and necessary for the public good.

He has forbidden his governors to pass laws of immediate and pressing importance, unless suspended in their operation till his assent should be obtained; and, when so suspended, he has utterly neglected to attend to them.

He has refused to pass other laws for the accommodation of large districts of people, unless those people would relinquish the right of representation in the legislature, a right inestimable to them, and formidable to tyrants only.

He has called together legislative bodies at places unusual, uncomfortable, and distant from the depository of their public records, for the sole purpose of fatiguing them into compliance with his measures.

He has dissolved representative houses repeatedly and continually for opposing with manly firmness his invasions on the rights of the people.

He has refused for a long time after such dissolutions to cause others to be elected, whereby the legislative powers, incapable of annihilation, have returned to the people at large for their exercise, the state remaining, in the meantime, exposed to all the dangers of invasion from without and convulsions within.

He has endeavored to prevent the population of these states; for that purpose obstructing the laws for naturalization of foreigners, refusing to pass others to encourage their migrations hither, and raising the conditions of new appropriations of lands.

He has suffered the administration of justice totally to cease in some of these states, refusing his assent to laws for establishing judiciary powers.

He has made our judges dependent on his will alone for the tenure of their offices, and the amount and payment of their salaries.

He has erected a multitude of new offices, by a self-assumed power, and sent hither swarms of new officers to harass our people and eat out their substance.

He has kept among us in times of peace standing armies and ships of war without the consent of our legislatures.

He has affected to render the military independent of, and superior to, the civil power.

He has combined with others to subject us to a jurisdiction foreign to our constitutions and unacknowledged by our laws, giving his assent to their acts of pretended legislation for quartering large bodies of armed troops among us; for protecting them by a mock trial from punishment for any murders which they should commit on the inhabitants of these states; for cutting off our trade with all parts of the world; for imposing taxes on us without our consent; for depriving us of the benefits of trial by jury; for transporting us beyond seas to be tried for pretended offenses; for abolishing the free system of English laws in a neighboring province, establishing therein an arbitrary government, and enlarging its boundaries, so as to render it at once an example and fit instrument for introducing the same absolute rule into these states; for taking away our charters, abolishing our most valuable laws, and altering fundamentally the forms of our governments; for suspending our own legislatures, and declaring themselves invested with power to legislate for us in all cases whatsoever.

He has abdicated government here withdrawing his governors, and declaring us out of his allegiance and protection.

He has plundered our seas, ravaged our coasts, burnt our towns, and destroyed the lives of our people.

He is at this time transporting large armies of foreign mercenaries to complete the works of death, desolation, and tyranny already begun with circumstances of cruelty and perfidy unworthy the head of a civilized nation.

He has constrained our fellow citizens taken captive on the high seas, to bear arms against their country, to become the executioners of their friends and brethren, or to fall themselves by their hands.

He has endeavored to bring on the inhabitants of our frontiers, the merciless Indian savages, whose known rule of warfare is an undistinguished destruction of all ages, sexes, and conditions of existence.

He has incited treasonable insurrections of our fellow citizens, with the allurements of forfeiture and confiscation of our property.

He has waged cruel war against human nature itself, violating its most sacred rights of life and liberty in the persons of a distant people who never offended him, captivating and carrying them into slavery in another hemisphere, or to incur miserable death in their transportation thither. This piratical warfare, the opprobrium of infidel powers, is the warfare of the Christian king of Great Britain. Determined to keep open a market where men should be bought and sold, he has prostituted his negative for suppressing every legislative attempt to prohibit or to restrain this execrable commerce. And that this assemblage of horrors might want no fact of distinguished die, he is now exciting those very people to rise in arms among us, and to purchase that liberty of which he has deprived them, by murdering the people on whom he also obtruded them: thus paying off former crimes committed against the liberties of one people, with crimes which he urges them to commit against the lives of another.

In every stage of these oppressions we have petitioned for redress in the most humble terms: our repeated petitions have been answered only by repeated injuries.

A prince whose character is thus marked by every act which may define a tyrant is unfit to be the ruler of a people who mean to be free. Future ages will scarcely believe that the hardiness of one man adventured, within the short compass of twelve years only, to lay a foundation so broad and so undisguised for tyranny over a people fostered and fixed in principles of freedom.

Nor have we been wanting in attentions to our British brethren. We have warned them from time to time of attempts by their legislature to extend a jurisdiction over these our states. We have reminded them of the circumstances of our emigration and settlement here, no one of which could warrant so strange a pretension; that these were effected at the expense of our own blood and treasure, unassisted by the wealth or the strength of Great Britain; that in constituting indeed our several forms of government, we had adopted one common king, thereby laying a foundation for perpetual league and amity with them; but that submission to their Parliament was no part of our constitution, nor ever in idea, if history may be credited; and, we appealed to their native justice and magnanimity as well as to the ties of our common kindred to disavow these usurpations which were likely to interrupt our connection and correspondence. They too have been deaf to the voice of justice and of consanguinity, and when occasions have been given them, by the regular course of their laws, of removing from their councils the disturbers of our harmony, they have, by their free election, re-established them in power. At this very time too, they are permitting their chief magistrate to send over not only soldiers of our common blood, but Scots and foreign mercenaries to invade and destroy us. These facts have given the last stab to agonizing affection, and manly spirit bids us to renounce forever these unfeeling brethren. We must endeavor to forget our former love for them, and hold them as we hold the rest of mankind, enemies in war, in peace friends. We might have been a free and a great people together; but a communication of grandeur and of freedom, it seems, is below their dignity. Be it so, since they will have it. The road to happiness and to glory is open to us, too. We will tread it apart from them, and acquiesce in the necessity which denounces our eternal separation.

We, therefore, the representatives of the United States of America in General Congress assembled, do, in the name and by the authority of the good people of these states, reject and renounce all allegiance and subjection to the kings of Great Britain and all others who may hereafter claim by, through, or under them; we utterly dissolve all political connection which may heretofore have subsisted between us and the people or Parliament of Great Britain; and finally we do assert and declare these colonies to be free and independent states, and that as free and independent states, they have full power to levy war, conclude peace, contract alliances, establish commerce, and to do all other acts and things which independent states may of right do.

And for the support of this declaration, we mutually pledge to each other our lives, our fortunes, and our sacred honor.

HUGH H. BRACKENRIDGE

—— ★ ——

The Whiskey Rebellion

From a Letter to Tench Cox, August 8, 1794

*After the passage in 1791 of a federal law imposing an excise tax
on whiskey, opposition by the grain farmers of western Pennsylvania—who were also distillers—developed into a full-fledged
regional rebellion. The organized resistence, centering around
Pittsburgh, continued—despite presidential proclamations, arrest warrants, riots, and negotiations—until October 14, 1794,
when President Washington finally ordered a militia of contin-
gents from four states to march into the area. There was little
regional resistence to this first national test of the federal government's power to enforce its laws. Hugh H. Brackenridge
(1755–1816), a prominent Pittsburgh lawyer and Pennsylvania
legislator, was a leader of the insurgent citizens, but he ultimately negotiated with the federal authorities to avoid a serious
confrontation. In 1795 he published* Incidents of the Western
Insurrection, *his account of the conflict.*

I take the opportunity to give . . . a summary of the present
state of this country, with respect to the opposition that exists
to the excise law. It has its origin not in any antifederal spirit. . . . It is chiefly the principles and operations of the law itself
that renders it obnoxious. Be this as it may, the facts are these.

The opposition which for some time showed itself in resolves of committees, in representations to government, in
masked attacks on insignificant deputy excise officials—for
only such would accept the appointment—did at length, on the
appearance of the marshal in this county to serve process, break
out into an open and direct attack on the inspector of the
revenue himself, General Neville. . . .

Subsequent to their departure from the country, notice was

given of a meeting on the Monongahela River, about eighteen miles from the town of Pittsburgh. Six delegates, of whom I was one, were sent from this town. Nothing material was done at this meeting, but the measure agreed upon of a more general meeting, on the fourteenth of August, near the same place, to take into view the present state of affairs of the country.

Subsequent to this the mail was intercepted, characters in Pittsburgh became obnoxious by letters found, in which sentiments construed to evince a bias in favor of the excise law were discovered.

In consequence of this, it was thought necessary to demand of the town that those persons should be delivered up, or expelled, or any other obnoxious character that might reside there; also, that the excise office, still kept in Pittsburgh, or said to be kept there, should be pulled down; the house of Abraham Kirkpatrick burned or pulled down; other houses also, that were the property of persons unfavorable to the cause.

For this purpose, circular letters were sent to the battalions of the counties, detachments from which met on Braddock's Field, to the amount of at least five thousand men, on the second of the month. It was dreaded on the part of the town that from the rage of the people involving the town in the general odium of abetting the excise law, it would be laid in ashes. And I aver that it would have been the case, had it not been for the prompt and decisive resolutions of the town to march out and meet them as brethren and comply with all demands.

This had the effect, and the battalions marched into town on the third, and during their delay there, and cantonment in the neighborhood, with a trifling exception of a slight damage done to the property of Abraham Kirkpatrick, in the possession of his tenant, which was afterward compensated, behaved with all the regularity and order of the French or American armies in their march through a town during the revolution with Great Britain.

The town of Pittsburgh will send delegates to the meeting of the fourteenth instant. What the result will be, I know not. I flatter myself nothing more than to send commissioners to the president with an address proposing that he shall delay any attempt to suppress this insurrection, as it will be styled, until the meeting of Congress. This will be the object, simply and alone, with all that labor to avert a civil war. On the part of the government, I would earnestly pray a delay, until such address and commissioners may come forward. . . .

It will be said this insurrection can be easily suppressed—it is but that of a part of four counties. Be assured it is that of the greater part—and I am induced to believe the three Virginia counties this side the mountain will fall in. The first measure, then, will be the reorganization of a new government, comprehending the three Virginia counties, and those of Pennsylvania to the westward, to what extent I know not. This event, which I contemplate with great pain, will be the result of the necessity of self-defense. For this reason, I earnestly and anxiously wish that delay on the part of the government may give time to bring about, if practicable, good order and subordination. By the time the Congress meets, there may be a favorable issue to the negotiation with regard to the navigation of the Mississippi, the western posts, etc. A suspension of the excise law during the Indian war, a measure I proposed in a publication three years ago, in Philadelphia, may perhaps suffice. Being then on an equal footing with other parts of the Union, if they submitted to the law, this country might also submit.

I anticipate all that can be said with regard to example, etc. I may be mistaken, but I am decisive in opinion that the United States cannot effect the operation of the law in this country. It is universally odious in the neighboring parts of all the neighboring states, and the militia under the law in the hands of the president cannot be called out to reduce an opposition. The midland counties, I am persuaded, will not even suffer the militia of more distant parts of the Union to pass through them.

But the excise law is a branch of the funding system, detested and abhorred by all the philosophic men, and the yeomanry of America, those that hold certificates excepted. There is a growling, lurking discontent at this system that is ready to burst out and discover itself everywhere. . . .

Should an attempt be made to suppress these people, I am afraid . . . they will march to Philadelphia, accumulating in their course, and swelling over the banks of the Susquehanna like a torrent—irresistible, and devouring in its progress. There can be no equality of contest between the rage of a forest and the abundance, indolence, and opulence of a city. If the president has evinced a prudent and approved delay in the case of the British spoliation, in the case of the Indian tribes, much more humane and politic will it be to consult the internal peace of the government, by avoiding force until every means of accommodation are found unavailing. I deplore my personal situation; I deplore the situation of this country, should a civil war ensue.

JAMES MADISON

———— ★ ————

The Virginia Resolutions

December 24, 1798

James Madison (1751–1836), who became the fourth president of the United States, is often considered the Father of the Constitution. With Alexander Hamilton and John Jay he wrote a famed series of papers urging the ratification of the new Constitution, published as The Federalist *(1787–1788). During the presidency of John Adams, Madison drafted the Virginia Resolutions in response to the Alien and Sedition Acts of 1798. Like Thomas Jefferson's Kentucky Resolutions, Virginia's document was a protest by a state legislature that challenged the federal government's authority, by virtue of the 1798 acts, to usurp the powers of the states, stiffen citizenship requirements, deport aliens by executive order, and curtail freedom of speech.*

R*esolved*, That the General Assembly of Virginia doth unequivocally express a firm resolution to maintain and defend the Constitution of the United States, and the Constitution of this state, against every aggression either foreign or domestic; and that they will support the government of the United States in all measures warranted by the former.

That this Assembly most solemnly declares a warm attachment to the union of the states, to maintain which it pledges all its powers; and that, for this end, it is their duty to watch over and oppose every infraction of those principles which constitute the only basis of that union, because a faithful observance of them can alone secure its existence and the public happiness.

That this Assembly doth explicitly and peremptorily declare that it views the powers of the federal government as resulting from the compact to which the states are parties, as limited by the plain sense and intention of the instrument constituting that compact; as no further valid than they are authorized by the grants enumerated in that compact; and that, in case of a deliberate, palpable, and dangerous exercise of other powers not granted by the said compact, the states, who are parties thereto, have the right and are in duty bound to interpose for arresting the progress of the evil, and for maintaining within their respective limits the authorities, rights, and liberties appertaining to them.

That the General Assembly doth also express its deep regret that a spirit has in sundry instances been manifested by the federal government to enlarge its powers by forced constructions of the constitutional charter which defines them; and that indications have appeared of a design to expound certain general phrases (which, having been copied from the very limited grant of powers in the former Articles of Confederation, were the less liable to be misconstrued) so as to destroy the meaning and effect of the particular enumeration which necessarily explains and limits the general phrases; and so as to consolidate the states, by degrees, into one sovereignty, the obvious tendency and inevitable result of which would be to transform the present republican system of the United States into an absolute, or at best, a mixed, monarchy.

That the General Assembly doth particularly protest against the palpable and alarming infractions of the Constitution in the two late cases of the Alien and Sedition Acts, passed at the last session of Congress; the first of which exercises a power nowhere delegated to the federal government and which, by uniting legislative and judicial powers to those of [the] executive, subvert the general principles of free government, as well as the particular organization and positive provisions of the federal Constitution; and the other of which acts exercises, in like manner, a power not delegated by the Constitution, but, on the contrary, expressly and positively forbidden by one of the amendments thereto, a power which more than any other ought to produce universal alarm, because it is leveled against the right of freely examining public characters and measures, and of free communication among the people thereon, which has ever been justly deemed the only effectual guardian of every other right.

That this state having, by its convention which ratified the federal Constitution, expressly declared that, among other essential rights, "the liberty of conscience and of the press cannot be canceled, abridged, restrained, or modified by any authority of the United States," and from its extreme anxiety to guard these rights from every possible attack of sophistry or ambition, having, with other states, recommended an amendment for that purpose, which amendment was in due time annexed to the Constitution—it would mark a reproachful inconsistency and criminal degeneracy if an indifference were now shown to the palpable violation of one of the rights thus declared and secured, and to the establishment of a precedent which may be fatal to the other.

That the good people of this commonwealth, having ever felt and continuing to feel the most sincere affection for their brethren of the other states, the truest anxiety for establishing and perpetuating the union of all and the most scrupulous fidelity to that Constitution, which is the pledge of mutual friendship, and the instrument of mutual happiness, the General Assembly doth solemnly appeal to the like dispositions of the other states, in confidence that they will concur with this commonwealth in declaring, as it does hereby declare, that the acts aforesaid are unconstitutional; and that the necessary and proper measures will be taken by each for cooperating with this state, in maintaining unimpaired the authorities, rights, and liberties reserved to the states respectively, or to the people.

That the governor be desired to transmit a copy of the foregoing resolutions to the executive authority of each of the other states, with a request that the same may be communicated to the legislature thereof; and that a copy be furnished to each of the senators and representatives representing this state in the Congress of the United States.

TECUMSEH

— ★ —

Land Rights of the Indian Nations

Speech at a Council with Indiana Territory
Governor William Henry Harrison,
Vincennes, August 20, 1810

---

*Tecumseh (1768–1813) was born in western Ohio, the son of a
Shawnee warrior. During the 1790s and early 1800s he led raids
against white settlements and emerged as an important war
chief. By 1806, his brother, a religious leader who was known as
the Prophet, had developed a large following; from this, Tecumseh built a political movement that attracted numerous Indians
to Prophetstown, the brothers' settlement at the juncture of the
Wabash and Tippecanoe rivers in Indiana. Tecumseh envisioned
a vast Indian confederacy to oppose the white Americans. He
traveled throughout the Midwest and the South meeting with
various tribal councils to urge unification. As governor of the
Indiana Territory, William Henry Harrison negotiated many
treaties with the tribes and in 1811 led U.S. forces against Prophetstown, which was destroyed in the Battle of Tippecanoe.
Tecumseh's warriors aided the British during the War of 1812,
and Harrison, in command of the American forces in the Northwest, won a decisive victory over the British and Indians in
Canada at the Battle of Thames, where Tecumseh was killed.*

I t is true I am a Shawnee. My forefathers were warriors. Their
son is a warrior. From them I only take my existence; from
my tribe I take nothing. I am the maker of my own fortune; and
oh! that I could make that of my red people, and of my country,
as great as the conceptions of my mind, when I think of the
Spirit that rules the universe. I would not then come to Governor Harrison, to ask him to tear the treaty and to obliterate the
landmark; but I would say to him: Sir, you have liberty to return

to your own country. The being within, communing with past ages, tells me that once, nor until lately, there was no white man on this continent. That it then all belonged to red men, children of the same parents, placed on it by the Great Spirit that made them, to keep it, to traverse it, to enjoy its productions, and to fill it with the same race. Once a happy race—since made miserable by the white people, who are never contented, but always encroaching. The way, and the only way, to check and to stop this evil is for all the red men to unite in claiming a common and equal right in the land, as it was at first, and should be yet; for it never was divided, but belongs to all for the use of each. That no part has a right to sell, even to each other, much less to strangers—those who want all, and will not do with less.

The white people have no right to take the land from the Indians, because they had it first; it is theirs. They may sell, but all must join. Any sale not made by all is not valid. The late sale is bad. It was made by a part only. Part do not know how to sell. It requires all to make a bargain for all. All red men have equal rights to the unoccupied land. The right of occupancy is as good in one place as in another. There cannot be two occupations in the same place. The first excludes all others. It is not so in hunting or traveling; for there the same ground will serve many, as they may follow each other all day; but the camp is stationary, and that is occupancy. It belongs to the first who sits down on his blanket or skins which he has thrown upon the ground; and till he leaves it, no other has a right.

WILLIAM LLOYD GARRISON

— ★ —

An Immediate End to Slavery

Editorial in the *Liberator*, January 1, 1831

William Lloyd Garrison (1805–1879) was the leading abolitionist of his day and perhaps the archetypal American firebrand reformer of the nineteenth century. In Newburyport, Massachusetts, while he was still in his teens, Garrison worked for and wrote antislavery articles for the Herald *newspaper. In his twenties he joined with Benjamin Lundy to publish a monthly periodical, the* Genius of Universal Emancipation, *in Baltimore. After being sued for libel and serving time in prison for not being able to pay his fine, Garrison returned to Massachusetts, launching his famous abolitionist newspaper, the* Liberator, *in 1831. He spoke throughout the North demanding immediate freedom for slaves and helped to establish the New England Anti-Slavery Society in 1832 and the American Anti-Slavery Society in 1833. Garrison went so far as to denounce the Constitution as an immoral document because of its toleration of slavery, and he advocated separation of the free states from the slave states. Garrison finally supported Lincoln after the president's Emancipation Proclamation, and when the Civil War ended he turned his energies to other causes, including women's suffrage, American Indian rights, and prohibition.*

In the month of August, I issued proposals for publishing the *Liberator* in Washington City; but the enterprise, though hailed in different sections of the country, was palsied by public indifference. Since that time, the removal of the *Genius of Universal Emancipation* to the seat of government has rendered less imperious the establishment of a similar periodical in that quarter.

During my recent tour for the purpose of exciting the minds of the people by a series of discourses on the subject of slavery, every place that I visited gave fresh evidence of the fact that a greater revolution in public sentiment was to be effected in the free states—*and particularly in New England*—than at the South. I found contempt more bitter, opposition more active, detraction more relentless, prejudice more stubborn, and apathy more frozen than among slave owners themselves. Of course, there were individual exceptions to the contrary. This state of things afflicted but did not dishearten me. I determined, at every hazard, to lift up the standard of emancipation in the eyes of the nation, *within sight of Bunker Hill and in the birthplace of liberty*. That standard is now unfurled; and long may it float, unhurt by the spoliations of time or the missiles of a desperate foe—yea, till every chain be broken, and every bondman set free! Let Southern oppressors tremble—let their secret abettors tremble—let their Northern apologists tremble—let all the enemies of the persecuted blacks tremble.

I deem the publication of my original prospectus unnecessary, as it has obtained a wide circulation. The principles therein inculcated will be steadily pursued in this paper, excepting that I shall not array myself as the political partisan of any man. In defending the great cause of human rights, I wish to derive the assistance of all religions and of all parties.

Assenting to the "self-evident truth" maintained in the American Declaration of Independence, "that all men are created equal, and endowed by their Creator with certain inalienable rights, among which are life, liberty and the pursuit of happiness," I shall strenuously contend for the immediate enfranchisement of our slave population. In Park Street Church, on the Fourth of July 1829, in an address on slavery, I unreflectingly assented to the popular but pernicious doctrine of *gradual* abolition. I seize this opportunity to make a full and unequivocal recantation and thus publicly to ask pardon of my God, of my country, and of my brethren the poor slaves, for having uttered a sentiment so full of timidity, injustice, and absurdity. A similar recantation, from my pen, was published in the *Genius of Universal Emancipation* at Baltimore, in September 1829. My conscience is now satisfied.

I am aware that many object to the severity of my language; but is there not cause for severity? I *will be* as harsh as truth and as uncompromising as justice. On this subject I do not wish to think, or speak, or write, with moderation. No! No! Tell a man whose house is on fire, to give a moderate alarm; tell him to moderately rescue his wife from the hands of the ravisher; tell the mother to gradually extricate her babe from the fire into which it has fallen; but urge me not to use moderation in a cause like the present. I am in earnest—I will not equivocate—I will not excuse—I will not retreat a single inch—*and I will be heard*. The apathy of the people is enough to make every statue leap from its pedestal and to hasten the resurrection of the dead.

It is pretended that I am retarding the cause of emancipation by the coarseness of my invective and the precipitancy of my measures. The charge is not true. On this question my influence—humble as it is—is felt at this moment to a considerable extent, and shall be felt in coming years—not perniciously, but beneficially—not as a curse, but as a blessing; and posterity will bear testimony that I was right. I desire to thank God, that he enables me to disregard "the fear of man which bringeth a snare," and to speak his truth in its simplicity and power.

RALPH WALDO EMERSON

——— ★ ———

The Utopian Community of Brook Farm, 1841-1846

From the *Atlantic Monthly*, October 1883

America has had a long history of providing fertile ground for utopian communities, hundreds of which sprung up during the nineteenth century. The majority of these were small religious groups organized in community-oriented settlements. The most famous, perhaps, was the Shakers, established in 1774. More secular communities, based on new economic, property, and labor relationships, began appearing with the founding of Robert Owen's community in New Harmony, Indiana, in 1824. In the 1840s, the North American Phalanx in Red Bank, New Jersey, and Brook Farm in West Roxbury, Massachusetts, adopted the communitarian ideas of Charles Fourier. Nathaniel Hawthorne was a member of Brook Farm, which attracted the attention of many other New England literary figures, including Ralph Waldo Emerson (1803–1882), the great essayist, lecturer, and transcendentalist philosopher.

The West Roxbury association was formed in 1841, by a society of members, men and women, who bought a farm in West Roxbury, of about two hundred acres, and took possession of the place in April. Mr. George Ripley was the president, and I think Mr. Charles Dana (afterwards well known as one of the editors of the New York *Tribune*) was the secretary. Many members took shares by paying money; others held shares by their labors. An old house on the place was enlarged, and three new houses built.

William Allen was at first and for some time the head farmer, and the work was distributed in orderly committees to men and women. There were many employments, more or less lucrative, found for, or brought hither by, these members—shoemakers, joiners, seamstresses. They had good scholars among them, and so received pupils for their education. The parents of the children in some instances wished to live there, and were received as boarders. Many persons, attracted by the beauty of the place and the culture and ambition of the community, joined them as boarders, and lived there for years. I think the numbers of this mixed community soon reached eighty or ninety souls.

It was a noble and generous movement in the projectors to try an experiment of better living. They had the feeling that our ways of living were too conventional and expensive, not allowing each to do what he had a talent for, and not permitting men to combine cultivation of mind and heart with a reasonable amount of daily labor. At the same time, it was an attempt to lift others with themselves, and to share the advantages they should attain with others now deprived of them.

There was, no doubt, great variety of character and purpose in the members of the community. It consisted in the main of young people; few of middle age, and none old. Those who inspired and organized it were persons impatient of the routine, the uniformity, perhaps they would say the squalid contentment, of society around them, which was so timid and skeptical of any progress. One would say then that impulse was the rule in the society, without centripetal balance; perhaps it would not be severe to say, intellectual sans-culottism, an impatience of the formal, routinary character of our educational, religious, social and economical life in Massachusetts. Yet there was immense hope in these young people. There was nobleness; there were self-sacrificing victims who compensated for the levity and rashness of their companions. The young people lived a great deal in a short time, and came forth, some of them, perhaps, with shattered constitutions. And a few grave sanitary influences of character were happily there, which, I was assured, were always felt.

George W. Curtis, of New York, and his brother, of English

Oxford, were members of the family from the first. Theodore Parker, the near neighbor of the farm and the most intimate friend of Mr. Ripley, was a frequent visitor. Mr. Ichabod Morton of Plymouth, a plain man, formerly engaged through many years in the fisheries with success—eccentric, with a persevering interest in education, and of a very democratic religion—came and built a house on the farm, and he, or members of his family, continued there to the end. Margaret Fuller, with her joyful conversation and large sympathy, was often a guest, and always in correspondence with her friends. Many ladies, whom to name were to praise, gave character and varied attraction to the place.

In and around Brook Farm, whether as members, boarders, or visitors, were many remarkable persons, for character, intellect, or accomplishments. I recall one youth of the subtlest mind—I believe I must say the subtlest observer and diviner of character I ever met, living, reading, writing, talking, there, perhaps, as long as the colony held together; his mind fed and overfed by whatever is exalted in genius, whether in poetry or art, in drama or music, or in social accomplishment and elegancy; a man of no employment or practical aims; a student and philosopher, who found his daily enjoyment not with the elders or his exact contemporaries so much as with the fine boys who were skating and playing ball or bird-hunting; forming the closest friendships with such, and finding his delight in the petulant heroisms of boys. Yet was he the chosen counselor to whom the guardians would repair on any hitch or difficulty that occurred, and drew from him a wise counsel—a fine, subtle, inward genius, puny in body and habit as a girl, yet with an aplomb like a general, never disconcerted. He lived and thought in 1842, such worlds of life; all hinging on the thought of being or reality as opposed to consciousness; hating intellect with the ferocity of a Swedenborg. He was the abbé, or spiritual father, from his religious bias. His reading lay in Aeschylus, Plato, Dante, Calderon, Shakespeare, and in modern novels and romances of merit.

There too was Hawthorne, with his cold yet gentle genius,

if he failed to do justice to this temporary home. There was the accomplished Doctor of Music, who has presided over its literature ever since in our metropolis. The Reverand William Henry Channing, now of London, was from the first a student of socialism in France and England, and in perfect sympathy with this experiment. An English baronet, Sir John Caldwell, was a frequent visitor, and more or less directly interested in the leaders and the success.

Hawthorne drew some sketches, not happily, as I think; I should rather say, quite unworthy of his genius. No friend who knew Margaret Fuller could recognize her rich and brilliant genius under the dismal mask which the public fancied was meant for her in that disagreeable story.

The founders of Brook Farm should have this praise: that they made what all people try to make, an agreeable place to live in. All comers, even the most fastidious, found it the pleasantest of residences. It is certain that freedom from household routine, variety of character and talent, variety of work, variety of means, of thought and instruction, art, music, poetry, reading, masquerade, did not permit sluggishness or despondency, broke up routine. There is agreement in the testimony that it was, to most of the associates, education; to many, the most important period of their life, the birth of valued friendships, their first acquaintance with the riches of conversation, their training in behavior. The art of letter writing, it is said, was immensely cultivated. Letters were always flying not only from house to house, but from room to room. It was a perpetual picnic, a French Revolution in small, an age of reason in a patty-pan.

In the American social communities, the gossip found such vent and sway as to become despotic. The institutions were whispering-galleries, in which the adored Saxon privacy was lost. Married women, I believe, uniformly decided against the community. It was to them like the brassy and lacquered life in hotels. The common school was well enough, but to the common nursery they had grave objections. Eggs might be hatched in ovens, but the hen on her own account much preferred the old way. A hen without her chickens was but half a hen.

It was a curious experience of the patrons and leaders of this noted community—in which the agreement with many parties was that they should give so many hours of instruction in mathematics, in music, in moral and intellectual philosophy, and so forth—that in every instance the newcomers showed themselves keenly alive to the advantages of the society, and were sure to avail themselves of every means of instruction; their knowledge was increased, their manners refined, but they became in that proportion averse to labor and were charged by the heads of the departments with a certain indolence and selfishness.

In practice it is always found that virtue is occasional, spotty, and not linear or cubic. Good people are as bad as rogues, if steady performance is claimed; the conscience of the conscientious runs in veins, and the most punctilious in some particulars are latitudinarian in others. It was very gently said that people on whom beforehand all persons would put the utmost reliance were not responsible. They saw the necessity that the work must be done, and did it not, and it of course fell to be done by the few religious workers. No doubt there was in many a certain strength drawn from the fury of dissent. Thus Mr. Ripley told Theodore Parker, "There is your accomplished friend: he would hoe corn all Sunday, if I would let him, but all Massachusetts could not make him do it on Monday."

Of course every visitor found that there was a comic side to this paradise of shepherds and shepherdesses. There was a stove in every chamber, and everyone might burn as much wood as he or she would saw. The ladies took cold on washing-day; so it was ordained that the gentlemen shepherds should wring and hang out clothes, which they punctually did. And it would sometimes occur that when they danced in the evening, clothespins dropped plentifully from their pockets. The country members naturally were surprised to observe that one man plowed all day, and one looked out of the window all day, and perhaps drew his picture, and both received at night the same wages.

One would meet also some modest pride in their advanced condition, signified by a frequent phrase, "Before we came out of civilization." The question which occurs to you had occurred much earlier to Fourier: "How, in this charming Elysium, is the dirty work to be done?" And long ago Fourier had exclaimed, "Ah, I have it!" and jumped with joy. "Don't you see," he cried, "that nothing so delights the young Caucasian child as dirt? See the mud-pies that all children will make, if you will let them. See how much more joy they find in pouring their pudding on the tablecloth than into their beautiful mouths. The children from six to eight, organized into companies, with flags and uniforms, shall do this last function of civilization."

In Brook Farm was this peculiarity, that there was no head. In every family is the father; in every factory, a foreman; in a shop, a master; in a boat, the skipper—But in this farm, no authority; each was master or mistress of their own actions; happy, hapless anarchists. They expressed, after much perilous experience, the conviction that plain dealing was the best defense of manners and morals between the sexes. People cannot live together in any but necessary ways. The only candidates who will present themselves will be those who have tried the experiment of independence and ambition, and have failed; and none others will barter for the most comfortable equality the chance of superiority. Then all communities have quarreled. Few people can live together on their merits. There must be kindred, or mutual economy, or a common interest in their business, or other external tie.

The society at Brook Farm existed, I think, about six or seven years, and then broke up; the farm was sold, and I believe all the partners came out with pecuniary loss. Some of them had spent on it the accumulations of years. I suppose they all, at the moment, regarded it as a failure. I do not think they can so regard it now, but probably as an important chapter in their experience which has been of lifelong value. What knowledge of themselves and of each other, what various practical wisdom, what personal power, what studies of character, what accumulated culture, many of the members owed to it! What mutual measure they took of each other! It was a close union, like that in a ship's cabin, of clergymen, young collegians, merchants, mechanics, farmers' sons and daughters, with men and women of rare opportunities and delicate culture, yet assembled there by a sentiment which all shared, some of them hotly shared, of the honesty of a life of labor and of the beauty of a life of humanity. The yeoman saw refined manners in persons who were his friends; and the lady or the romantic scholar saw the continuous strength and faculty in people who would have disgusted them but that these powers were now spent in the direction of their own theory of life.

I recall these few selected facts, none of them of much independent interest, but symptomatic of the times and country. I please myself with the thought that our American mind is not now eccentric or rude in its strength, but is beginning to show a quiet power, drawn from wide and abundant sources, proper to a continent and to an educated people. If I have owed much to the special influences I have indicated, I am not less aware of that excellent and increasing circle of masters in arts and in song and in science, who cheer the intellect of our cities and this country today; whose genius is not a lucky accident, but normal, and with broad foundation of culture, and so inspires the hope of steady strength advancing on itself, and a day without night.

John McLean

──── ★ ────

Against the Forcible Abduction of Fugitive Slaves

Dissenting Opinion, U.S. Supreme Court, *Prigg v. Commonwealth of Pennsylvania*, 1842

*One of the many issues that swirled around the immense prob-
lem of slavery in America was the question of ownership of
slaves after they had escaped to a free state and the validity of
state laws prohibiting the forced return of slaves to a Southern
state. Justice Joseph Story wrote the opinion of the U.S. Supreme
Court in the case of* Prigg v. Commonwealth of Pennsylvania
*that federal laws take precedence over state laws, "that the right
to seize and retake fugitive slaves and the duty to deliver them
up, in whatever state of the Union they may be found . . . derive
their whole validity and obligation exclusively from the Constitution of the United States." Justice John McLean (1785–1861),
however, wrote in his dissenting opinion that the state of Pennsylvania "to preserve the peace of its citizens . . . has prohibited
the forcible abduction of persons of color. Does this law conflict
with the Constitution? It clearly does not."*

The slave is found in a state where every man, black or white, is presumed to be free; and this state, to preserve the peace of its citizens, and its soil and jurisdiction from acts of violence, has prohibited the forcible abduction of persons of color. Does this law conflict with the Constitution? It clearly does not in its terms. . . .

No conflict can arise between the act of Congress and this state law. The conflict can only arise between the forcible acts of the master and the law of the state. The master exhibits no proof of right to the services of the slave, but seizes him and is about to remove him by force. I speak only of the force exerted on the slave. The law of the state presumes him to be free and prohibits his removal. Now, which shall give way, the master or the state? The law of the state does in no case discharge, in the language of the Constitution, the slave from the service of his master.

It is a most important police regulation. And if the master violate it, is he not amenable? The offense consists in abduction of a person of color. And this is attempted to be justified upon the simple ground that the slave is property. That a slave is property must be admitted. The state law is not violated by the seizure of the slave by the master—for this is authorized by the act of Congress—but by removing him out of the state by force, and without proof of right, which the act does not authorize. Now, is not this an act which a state may prohibit? . . .

The important point is: Shall the presumption of right set up by the master, unsustained by any proof, or the presumption which arises from the laws and institutions of the state, prevail? This is the true issue. The sovereignty of the state is on one side, and the asserted interest of the master on the other. That interest is protected by the paramount law, and a special, a summary, and an effectual mode of redress is given. But this mode is not pursued, and the remedy is taken into his own hands by the master.

The presumption of the state that the colored person is free may be erroneous in fact; and if so, there can be no difficulty in proving it. But may not the assertion of the master be erroneous also? And if so, how is his act of force to be remedied? The colored person is taken, and forcibly conveyed beyond the jurisdiction of the state. This force, not being authorized by the act of Congress nor by the Constitution, may be prohibited by the state. As the act covers the whole power in the Constitution, and carries out, by special enactments, its provisions, we are, in my judgment, bound by the act. We can no more, under such circumstances, administer a remedy under the Constitution in disregard of the act than we can exercise a commercial or other power in disregard of an act of Congress on the same subject.

This view respects the rights of the master and the rights of the state. It neither jeopardizes nor retards the reclamation of the slave. It removes all state action prejudicial to the rights of the master, and recognizes in the state a power to guard and protect its own jurisdiction, and the peace of its citizens.

DOROTHEA DIX

—— ★ ——

Conditions in New Jersey Asylums, Jails, and Almshouses

Memorial to the State Legislature of New Jersey,
January 23, 1845

---

*During the 1820s and 1830s Dorothea Lynde Dix (1802–1887)
headed a school for girls in Boston. In 1841, after a visit to a
Cambridge, Massachusetts, jail to teach a Sunday-school class,
she bristled at the conditions and the confinement of the mentally ill with criminals. She began agitating for reform and the
establishment of separate facilities for those with mental illness.
She reported to state legislatures on her findings after investigating poorhouses and jails, first in Massachusetts, and then in
nearly every other state. Her efforts on behalf of the mentally ill
and improved prison conditions resulted in widespread institutional reforms in the United States, Canada, and Europe. During
the Civil War, Dorothea Dix served as superintendent of nurses
for the Union army.*

To the Honorable the Senate and General Assembly of the
State of New Jersey: I come to solicit your attention to the
condition and necessities of idiots, epileptics, and the insane
poor, in the state of New Jersey.

I ask your consideration of the *claims* of this large and much
neglected class of sufferers, and such effective legislative action
as shall check that tide of misery, the destroying force of which
each year witnesses the increase. I do not come here to quicken
your generous impulses, and move you to emotion, by showing
the existence of terrible abuses, revealing scenes of almost in-
credible sufferings. I come to ask *justice* of the legislature of
New Jersey, for those who, in the providence of God, are inca-

pable of pleading their own cause, and of claiming redress for their own grievances. Be patient with me—it is for your own citizens I plead; it is for helpless, friendless men and women, in your very midst, I ask succor—into whose broken minds hope and consolation find no entrance—the foul air of whose dreary cells still oppresses my breath—the clanking of whose heavy chains still sounds upon my ear. Have pity upon them! . . . their grievous, forlorn estate may be shared by yourselves or your children. A solemn responsibility is entrusted to you: it is for you to put a termination to evils and miseries which may yet be remedied or alleviated; it is for you to surround these unfortunate beings with such protecting influences as their incapacity for self-care demands, and to guard against the aggravation of like evils and miseries for the future.

Within the last few months, I have traversed a considerable portion of your state, and have found, in jails and poorhouses, and wandering at will over the country, large numbers of insane and idiotic persons, whose irresponsibility and imbecility render them objects of deep commiseration. These, whether the subjects of public bounty or of private charity, are inappropriately treated for recovery, or injudiciously managed, through ignorance or limitation of suitable means; thus they are left to exposures and sufferings, at once pitiable and revolting, and however in detail strongly represented, incapable of being exaggerated. I appeal to the public to sustain this strong assertion, and I appeal to medical men, whose professional duties conduct them amidst every form of painful disease, to unite their testimony with mine, and to aid in showing how great is the need, how important the demand, for a State Asylum for Insane Persons.

It is my duty to speak explicitly upon this subject. I shall be sorry to wound the feelings of any individual; I disclaim all personality—calling attention to defective systems, not to those who are officially appointed to carry them out. I shall not attempt to detail full histories, nor to refer directly to all cases embraced in the class of insane and idiots; but shall confine myself chiefly, to facts at present existing, and scenes to which I lately have been witness. . . .

I proceed to show the actual condition of those jails and poorhouses which I have visited. . . .

MONMOUTH COUNTY JAIL, at Freehold, is tolerably well arranged, and the apartments are sufficiently large and numerous to admit, in some sort, a classification of the prisoners. The only individual held there at the time of my visit was a colored man, who is represented not only as dangerous to be at large, but dangerous to "his keeper," being of late years subject to violent paroxysms, and when suffering under any injury, real or imaginary, both threatens and attempts personal violence. His history, as related by citizens in the county, is briefly this: He was from infancy of an eccentric and excitable temper, and was brought up by a family to which he was much attached, the master of which, perceiving a mental defect, avoided what disturbed his quiet, and by skillful management made him a faithful and useful servant. Death deprived him of this judicious guardian: he remained with the family; but the son-in-law of his late master less well understood his mental disabilities, and how to manage him: the result was that in dealing him a blow for some supposed neglect of duty, he instantly returned the attack, and was roused to a terrible excitement. The master, through fear, caused him to be committed on a charge of assault and battery, with intent to kill: he proved very ungovernable in the county jail, and, after a considerable time had passed, was tried, convicted, and sentenced to *ten years imprisonment* in the state penitentiary. During all this dreary period, he was considered a "very crazy man," and of course, as the warden himself told me, came out worse than when he entered. "For how can we," continued he, "bring madmen under curative treatment in the prison, even if they are curable at all?" He received his discharge, poor fellow! What was he now to do? His heart yearned for his old home—the home of his "dear old master, who was dead and gone." True to the instincts of his nature, thither he wandered, for neither friends nor home had he beside; he was received, but his obvious insanity made him feared: indeed he was a dangerous inmate at times. He roamed over the fields and through the old familiar woodlands, gathering into heaps old wood, that "nothing should be wasted." On this ground, occasion was made to charge him with petty depredations: he was again committed to the county jail, and there I found him. The keeper said he was often "dangerous to approach, especially if long kept close." I have refrained from giving the details of this painful history: they are known to many of your citizens.

We have not dwelt upon his sufferings in the jail; we have not followed him to his dreary prison, and there looked into his cell, cheerless and lonely, as month after month, and year after year, the crazy man, incapable of occupation, and beyond the reach of appropriate care, wore away time till ten times twelve months were numbered. It is possible it may seem no great evil, such a life as this, just as here it is briefly touched upon, but it is terrible in its reality. The poorhouse pauper, the wandering beggar, find the relief they seek, the aid they ask; but who are the friends of the insane poor, and what is the meed rendered to their necessities? What do our investigations reveal? Kindly care, skillful remedies, guardian protection, or chains, bondage, and long imprisonment? Mitigated suffering or unmitigated woe? Where is the hospital? For a hospital, behold I show you the cells of the poorhouse, the dungeons of the prisons. I have asked who are the friends of the insane poor? Few can effectually befriend them; this affecting christian duty devolves on the state; and the state will cancel this sacred obligation, only by acknowledging the wardship of these, the pariahs of our country, and establishing an asylum for their protection.

Attached to the SHARK RIVER POORHOUSE, in Monmouth County, is a farm of nine hundred acres, one hundred of which are cultivated. The cost of supporting the poor is about sixty cents per week for each individual; the supplies appeared to me sufficient and of good quality, although the system of the distribution of provisions, and separate cooking in the lodging-rooms, is very objectionable; and the more so, as there is no infirmary or hospital department connected with the establishment. The sick, the infirm, and the imbecile, are indiscriminately distributed and associated. The house, which is built of wood, is very old and inconveniently constructed for the purpose for which it is occupied. It contains, in winter, about sixty paupers, gathered from three townships: in the spring, a portion of these seek maintenance elsewhere. At this poorhouse I found, in November, forty inmates, chiefly aged and infirm persons, imbeciles, idiots, and insane: of the latter there are seven idiotic, two whole idiots, two very insane, and several demented.

In the vicinity of the main dwelling is a small brick building, containing on the first floor two poor cells, from eight to nine feet square, warmed in cold weather by a stove set into the dividing wall, or partition. A straw bed and blanket, spread upon the floor, constitute the furniture, if one excepts the *ringbolts* and *iron chains for securing the patients!* Ventilation by a small window is quite deficient. At the time of my visit, there was but one cell occupied: the crazy man was allowed to go abroad during the day, for it was "his calm time," and it was deemed necessary to fasten him up only at night; at present, too, the chains were disused. Over these cells was a third, which could be reached only by a ladder, "quite unfit," as I was told, "for anyone to be kept in." A kind and considerate master and mistress directed this establishment.

I heard in this township, of three wandering insane persons, but learned nothing special of their history; little interest was expressed for them. Where they belonged, to whom they were allied, or what their name and degree, were facts equally obscure and equally uncared for. . . .

MIDDLESEX COUNTY JAIL, in New Brunswick, is in decent order, contains two apartments on the first floor and a dungeon below. I found here but one prisoner; he occupied the same room with an idiotic or demented man, who had been committed here, either for his own safety, or the safety of others. Of his history, I could learn only this: He was found wandering from place to place, and incapable of rendering any account of himself; the *jail* opened its strong doors to receive and *protect* him! I was informed that insane persons were often brought to the jail, "and," added the speaker, "we should be glad to use them well, but this is a hard place for such; we can't deal justly by them here."

The TOWNSHIP POORHOUSE, in North Brunswick, contained sixteen paupers, several being of feeble and imbecile minds. Here were four children; no school; religious meetings held usually once a month. The house is neat and comfortable, but not sufficiently ventilated. A wooden building, opposite the dwelling-house, is appropriated to the insane: a passage ranges the entire length, on one side of which are the "crazy cells," which were four in number. These could, in moderate weather, be sufficiently warmed by a stove, which was placed in the passage opposite the wooden gratings, or barred doors of the cells. One cell was occupied by a crazy man, who at times was subject to furious madness. He was chained, and lying in a sort of box on the floor: as far as I could see, this was a sort of narrow pen, made by nailing two boards of unequal length to the floor and partition; it contained some straw and sufficient coverings. The condition of this man was repulsive and filthy: one of the paupers had charge of him, and lodged in one of the cells to guard against fire—a needful precaution. I believe the superintendents of the poorhouse do as well for him as they are able; it is a difficult task to change his garments, and wash, and shave him: there are times when this is considered quite impracticable. I saw him, they said, "at the best"; sometimes he was outrageous, uttering the most furious imprecations—threatening, by word and act, all who approached him. The cells measured six feet by ten, were lighted by a grated window, and could be tolerably ventilated. . . .

ESSEX COUNTY JAIL, at Newark, is well built of stone, and adapted to carry out, by its construction, "the separate system"; but the county does not require either order, or classification, or the employment of offenders. Persons waiting trial, prisoners sentenced, of both sexes and all colors, the young, the children, old men, and men of middle age all are promiscuously associated during the day, and can talk from their cells by night. This intercourse is not for better or worse, for good or evil, for of the good there can be no trait ordinarily manifested here: the adept in crime, whose cunning and adroitness made him for a time successful, finds delight in initiating the juvenile offender, or the tyro, in the arts of larceny and burglary. Time must be killed somehow; here is no employment, and for those who read, nothing to read. "We amuse ourselves in the only way we can," said a prisoner, " 'cutting up' whenever we've a chance," "and telling good stories of our adventures and escapes—oh, that is good fun." How far imprisonment benefits society when offenders are thrown together under such circumstances, or how far their morals are improved, is not so fitly the question as: What is the harm done to society? What the increase of knowledge in guilt and sin to the prisoner? Most county jails in the United States are not places of reform, not places where the offender pauses in his career of evil—*they are positively and certainly schools of vice:* they confirm the vicious in vicious propensities; they educate the criminal to more successful criminal enterprises. In short, we cause transgressors to be for a time held in restraint, only to enlarge them, by-and-by, more thoroughly trained—to enter upon a new career of crime. Our county jails, in effect, are the primary schools and the normal schools for the state prisons. In the jail at Newark, I particularly remarked a child, who was charged with a larceny, listening with delight to several adult prisoners, his seniors in crime as well as years: he was committed in November, and was to have his trial in January. He *had* learned his daily task without urging, and will need, by-and-by, no prompter when he brings the lessons he gets here by theory into practice. Who is blameworthy if this boy becomes an accomplished rogue? himself or the community? the whole, or the integral members of society?

In this jail are two madmen, so furious and troublesome at times, that it is a labor of great difficulty to keep them in any degree of order. They appear almost incapable of self-care, and whether we consider the office of the warden, the prisoners who are waiting trial, or the insane themselves, we feel the positive injustice to all parties in the jail detention of these maniacs. They certainly are, at all times, unfit and unsafe to be at large, manifesting both property-destroying and homicidal propensities; they have already jeopardized the life of the warden. . . .

In BERGEN COUNTY JAIL, at Hackensack, I found two prisoners—no insane. This jail has been much complained of. I saw it in tolerable order, but of the food and treatment of the prisoners I had no means of judging. On the first floor were four rooms of good size—the dungeons below are seldom used. I heard of several idiots and insane in the county, but did not see them. A case of moral insanity was related to me by an intelligent and able lawyer of Hackensack, who lamented there was no state asylum, as the courts, for the public security, were often compelled to send irresponsible offenders to the penitentiary, who in fact were only fit subjects for an insane hospital. The man above referred to was totally incapable of applying his faculties to procure the means of self-support, was also of feeble health, and when through moral perversity, committing petty depredations, had not sense enough to apply them for his own advantage, nor any interest in promoting the bad or mischievous purposes of others. He is at present in the penitentiary at Trenton, for the third time.

There is no poorhouse in Bergen County. The poor are placed in those families who agree to receive them at the lowest prices. "Sometimes they fare tolerably well," said a citizen. "Oftener, I am afraid, their condition is of the hardest." The infirm and sick (the very class who most claim care and kindness) suffer most under such a system. . . .

MORRIS COUNTY JAIL, at Morristown, seemed to be well ordered, and was in general clean; there were several prisoners in November, but at present no insane. One some time since was removed, and is, I am informed, cared for, not readily and willingly by his kindred, who would, I assert it upon authority, have preferred his incarceration in the state penitentiary to the trouble of taking care of him, and the expense superadded!

The MORRIS COUNTY POORHOUSE, is in Hanover Township, several miles from Morristown, and in November numbered one hundred and ten inmates. It was generally clean and decently furnished, and so far as I had the opportunity of learning, was well conducted by the superintendents in all its general arrangements. A separate building for the sick and infirm is much needed. There was here no school for the children, but religious exercises sometimes. Here were several imbeciles, five insane, and one of the latter class who had lately absconded, it was supposed, might be returned. Sometimes there are cases of violently excited maniacs here. For such I found two cells in a cellar, constructed of plank and boards. These dreary places were seven and a half feet high, by eight square; dark, damp, and unfurnished, unwarmed and unventilated. One would not hesitate but refuse to shut up here a worthless dog even—and so felt the master of the house and physician, who prefer *the alternative of chaining the patients with clogs and fetters* to the responsibility and inhumanity of putting them into these savage dens. A small aperture cut at the end of one of these cells some time ago occasioned the involuntary death of the crazy tenant, who thrusting his head through in his eagerness to escape, could not withdraw it, and hanging there died. A female maniac died in the adjoining cell, since which I believe they have been disused. "This," said the keeper, "is not the place for crazy people; we have no means of properly controlling the outrageous, or of taking fit care of those who are more quiet." The physician, who was present, expressed in strong terms his conviction of the need of a state hospital. . . .

The cases of insanity in private families, some of which are blessed with affluence, and others borne down by the depressing influences of poverty and misfortune conjoined, are numerous. Many painful details have reached me, which I have not felt at liberty to record with other cases represented in this memorial, since I have no right to give precision to my facts, by designating

names and locations. Almost daily some new history reaches
me, and there must be a far greater number of which I know
nothing. . . .

Of the insane in the state penitentiary, I have ascertained
satisfactorily, that the largest part *have been committed in that
condition.* I have myself seen and traced the history of some of
those who have been sent from the counties of Gloucester,
Salem, Burlington, Monmouth, Mercer, Essex, and Bergen.
These all had propensities which ranked them with the most
dangerous class of patients, and altogether unfit to be at large.
Some were homicidal, others disposed to destroy buildings by
fire, others again coveted property belonging to others, which
when possessed, was no longer desirable, and applied in no way
to their personal use. . . .

The inconsistencies of the jurisprudence of insanity are beginning to clear away. We have too long followed the absurdi-
ties of the English law, which, equally unphilosophical and
contradictory, has, while professing to extend its protection to
the insane, at the same time condemned them to jails and penitentiaries, to transportation or the gallows. Strange to say, the
French are here again in advance of us. How humane and clear
this simple principle of their code: . . . Neither is there crime nor
offense when the accused, at the time of the act, was in a state
of insanity. In the penal code of Louisiana, compiled by the
Honorable Edward Livingston, we find a similar clearness
and precision. In the criminal code of New York the same dis-
tinctness is preserved: "No act done by a person in a state of
insanity can be punished as an offense, and *no insane person can
be tried and sentenced to any punishment,* or punished for any
crime or offense committed in that state." Why should not these
sound principles be adopted into all our statute books? Why
should any enlightened state retain this remnant of a bar-
barous age? . . .

The provincial parliament of Canada has accepted memori-
als, giving the subject full and fair discussion, and, as a measure
towards abolishing this harsh feature of their criminal jurispru-

dence, has made liberal appropriations for the erection and endowment of a lunatic hospital, which shall gather the unfortunate patients from the jails and provincial prisons, where I have seen them reduced to the most forlorn and abject conditions. Here, in the United States, we annually witness progress: one state after another is detecting the errors of their several penal codes, and reforming them upon a more humane plan. The custom of sending insane prisoners for a term of years to your state penitentiary, has brought, and is still bringing, reproach upon a system wisely and humanely conceived, and which, if carried into practice with fidelity on the part of all the officers of the institution, is capable of producing benefits to society and individuals, beyond any plan for prison government ever yet adopted. But the discipline of your prison is perpetually interfered with through the presence of insane prisoners, whose wants and peculiarities cannot be ministered to by officers whose principal duties require quite an opposite order of qualifications. The extreme injustice and cruelty of this practice to the insane themselves, will hardly bear comment, but demands redress.

The establishment of hospitals for the insane has, within the last century, become so general among all civilized and christianized nations, that the neglect of this duty seems to involve aggravated culpability, and a just appreciation of the claims of humanity, which can find neither justification nor apology. . . .

The rapid diffusion of correct principles and improved modes of treating the insane in the United States, within the last twenty years, is too well known to render any historical detail of our asylums necessary here. New hospitals are annually founded, and old establishments remodeled, and made to keep pace with the rapid improvements of the age. They are superintended by skillful physicians of intelligent minds, and most of them distinguished in their profession, who spend the strength of their best years in advancing the cause of humanity. They "spend and are spent" in the noble effort to heal or mitigate those diseases which derange the healthful functions of the brain, and thus disturb the reasoning faculties and perceptions. The very onerous duties of the superintending physician of a hospital for the insane, and, indeed, of all official persons connected with these institutions, can be appreciated only by those who are very familiar with the routine of their daily duties. We may, with a just pride, rejoice that we have hospitals which will bear a close and very favorable comparison with any in the Old World, and these directed by men whose abilities give distinction to the institutions over which they preside.

I have confidence in hospital care for the insane, and in no other care, which, under the most favorable circumstances even, can be brought to surround the patient. Insanity is a malady which requires treatment appropriate to its peculiar and varied forms; the most skillful physicians in general practice, are among the first to recommend their patients to hospital treatment, and however painful it may be to friends to yield up the sufferer to the care of strangers, natural tenderness and sensibilities never should stand in the way of ultimate benefit to the patient. And if this care is needed for the rich, for those whose homes abound in every luxury which wealth can purchase, and refined habits covet, how much more is it needed for those who are brought low by poverty, and are destitute of friends? for those who find refuge under this calamitous disease only in jails and poorhouses, or perchance, in the cells of a state penitentiary?

But suppose the jail to afford comfortable apartments, decently furnished, and to be directed by an intelligent and humane keeper—advantages not frequently brought together—what then? Is not a jail built to detain *criminals,* bad persons, who willingly and wilfully transgressing the civil and social laws, are for these offenses, for a time imprisoned? Where is the propriety, where the justice, of bringing under the same condemnation, conscious offenders, and persons *not guilty of crime, but laboring under disease?* There is as much justice in conveying to our prisons a man lingering in a consumption, or pining under a consuming fever, as in taking there one who has lesion of the brain, or organic malconstruction. . . .

The disposition to annoy and distress insane and imbecile persons is not confined to our jails; it is exhibited in the poorhouses, and often witnessed, sometimes accompanied by fatal consequences, on the streets and highways.

If prisons are unfit for the insane, under ordinary circumstances, poorhouses are certainly not less so. Overseers of the poor, the superintendents of the poorhouses, and the poor themselves, are all perplexed and disturbed by the difficulties, the inconvenience, and the impropriety of such a residence for the insane.

Poorhouses, which have for their object the comfort of the aged, the helpless, and the invalid poor, are often so complex in their arrangements and objects that the purpose of their establishment is lost sight of. Seldom planned with a view to the proper separation and classification of the inmates, order and morality are with difficulty maintained. When to the care of providing for a large and miscellaneous family is joined the charge of a farm, on the part of the master, and the most various and burdensome duties on that of the mistress of the house, it is not surprising that the difficult task of managing the insane and the idiots should soonest be neglected, and soonest produce troubles which few have the patience and skill to sustain. Besides, it should be remembered, that while many are capable of judiciously directing an extensive poorhouse establishment, very few have either the tact or experience requisite for rightly managing the insane. While in all the Northern states, and some of the middle and Southern—that is to say, in all the states I have yet visited—I have found almost every form and variety of misery, produced by what many would term abuse, and outrage, and the grossest neglects, I can say, with sincerity, that most of the sufferings and neglects to which I have found the insane exposed have been not so much the result of hard-hearted brutality, as of ignorance, and want of qualification for discharging those duties, and absolute perplexity as to the mode of

rendering the objects of their cares, either tranquil or comfortable. Many have truly believed that an insane man or woman
was no better than a mere brute, and less easy to take care of;
they have not supposed them susceptible of emotions of pain or
pleasure, capable of being controlled through kind influences, or
of being restored through any cares they could bestow. It is very
frequent, I have found it so, especially in the county-houses of
this state, and many in Pennsylvania, that almost the only objections which could be advanced against them, under the present
general system, were to be found in the truly deplorable condition of the insane and idiotic inmates. We repeat of poorhouses
what we have asserted of prisons—the insane *cannot* be suit-
ably cared for in any such establishments.

Perhaps one cause for the unwillingness felt by some to
promote the establishment of hospitals for the insane is a doubt
of the curability of the malady, or of the superior advantage of
hospital treatment over private practice. Such doubts are fast
passing from the public mind. Thirty years since, in our country,
they might have had plausibility, sustained by want of an experience of benefits resulting from judicious management. A new
era has dawned on this department of medical science, and we
daily witness the most gratifying results, in the large number of
patients restored to their friends, confirmed in bodily and mental health. The twenty-third annual report of the McLean Asylum, at Sommerville, near Charlestown, Massachusetts, by Dr.
Bell, shows that "the records of the asylum justify the declaration, that *all cases certainly recent,* that is, whose origin does not
directly or obscurely run back more than a year, *recover under
a fair trial.* This is the general law, the occasional instances to
the contrary are the exceptions." In this opinion Dr. Ray, of the
Maine State Hospital, concurs. . . .

Dr. Chandler, superintendent of the New Hampshire Asylum, says, in the report for 1843, that "it is well established that
the *earlier* patients are placed under curative treatment, in hospitals, *the more speedy and sure is the recovery.*"

Dr. Brigham, superintendent of the New York State Asylum, writes as follows, in his first report of that institution: "Few things relating to the management and treatment of the insane, are so well established as the necessity of their *early* treatment, and their removal from home, in order to effect recovery. There are exceptions, no doubt. By examining the records of well conducted lunatic asylums, it appears that more than eight out of ten of the recent cases recover, while not more than one in six of the old cases are cured." . . .

Dr. Brigham, speaking of the benefit of labor for the insane, especially in the open air, adds that "incurable cases, instead of being immured in jails, and in town and county houses, without employment, where they are continually losing mind, and becoming worse, should be placed in good asylums, and have employment on the farm or in shops. In this way they would in general be rendered much happier, and some would probably recover. . . . A broad distinction should be made between the *sane* and the *insane* poor, as regards providing for their comfort. The former may have in a good county poorhouse most essential comforts, *provided the insane are not kept in it;* but the insane themselves, unless they have *special* care in reference to their disordered minds, have little or none." . . .

The propriety of providing for *all* those who suffer under the various forms of mental disease, or, more accurately speaking, of physical disease affecting and disturbing the natural and healthful functions of the brain, is found in the daily experience of society, and confirmed by the opinion of medical men. . . .

Permit me, in conclusion, to urge that the delay to provide suitable asylums for the insane produces miseries to individuals, and evils to society, inappreciable in their utmost influence, except by those who have given time to the examination of the subject, and who have witnessed the appalling degradation of these wretched sufferers in the poorhouses, and jails, and penitentiaries of our land.

Shall New Jersey be last of "the Thirteen Sisters" to respond to the claims of humanity, and to acknowledge the demands of justice?

HENRY DAVID THOREAU

— ★ —

The Best Government
Governs Not at All

From "Civil Disobedience," 1849

*The great American naturalist, philosopher, and writer Henry
David Thoreau (1817–1862) began his keen observances of the
New England landscape with a journal of his boating trip of
1839, which was published ten years later as* A Week on the
Concord and Merrimack Rivers. *Under the influence of his
friend Ralph Waldo Emerson, Thoreau sharpened his meta-
physical response to nature, ultimately living alone, from 1845 to
1847, in a hut he himself built on the shore of Walden Pond, near
Concord, Massachusetts. While Thoreau's paean to the self-
reliant, contemplative life in relation to nature is found in*
Walden (1854), *this philosophy in relation to politics and the
state is forcibly expressed in his famous essay "Civil Disobedience," first published in a periodical in 1849. The tone of the
essay is straightforward, reasonable, and full of common-sense
conviction, but the call is essentially to anarchy—against government itself, for rejection of unjust laws and for rebellion
when necessary, and in favor of the primacy of the individual.*

I heartily accept the motto "Government is best which governs
least," and I should like to see it acted up to more rapidly and
systematically. Carried out, it finally amounts to this, which
also I believe: "Government is best which governs not at all";
and when men are prepared for it, that will be the kind of
government which they will have. Government is at best but an
expedient; but most governments are usually, and all governments are sometimes, inexpedient. The objections which have
been brought against a standing army, and they are many and
weighty, and deserve to prevail, may also at last be brought

against a standing government. The standing army is only an arm of the standing government. The government itself, which is only the mode which the people have chosen to execute their will, is equally liable to be abused and perverted before the people can act through it. Witness the present Mexican War, the work of comparatively a few individuals using the standing government as their tool; for, in the outset, the people would not have consented to this measure.

This American government—what is it but a tradition, though a recent one, endeavoring to transmit itself unimpaired to posterity, but each instant losing some of its integrity? It has not the vitality and force of a single living man; for a single man can bend it to his will. It is a sort of wooden gun to the people themselves. But it is not the less necessary for this; for the people must have some complicated machinery or other, and hear its din, to satisfy that idea of government which they have. Governments show thus how successfully men can be imposed on, even impose on themselves, for their own advantage. It is excellent, we must all allow. Yet this government never of itself furthered any enterprise, but by the alacrity with which it got out of its way. *It* does not keep the country free. *It* does not settle the West. *It* does not educate. The character inherent in the American people has done all that has been accomplished; and it would have done somewhat more if the government had not sometimes got in its way. For government is an expedient by which men would fain succeed in letting one another alone; and, as has been said, when it is most expedient, the governed are most let alone by it. Trade and commerce, if they were not made of india-rubber, would never manage to bounce over the obstacles which legislators are continually putting in their way; and, if one were to judge these men wholly by the effects of their actions and not partly by their intentions, they would deserve to be classed and punished with those mischievous persons who put obstructions on the railroads.

But, to speak practically and as a citizen, unlike those who call themselves no-government men, I ask for, not at once no government, but at once a better government. Let every man make known what kind of government would command his respect, and that will be one step toward obtaining it.

After all, the practical reason why, when the power is once in the hands of the people, a majority are permitted, and for a long period continue, to rule is not because they are most likely to be in the right, nor because this seems fairest to the minority, but because they are physically the strongest. But a government in which the majority rule in all cases cannot be based on justice, even as far as men understand it. Can there not be a government in which majorities do not virtually decide right and wrong, but conscience?—in which majorities decide only those questions to which the rule of expediency is applicable? Must the citizen ever for a moment, or in the least degree, resign his conscience to the legislator? Why has every man a conscience, then? I think that we should be men first, and subjects afterward. It is not desirable to cultivate a respect for the law, so much as for the right. The only obligation which I have a right to assume is to do at any time what I think right.

It is truly enough said that a corporation has no conscience; but a corporation of conscientious men is a corporation *with* a conscience. Law never made men a whit more just; and, by means of their respect for it, even the well-disposed are daily made the agents of injustice. A common and natural result of an undue respect for law is that you may see a file of soldiers, colonel, captain, corporal, privates, powder-monkeys, and all, marching in admirable order over hill and dale to the wars, against their wills, ay, against their common sense and consciences, which makes it very steep marching indeed, and produces a palpitation of the heart. They have no doubt that it is a damnable business in which they are concerned; they are all peaceably inclined. Now, what are they? Men at all? or small movable forts and magazines, at the service of some unscrupulous man in power? . . .

How does it become a man to behave toward this American government today? I answer that he cannot without disgrace be associated with it. I cannot for an instant recognize that political organization as *my* government which is the *slave's* government also.

All men recognize the right of revolution; that is, the right to refuse allegiance to, and to resist, the government, when its tyranny or its inefficiency are great and unendurable. But almost all say that such is not the case now. But such was the case, they think, in the Revolution of '75. If one were to tell me that this was a bad government because it taxed certain foreign commodities brought to its ports, it is most probable that I should not make an ado about it, for I can do without them. All machines have their friction; and possibly this does enough good to counterbalance the evil. At any rate, it is a great evil to make a stir about it. But when the friction comes to have its machine, and oppression and robbery are organized, I say let us not have such a machine any longer. In other words, when a sixth of the population of a nation which has undertaken to be the refuge of liberty are slaves, and a whole country is unjustly overrun and conquered by a foreign army, and subjected to military law, I think that it is not too soon for honest men to rebel and revolutionize. What makes this duty the more urgent is the fact that the country so overrun is not our own, but ours is the invading army. . . .

All voting is a sort of gaming, like checkers or backgammon, with a slight moral tinge to it, a playing with right and wrong, with moral questions; and betting naturally accompanies it. The character of the voters is not staked. I cast my vote, perchance, as I think right; but I am not vitally concerned that that right should prevail. I am willing to leave it to the majority. Its obligation, therefore, never exceeds that of expediency. Even *voting* for the right is *doing* nothing for it. It is only expressing to men feebly your desire that it should prevail. A wise man will not leave the right to the mercy of chance, nor wish it to prevail through the power of the majority. There is but little virtue in the action of masses of men. When the majority shall at length vote for the abolition of slavery, it will be because they are indifferent to slavery, or because there is but little slavery left to be abolished by their vote. *They* will then be the only slaves. Only his vote can hasten the abolition of slavery who asserts his own freedom by his vote. . . .

It is not a man's duty, as a matter of course, to devote himself to the eradication of any, even the most enormous, wrong; he may still properly have other concerns to engage him; but it is his duty, at least, to wash his hands of it, and, if he gives it no thought longer, not to give it practically his support. If I devote myself to other pursuits and contemplations, I must first see, at least, that I do not pursue them sitting upon another man's shoulders. I must get off him first, that he may pursue his contemplations too. See what gross inconsistency is tolerated. I have heard some of my townsmen say, "I should like to have them order me out to help put down an insurrection of the slaves, or to march to Mexico—see if I would go"; and yet these very men have each, directly by their allegiance, and so indirectly, at least, by their money, furnished a substitute. The soldier is applauded who refuses to serve in an unjust war by those who do not refuse to sustain the unjust government which makes the war—is applauded by those whose own act and authority he disregards and sets at naught—as if the state were penitent to that degree that it hired one to scourge it while it sinned, but not to that degree that it left off sinning for a moment. Thus, under the name of Order and Civil Government, we are all made at last to pay homage to and support our own meanness. After the first blush of sin comes its indifference; and from immoral it becomes, as it were, *un*moral, and not quite unnecessary to that life which we have made.

The broadest and most prevalent error requires the most disinterested virtue to sustain it. The slight reproach to which the virtue of patriotism is commonly liable, the noble are most likely to incur. Those who, while they disapprove of the character and measures of a government, yield to it their allegiance and support are undoubtedly its most conscientious supporters, and so frequently the most serious obstacles to reform. Some are petitioning the state to dissolve the Union, to disregard the requisitions of the president. Why do they not dissolve it themselves—the union between themselves and the state—and refuse to pay their quota into its treasury? Do not they stand in the same relation to the state that the state does to the Union? And have not the same reasons prevented the state from resisting the Union which have prevented them from resisting the state?

How can a man be satisfied to entertain an opinion merely, and enjoy it? Is there any enjoyment in it, if his opinion is that he is aggrieved? If you are cheated out of a single dollar by your neighbor, you do not rest satisfied with knowing that you are cheated, or with saying that you are cheated, or even with petitioning him to pay you your due; but you take effectual steps at once to obtain the full amount, and see that you are never cheated again. Action from principle, the perception and the performance of right, changes things and relations; it is essentially revolutionary, and does not consist wholly with anything which was. It not only divides states and churches, it divides families; ay, it divides the *individual,* separating the diabolical in him from the divine.

Unjust laws exist. Shall we be content to obey them, or shall we endeavor to amend them, and obey them until we have succeeded, or shall we transgress them at once? Men generally, under such a government as this, think that they ought to wait until they have persuaded the majority to alter them. They think that, if they should resist, the remedy would be worse than the evil. But it is the fault of the government itself that the remedy *is* worse than the evil. *It* makes it worse. Why is it not more apt to anticipate and provide for reform? Why does it not cherish its wise minority? Why does it cry and resist before it is hurt? Why does it not encourage its citizens to be on the alert to point out its faults, and *do* better than it would have them? Why does it always crucify Christ, and excommunicate Copernicus and Luther, and pronounce Washington and Franklin rebels? . . .

As for adopting the ways which the state has provided for remedying the evil, I know not of such ways. They take too much time, and a man's life will be gone. I have other affairs to attend to. I came into this world not chiefly to make this a good place to live in but to live in it, be it good or bad. A man has not everything to do, but something; and because he cannot do *everything,* it is not necessary that he should do *something* wrong. It is not my business to be petitioning the governor or the legislature any more than it is theirs to petition me; and if they should not hear my petition, what should I do then? But in this case the state has provided no way: its very constitution is the evil. This may seem to be harsh and stubborn and unconciliatory; but it is to treat with the utmost kindness and consideration the only spirit that can appreciate or deserves it. So is all change for the better, like birth and death, which convulse the body.

I do not hesitate to say, that those who call themselves abolitionists should at once effectually withdraw their support, both in person and property, from the government of Massachusetts, and not wait till they constitute a majority of one before they suffer the right to prevail through them. I think that it is enough if they have God on their side, without waiting for that other one. Moreover, any man more right than his neighbors constitutes a majority of one already.

I meet this American government, or its representative, the state government, directly, and face to face, once a year—no more—in the person of its tax-gatherer; this is the only mode in which a man situated as I am necessarily meets it; and it then says distinctly, Recognize me. And the simplest, the most effectual, and, in the present posture of affairs, the indispensablest mode of treating with it on this head, of expressing your little satisfaction with and love for it, is to deny it then. My civil neighbor, the tax-gatherer, is the very man I have to deal with—for it is, after all, with men and not with parchment that I quarrel—and he has voluntarily chosen to be an agent of the government. How shall he ever know well what he is and does as an officer of the government, or as a man, until he is obliged to consider whether he shall treat me, his neighbor, for whom he has respect, as a neighbor and well-disposed man or as a maniac and disturber of the peace, and see if he can get over this obstruction to his neighborliness without a ruder and more impetuous thought or speech corresponding with his action. I know this well, that if one thousand, if one hundred, if ten men whom I could name—if *ten honest men* only—ay, if *one honest man,* in this state of Massachusetts, *ceasing to hold slaves,* were actually to withdraw from this copartnership, and be locked up in the county jail therefore, it would be the abolition of slavery in America. For it matters not how small the beginning may seem to be: what is once well done is done forever. But we love better to talk about it: that we say is our mission. Reform keeps many scores of newspapers in its service, but not one man. . . .

Under a government which imprisons any unjustly, the true place for a just man is also a prison. The proper place today, the only place which Massachusetts has provided for her freer and less desponding spirits, is in her prisons, to be put out and locked out of the state by her own act, as they have already put themselves out by their principles. It is there that the fugitive slave, and the Mexican prisoner on parole, and the Indian come to plead the wrongs of his race should find them; on that separate, but more free and honorable, ground, where the state places those who are not *with* her, but *against* her—the only house in a slave state in which a free man can abide with honor. If any think that their influence would be lost there, and their voices no longer afflict the ear of the state, that they would not be as an enemy within its walls, they do not know by how much truth is stronger than error, nor how much more eloquently and effectively he can combat injustice who has experienced a little in his own person.

Cast your whole vote, not a strip of paper merely, but your whole influence. A minority is powerless while it conforms to the majority; it is not even a minority then; but it is irresistible when it clogs by its whole weight. If the alternative is to keep all just men in prison, or give up war and slavery, the state will not hesitate which to choose. If a thousand men were not to pay their tax bills this year, that would not be a violent and bloody measure, as it would be to pay them and enable the state to commit violence and shed innocent blood. This is, in fact, the definition of a peaceable revolution, if any such is possible. If the tax-gatherer, or any other public officer, asks me, as one has done, "But what shall I do?" my answer is, "If you really wish to do anything, resign your office." When the subject has refused allegiance, and the officer has resigned his office, then the revolution is accomplished. But even suppose blood should flow. Is there not a sort of bloodshed when the conscience is wounded? Through this wound a man's real manhood and immortality flow out, and he bleeds to an everlasting death. I see this blood flowing now. . . .

When I converse with the freest of my neighbors, I perceive that, whatever they may say about the magnitude and seriousness of the question, and their regard for the public tranquillity, the long and the short of the matter is that they cannot spare the protection of the existing government, and they dread the consequences to their property and families of disobedience to it. For my own part, I should not like to think that I ever rely on the protection of the state. But, if I deny the authority of the state when it presents its tax bill, it will soon take and waste all my property, and so harass me and my children without end. This is hard. This makes it impossible for a man to live honestly, and at the same time comfortably, in outward respects. It will not be worth the while to accumulate property; that would be sure to go again. You must hire or squat somewhere, and raise but a small crop, and eat that soon. You must live within yourself, and depend upon yourself always tucked up and ready for a start, and not have many affairs. . . .

I have paid no poll tax for six years. I was put into a jail once on this account, for one night; and, as I stood considering the walls of solid stone, two or three feet thick, the door of wood and iron, a foot thick, and the iron grating which strained the light, I could not help being struck with the foolishness of that institution which treated me as if I were mere flesh and blood and bones, to be locked up. I wondered that it should have concluded at length that this was the best use it could put me to, and had never thought to avail itself of my services in some way. I saw that, if there was a wall of stone between me and my townsmen, there was a still more difficult one to climb or break through before they could get to be as free as I was. I did not for a moment feel confined, and the walls seemed a great waste of stone and mortar. I felt as if I alone of all my townsmen had paid my tax. They plainly did not know how to treat me, but behaved like persons who are underbred. In every threat and in every compliment there was a blunder; for they thought that my chief desire was to stand the other side of that stone wall. I could not but smile to see how industriously they locked the door on my meditations, which followed them out again without let or hindrance, and *they* were really all that was dangerous. As they could not reach me, they had resolved to punish my body; just as boys, if they cannot come at some person against whom they have a spite, will abuse his dog. I saw that the state was half-witted, that it was timid as a lone woman with her silver spoons, and that it did not know its friends from its foes, and I lost all my remaining respect for it, and pitied it.

Thus the state never intentionally confronts a man's sense, intellectual or moral, but only his body, his senses. It is not armed with superior wit or honesty, but with superior physical strength. I was not born to be forced. I will breathe after my own fashion. Let us see who is the strongest. What force has a multitude? They only can force me who obey a higher law than I. . . .

The night in prison was novel and interesting enough. The prisoners in their shirtsleeves were enjoying a chat and the evening air in the doorway when I entered. But the jailer said, "Come, boys, it is time to lock up"; and so they dispersed, and I heard the sound of their steps returning into the hollow apartments. My roommate was introduced to me by the jailer as "a first-rate fellow and a clever man." When the door was locked, he showed me where to hang my hat, and how he managed matters there. The rooms were whitewashed once a month; and this one, at least, was the whitest, most simply furnished, and probably the neatest apartment in the town. He naturally wanted to know where I came from, and what brought me there. And when I had told him, I asked him in my turn how he came there, presuming him to be an honest man, of course; and, as the world goes, I believe he was. "Why," said he, "they accuse me of burning a barn; but I never did it." As near as I could discover, he had probably gone to bed in a barn when drunk, and smoked his pipe there; and so a barn was burnt. He had the reputation of being a clever man, had been there some three months waiting for his trial to come on, and would have to wait as much longer; but he was quite domesticated and contented, since he got his board for nothing, and thought that he was well treated.

He occupied one window, and I the other; and I saw that if one stayed there long, his principal business would be to look out the window. I had soon read all the tracts that were left there, and examined where former prisoners had broken out, and where a grate had been sawed off, and heard the history of the various occupants of that room; for I found that even here there was a history and a gossip which never circulated beyond the walls of the jail. Probably this is the only house in the town where verses are composed, which are afterward printed in a circular form, but not published. I was shown quite a long list of verses which were composed by some young men who had been detected in an attempt to escape, who avenged themselves by singing them.

I pumped my fellow prisoner as dry as I could, for fear I should never see him again; but at length he showed me which was my bed, and left me to blow out the lamp.

It was like traveling into a far country, such as I had never expected to behold, to lie there for one night. It seemed to me that I never had heard the town clock strike before, nor the evening sounds of the village; for we slept with the windows open, which were inside the grating. It was to see my native village in the light of the Middle Ages, and our Concord was turned into a Rhine stream, and visions of knights and castles passed before me. They were the voices of old burghers that I heard in the streets. I was an involuntary spectator and auditor of whatever was done and said in the kitchen of the adjacent village inn—a wholly new and rare experience to me. It was a closer view of my native town. I was fairly inside of it. I never had seen its institutions before. This is one of its peculiar institutions; for it is a shire town. I began to comprehend what its inhabitants were about.

In the morning, our breakfasts were put through the hole in the door, in small oblong-square tin pans, made to fit, and holding a pint of chocolate, with brown bread, and an iron spoon. When they called for the vessels again, I was green enough to return what bread I had left; but my comrade seized it, and said that I should lay that up for lunch or dinner. Soon after he was let out to work at haying in a neighboring field, whither he went every day, and would not be back till noon; so he bade me good day, saying that he doubted if he should see me again.

When I came out of prison—for someone interfered, and paid that tax—I did not perceive that great changes had taken place on the common, such as he observed who went in a youth and emerged a tottering and grayheaded man; and yet a change had to my eyes come over the scene—the town, and state, and country—greater than any that mere time could effect. I saw yet more distinctly the state in which I lived. I saw to what extent the people among whom I lived could be trusted as good neighbors and friends; that their friendship was for summer weather only; that they did not greatly propose to do right; that they were a distinct race from me by their prejudices and superstitions. . . .

It was formerly the custom in our village, when a poor debtor came out of jail, for his acquaintances to salute him, looking through their fingers, which were crossed to represent the grating of a jail window, "How do ye do?" My neighbors did not thus salute me, but first looked at me, and then at one another, as if I had returned from a long journey. I was put into jail as I was going to the shoemaker's to get a shoe which was mended. When I was let out the next morning, I proceeded to finish my errand, and, having put on my mended shoe, joined a huckleberry party, who were impatient to put themselves under my conduct; and in half an hour—for the horse was soon tackled—was in the midst of a huckleberry field, on one of our highest hills, two miles off, and then the state was nowhere to be seen. . . .

I have never declined paying the highway tax, because I am as desirous of being a good neighbor as I am of being a bad subject; and as for supporting schools, I am doing my part to educate my fellow countrymen now. It is for no particular item in the tax bill that I refuse to pay it. I simply wish to refuse allegiance to the state, to withdraw and stand aloof from it effectually. I do not care to trace the course of my dollar, if I could, till it buys a man or a musket to shoot one with—the dollar is innocent— but I am concerned to trace the effects of my allegiance. In fact, I quietly declare war with the state, after my fashion, though I will still make what use and get what advantage of her I can, as is usual in such cases.

If others pay the tax which is demanded of me, from a sympathy with the state, they do but what they have already done in their own case, or rather they abet injustice to a greater extent than the state requires. If they pay the tax from a mistaken interest in the individual taxed, to save his property, or prevent his going to jail, it is because they have not considered wisely how far they let their private feelings interfere with the public good.

This, then, is my position at present. But one cannot be too much on his guard in such a case, lest his action be biased by obstinacy or an undue regard for the opinions of men. Let him see that he does only what belongs to himself and to the hour. . . .

I do not wish to quarrel with any man or nation. I do not wish to split hairs, to make fine distinctions, or set myself up as better than my neighbors. I seek rather, I may say, even an excuse for conforming to the laws of the land. I am but too ready to conform to them. Indeed, I have reason to suspect myself on this head; and each year, as the tax-gatherer comes round, I find myself disposed to review the acts and position of the general and state governments, and the spirit of the people, to discover a pretext for conformity.

No man with a genius for legislation has appeared in America. They are rare in the history of the world. There are orators, politicians, and eloquent men, by the thousand; but the speaker has not yet opened his mouth to speak who is capable of settling the much-vexed questions of the day. We love eloquence for its own sake, and not for any truth which it may utter, or any heroism it may inspire. Our legislators have not yet learned the comparative value of free trade and of freedom, of union, and of rectitude, to a nation. They have no genius or talent for comparatively humble questions of taxation and finance, commerce and manufactures and agriculture. If we were left solely to the wordy wit of legislators in Congress for our guidance, uncorrected by the seasonable experience and the effectual complaints of the people, America would not long retain her rank among the nations. For eighteen hundred years, though perchance I have no right to say it, the New Testament has been written; yet where is the legislator who has wisdom and practical talent enough to avail himself of the light which it sheds on the science of legislation?

The authority of government, even such as I am willing to submit to—for I will cheerfully obey those who know and can do better than I, and in many things even those who neither know nor can do so well—is still an impure one: to be strictly just, it must have the sanction and consent of the governed. It can have no pure right over my person and property but what I concede to it. The progress from an absolute to a limited monarchy, from a limited monarchy to a democracy, is a progress toward a true respect for the individual. Even the Chinese philosopher was wise enough to regard the individual as the basis of the empire. Is a democracy, such as we know it, the last improvement possible in government? Is it not possible to take a step further toward recognizing and organizing the rights of man?

There will never be a really free and enlightened state until the state comes to recognize the individual as a higher and independent power, from which all its own power and authority are derived, and treats him accordingly. I please myself with imagining a state at last which can afford to be just to all men, and to treat the individual with respect as a neighbor; which even would not think it inconsistent with its own repose if a few were to live aloof from it, not meddling with it, nor embraced by it, who fulfilled all the duties of neighbors and fellow men. A state which bore this kind of fruit, and suffered it to drop off as fast as it ripened, would prepare the way for a still more perfect and glorious state, which also I have imagined, but not yet anywhere seen.

—— ★ ——

Dred Scott: A Slave and a Citizen

Dissenting Opinion, U.S. Supreme Court,
Dred Scott v. Sandford, 1857

The Dred Scott *decision is perhaps the most famous U.S. Supreme Court case in American history. Scott was a slave from Missouri who resided for a while with his owner in Illinois and Wisconsin Territory and then returned to Missouri. According to the Missouri Compromise of 1820, while slavery was permitted in the state of Missouri it was forbidden in the territory. Scott claimed he—and his family—had become free while in the North and was from then on a citizen of his home state. Chief Justice Roger Taney, delivering the opinion of the Court, held that slaves could not be citizens and had no right to sue in the federal courts. In addition, Taney declared that the Missouri Compromise was unconstitutional, that slavery could not be prohibited in any of the territories, and that slaves were property and could be transported anywhere within U.S. jurisdiction without a change in their status. Justice John McLean, writing one of the two dissenting opinions, said that the Court's argument that Scott was " 'of African descent, his ancestors . . . sold as Negro slaves' . . . does not show that he is not a citizen of Missouri. . . . Being born under our Constitution and laws, no naturalization is required, as one of foreign birth, to make him a citizen."*

This case is before us on a writ of error from the circuit court for the district of Missouri.

An action of trespass was brought, which charges the defendant with an assault and imprisonment of the plaintiff, and also of Harriet Scott, his wife, Eliza and Lizzie, his two children, on the ground that they were his slaves, which was without right on his part, and against law.

The defendant filed a plea in abatement, "that said causes of action, and each and every of them, if any such accrued to the said Dred Scott, accrued out of the jurisdiction of this court, and exclusively within the jurisdiction of the courts of the state of Missouri, for that, to wit, said plaintiff, Dred Scott, is not a citizen of the state of Missouri, as alleged in his declaration, because he is a Negro of African descent, his ancestors were of pure African blood, and were brought into this country and sold as Negro slaves; and this the said Sandford is ready to verify; wherefore he prays judgment whether the court can or will take further cognizance of the action aforesaid."

To this a demurrer was filed, which, on argument, was sustained by the court, the plea in abatement being held insufficient; the defendant was ruled to plead over. Under this rule he pleaded: (1) not guilty; (2) that Dred Scott was a Negro slave, the property of the defendant; and (3) that Harriet, the wife, and Eliza and Lizzie, the daughters of the plaintiff, were the lawful slaves of the defendant. . . .

The parties agreed to the following facts: In the year 1834, the plaintiff was a Negro slave belonging to Dr. Emerson, who was a surgeon in the army of the United States. In that year, Dr. Emerson took the plaintiff from the state of Missouri to the post of Rock Island, in the state of Illinois, and held him there as a slave until the month of April or May 1836. At the time last mentioned, Dr. Emerson removed the plaintiff from Rock Island to the military post at Fort Snelling, situated on the west bank of the Mississippi River, in the territory known as Upper Louisiana, acquired by the United States from France, and situated north of latitude thirty-six degrees thirty minutes north, and north of the state of Missouri. Dr. Emerson held the plaintiff in slavery, at Fort Snelling, from the last-mentioned date until the year 1838.

In the year 1835, Harriet, who is named in the second count of the plaintiff's declaration, was the Negro slave of Major Taliaferro, who belonged to the army of the United States. In that year, Major Taliaferro took Harriet to Fort Snelling, a military post situated as hereinbefore stated, and kept her there as a slave until the year 1836, and then sold and delivered her as a slave, at Fort Snelling, unto Dr. Emerson, who held her in slavery, at that place, until the year 1838.

In the year 1836, the plaintiff and Harriet were married at Fort Snelling, with the consent of Dr. Emerson, who claimed to be their master and owner. Eliza and Lizzie, named in the third count of the plaintiff's declaration, are the fruit of that marriage. Eliza is about fourteen years old, and was born on board the steamboat *Gipsey,* north of the north line of the state of Missouri, and upon the river Mississippi. Lizzie is about seven years old, and was born in the state of Missouri, at the military post called Jefferson Barracks.

In the year 1838, Dr. Emerson removed the plaintiff and said Harriet and their daughter Eliza from Fort Snelling to the state of Missouri, where they have ever since resided.

Before the commencement of the suit, Dr. Emerson sold and conveyed the plaintiff, Harriet, Eliza, and Lizzie, to the defendant, as slaves, and he has ever since claimed to hold them as slaves.

At the times mentioned in the plaintiff's declaration, the defendant, claiming to be the owner, laid his hands upon said plaintiff, Harriet, Eliza, and Lizzie, and imprisoned them; doing in this respect, however, no more than he might lawfully do, if they were of right his slaves at such times.

In the first place, the plea to the jurisdiction is not before us, on this writ of error. A demurrer to the plea was sustained, which ruled the plea bad, and the defendant, on leave, pleaded over.

The decision on the demurrer was in favor of the plaintiff; and as the plaintiff prosecutes this writ of error, he does not complain of the decision on the demurrer. The defendant might have complained of this decision, as against him, and have prosecuted a writ of error, to reverse it. But as the case, under the instruction of the court to the jury, was decided in his favor, of course he had no ground of complaint.

But it is said, if the Court, on looking at the record, shall clearly perceive that the circuit court had no jurisdiction, it is a ground for the dismissal of the case. This may be characterized as rather a sharp practice, and one which seldom, if ever, occurs. No case was cited in the argument as authority, and not a single case precisely in point is recollected in our reports. The pleadings do not show a want of jurisdiction. This want of jurisdiction can only be ascertained by a judgment on the demurrer to the special plea. No such case, it is believed, can be cited. But if this rule of practice is to be applied in this case, and the plaintiff in error is required to answer and maintain as well the points ruled in his favor, as to show the error of those ruled against him, he has more than an ordinary duty to perform. Under such circumstances, the want of jurisdiction in the circuit court must be so clear as not to admit of doubt. Now, the plea which raises the question of jurisdiction, in my judgment, is radically defective. The gravamen of the plea is this: "That the plaintiff is a Negro of African descent, his ancestors being of pure African blood, and were brought into this country, and sold as Negro slaves."

There is no averment in this plea which shows or conduces to show an inability in the plaintiff to sue in the circuit court. It does not allege that the plaintiff had his domicile in any other state, nor that he is not a free man in Missouri. He is averred to have had a Negro ancestry, but this does not show that he is not a citizen of Missouri, within the meaning of the act of Congress authorizing him to sue in the circuit court. It has never been held necessary, to constitute a citizen within the act, that he should have the qualifications of an elector. Females and minors may sue in the federal courts, and so may any individual who has a permanent domicile in the state under whose laws his rights are protected, and to which he owes allegiance.

Being born under our Constitution and laws, no naturalization is required, as one of foreign birth, to make him a citizen. The most general and appropriate definition of the term citizen is "a freeman." Being a freeman, and having his domicile in a state different from that of the defendant, he is a citizen within the act of Congress, and the courts of the Union are open to him.

It has often been held, that the jurisdiction, as regards parties, can only be exercised between citizens of different states, and that a mere residence is not sufficient; but this has been said to distinguish a temporary from a permanent residence.

To constitute a good plea to the jurisdiction, it must negative those qualities and rights which enable an individual to sue in the federal courts. This has not been done; and on this ground the plea was defective, and the demurrer was properly sustained. . . .

The pleader has not the boldness to allege that the plaintiff is a slave, as that would assume against him the matter in controversy, and embrace the entire merits of the case in a plea to the jurisdiction. But beyond the facts set out in the plea, the court, to sustain it, must assume the plaintiff to be a slave, which is decisive on the merits. . . .

The defendant's counsel complains that if the court takes jurisdiction on the ground that the plaintiff is free, the assumption is against the right of the master. This argument is easily answered. In the first place, the plea does not show him to be a slave; it does not follow that a man is not free whose ancestors were slaves. The reports of the Supreme Court of Missouri show that this assumption has many exceptions; and there is no averment in the plea that the plaintiff is not within them. . . .

It has been argued that if a colored person be made a citizen of a state he cannot sue in the federal court. The Constitution declares that federal jurisdiction "may be exercised between citizens of different states," and the same is provided in the act of 1789. The above argument is properly met by saying that the Constitution was intended to be a practical instrument; and where its language is too plain to be misunderstood, the argument ends. . . .

There is no nation in Europe which considers itself bound to return to his master a fugitive slave, under the civil law or the law of nations. On the contrary, the slave is held to be free where there is no treaty obligation, or compact in some other form, to return him to his master. The Roman law did not allow freedom to be sold. An ambassador or any other public functionary could not take a slave to France, Spain, or any other country of Europe, without emancipating him. A number of slaves escaped from a Florida plantation, and were received on board of ship by Admiral Cochrane; by the King's Bench, they were held to be free. . . .

In the great and leading case of *Prigg v. The State of Pennsylvania,* . . . this Court said that, by the general law of nations, no nation is bound to recognize the state of slavery, as found within its territorial dominions, where it is in opposition to its own policy and institutions, in favor of the subjects of other nations where slavery is organized.

To the position that slavery can only exist except under the authority of law, it is objected that in few if in any instances has it been established by statutory enactment. This is no answer to the doctrine laid down by the Court. Almost all the principles of the common law had their foundation in usage. Slavery was introduced into the colonies of this country by Great Britain at an early period of their history, and it was protected and cherished, until it became incorporated into the colonial policy. It is immaterial whether a system of slavery was introduced by express law, or otherwise, if it have the authority of law. There is no slave state where the institution is not recognized and protected by statutory enactments and judicial decisions. Slaves are made property by the laws of the slave states, and as such are liable to the claims of creditors; they descend to heirs, are taxed, and in the South they are a subject of commerce. . . .

I will now consider the relation which the federal government bears to slavery in the states.

Slavery is emphatically a state institution. In the ninth section of the first article of the Constitution, it is provided "that the migration or importation of such persons as any of the states now existing shall think proper to admit, shall not be prohibited by the Congress prior to the year 1808, but a tax or duty may be imposed on such importation, not exceeding ten dollars for each person."

In the Convention, it was proposed by a committee of eleven to limit the importation of slaves to the year 1800, when Mr. Pinckney moved to extend the time to the year 1808. This motion was carried—New Hampshire, Massachusetts, Connecticut, Maryland, North Carolina, South Carolina, and Georgia, voting in the affirmative; and New Jersey, Pennsylvania, and Virginia, in the negative. In opposition to the motion, Mr. Madison said: "Twenty years will produce all the mischief that can be apprehended from the liberty to import slaves; so long a term will be more dishonorable to the American character than to say nothing about it in the Constitution." . . .

The provision in regard to the slave trade shows clearly that Congress considered slavery a state institution, to be continued and regulated by its individual sovereignty; and to conciliate that interest, the slave trade was continued twenty years, not as a general measure, but for the "benefit of such states as shall think proper to encourage it." . . .

The only connection which the federal government holds with slaves in a state arises from that provision of the Constitution which declares that "no person held to service or labor in one state, under the laws thereof, escaping into another, shall, in consequence of any law or regulation therein, be discharged from such service or labor, but shall be delivered up, on claim of the party to whom such service or labor may be due."

This being a fundamental law of the federal government, it rests mainly for its execution, as has been held, on the judicial power of the Union; and so far as the rendition of fugitives from labor has become a subject of judicial action, the federal obligation has been faithfully discharged. . . .

We need not refer to the mercenary spirit which introduced the infamous traffic in slaves to show the degradation of Negro slavery in our country. This system was imposed upon our colonial settlements by the mother country, and it is due to truth to say that the commercial colonies and states were chiefly engaged in the traffic. But we know as a historical fact that James Madison, that great and good man, a leading member in the federal Convention, was solicitous to guard the language of that instrument so as not to convey the idea that there could be property in man.

I prefer the lights of Madison, Hamilton, and Jay, as a means of construing the Constitution in all its bearings, rather than to look behind that period, into a traffic which is now declared to be piracy, and punished with death by Christian nations. I do not like to draw the sources of our domestic relations from so dark a ground. Our independence was a great epoch in the history of freedom; and while I admit the government was not made especially for the colored race, yet many of them were citizens of the New England states, and exercised the rights of suffrage when the Constitution was adopted, and it was not doubted by any intelligent person that its tendencies would greatly ameliorate their condition.

Many of the states, on the adoption of the Constitution, or shortly afterward, took measures to abolish slavery within their respective jurisdictions; and it is a well-known fact that a belief was cherished by the leading men, South as well as North, that the institution of slavery would gradually decline, until it would become extinct. The increased value of slave labor, in the culture of cotton and sugar, prevented the realization of this expectation. Like all other communities and states, the South's were influenced by what they considered to be their own interests.

But if we are to turn our attention to the dark ages of the world, why confine our view to colored slavery? On the same principles, white men were made slaves. All slavery has its origin in power, and is against right.

The power of Congress to establish territorial governments, and to prohibit the introduction of slavery therein, is the next point to be considered. . . .

The Ordinance of 1787 was passed, "for the government of the United States territory northwest of the river Ohio," with but one dissenting vote. This instrument provided there should be organized in the territory not less than three nor more than five states, designating their boundaries. It was passed while the federal Convention was in session, about two months before the Constitution was adopted by the Convention. The members of the Convention must therefore have been well acquainted with the provisions of the Ordinance. It provided for a temporary government, as initiatory to the formation of state governments. Slavery was prohibited in the territory.

Can anyone suppose that the eminent men of the federal Convention could have overlooked or neglected a matter so vitally important to the country, in the organization of temporary governments for the vast territory northwest of the river Ohio? In the third section of the fourth article of the Constitution, they did make provision for the admission of new states, the sale of the public lands, and the temporary government of the territory. Without a temporary government, new states could not have been formed, nor could the public lands have been sold. . . .

In the discussion of the power of Congress to govern a territory, in the case of the *Atlantic Insurance Company v. Canter* . . . Chief Justice Marshall, speaking for the Court, said, in regard to the people of Florida: "They do not, however, participate in political power; they do not share in the government till Florida shall become a state; in the meantime, Florida continues to be a territory of the United States, governed by virtue of that clause in the Constitution which empowers Congress 'to make all needful rules and regulations respecting the territory or other property belonging to the United States.' " And he adds, "Perhaps the power of governing a territory belonging to the United States, which has not, by becoming a state, acquired the means of self-government, may result necessarily from the fact that it is not within the jurisdiction of any particular state, and is within the power and jurisdiction of the United States. The right to govern may be the inevitable consequence of the right to acquire territory; whichever may be the source whence the power is derived, the possession of it is unquestioned." . . .

The power to establish post offices and post roads gives power to Congress to make contracts for the transportation of the mail, and to punish all who commit depredations upon it in its transit, or at its places of distribution. Congress has power to regulate commerce, and, in the exercise of its discretion, to lay an embargo, which suspends commerce; so, under the same power, harbors, lighthouses, breakwaters, etc., are constructed.

Did Chief Justice Marshall, in saying that Congress governed a territory, by exercising the combined powers of the federal and state governments, refer to unlimited discretion? A government which can make white men slaves? Surely, such a remark in the argument must have been inadvertently uttered. On the contrary, there is no power in the Constitution by which Congress can make either white or black men slaves. In organizing the government of a territory, Congress is limited to means appropriate to the attainment of the constitutional object. No powers can be exercised which are prohibited by the Constitution, or which are contrary to its spirit; so that, whether the object may be the protection of the persons and property of purchasers of the public lands, or of communities who have been annexed to the Union by conquest or purchase, they are initiatory to the establishment of state governments, and no more power can be claimed or exercised than is necessary to the attainment of the end. This is the limitation of all the federal powers.

But Congress has no power to regulate the internal concerns of a state, as of a territory; consequently, in providing for the government of a territory, to some extent, the combined powers of the federal and state governments are necessarily exercised.

If Congress should deem slaves or free colored persons injurious to the population of a free territory, as conducing to lessen the value of the public lands, or on any other ground connected with the public interest, they have the power to prohibit them from becoming settlers in it. This can be sustained on the ground of a sound national policy, which is so clearly shown in our history by practical results that it would seem no considerate individual can question it. And, as regards any unfairness of such a policy to our Southern brethren, as urged in the argument, it is only necessary to say that, with one-fourth of the federal population of the Union, they have in the slave states a larger extent of fertile territory than is included in the free states; and it is submitted, if masters of slaves be restricted from bringing them into free territory, that the restriction on the free citizens of nonslaveholding states, by bringing slaves into free territory, is four times greater than that complained of by the South. But, not only so; some three or four hundred thousand holders of slaves, by bringing them into free territory, impose a restriction on twenty millions of the free states. The repugnancy to slavery would probably prevent fifty or a hundred freemen from settling in a slave territory, where one slaveholder would be prevented from settling in a free territory.

This remark is made in answer to the argument urged that a prohibition of slavery in the free territories is inconsistent with the continuance of the Union. Where a territorial government is established in a slave territory, it has uniformly remained in that condition until the people form a state Constitution; the same course where the territory is free, both parties acting in good faith, would be attended with satisfactory results.

The sovereignty of the federal government extends to the entire limits of our territory. Should any foreign power invade our jurisdiction, it would be repelled. There is a law of Congress to punish our citizens for crimes committed in districts of country where there is no organized government. Criminals are brought to certain territories or states, designated in the law, for punishment. Death has been inflicted in Arkansas and in Missouri, on individuals, for murders committed beyond the limit of any organized territory or state; and no one doubts that such a jurisdiction was rightfully exercised. If there be a right to acquire territory, there necessarily must be an implied power to govern it. When the military force of the Union shall conquer a country, may not Congress provide for the government of such country? This would be an implied power essential to the acquisition of new territory. This power has been exercised, without doubt of its constitutionality, over territory acquired by conquest and purchase. . . .

The prohibition of slavery north of thirty-six degrees thirty minutes, and of the state of Missouri, contained in the act admitting that state into the Union, was passed by a vote of 134, in the House of Representatives, to 42. Before Mr. Monroe signed the act, it was submitted by him to his Cabinet, and they held the restriction of slavery in a territory to be within the constitutional powers of Congress. It would be singular if in 1804 Congress had power to prohibit the introduction of slaves in Orleans Territory from any other part of the Union, under the penalty of freedom to the slave, if the same power, embodied in the Missouri Compromise, could not be exercised in 1820.

But this law of Congress, which prohibits slavery north of Missouri and of thirty-six degrees thirty minutes, is declared to have been null and void by my brethren. And this opinion is founded mainly, as I understand, on the distinction drawn between the Ordinance of 1787 and the Missouri Compromise line. In what does the distinction consist? The ordinance, it is said, was a compact entered into by the confederated states before the adoption of the Constitution; and that in the cession of territory authority was given to establish a territorial government.

It is clear that the ordinance did not go into operation by virtue of the authority of the Confederation, but by reason of its modification and adoption by Congress under the Constitution. It seems to be supposed, in the opinion of the court, that the articles of cession placed it on a different footing from territories subsequently acquired. I am unable to perceive the force of this distinction. That the ordinance was intended for the government of the Northwestern Territory, and was limited to such territory, is admitted. It was extended to Southern territories, with modifications, by acts of Congress, and to some Northern territories. But the ordinance was made valid by the act of Congress, and without such act could have been of no force. It rested for its validity on the act of Congress, the same, in my opinion, as the Missouri Compromise line.

If Congress may establish a territorial government in the exercise of its discretion, it is a clear principle that a court cannot control that discretion. This being the case, I do not see on what ground the act is held to be void. It did not purport to forfeit property, or take it for public purposes. It only prohibited slavery; in doing which, it followed the Ordinance of 1787.

I will now consider the effect of taking slaves into a state or territory, and so holding them, where slavery is prohibited.

If the principle laid down in the case of *Prigg v. The State of Pennsylvania* is to be maintained, and it is certainly to be maintained until overruled, as the law of this Court, there can be no difficulty on this point. In that case, the court says: "The state of slavery is deemed to be a mere municipal regulation, founded upon and limited to the range of the territorial laws." If this be so, slavery can exist nowhere except under the authority of law, founded on usage having the force of law, or by statutory recognition. And the Court further says: "It is manifest, from this consideration, that if the Constitution had not contained the clause requiring the rendition of fugitives from labor, every nonslaveholding state in the Union would have been at liberty to have declared free all runaway slaves coming within its limits, and to have given them entire immunity and protection against the claims of their masters."

Now, if a slave abscond, he may be reclaimed; but if he accompany his master into a state or territory where slavery is prohibited, such slave cannot be said to have left the service of his master where his services were legalized. And if slavery be limited to the range of the territorial laws, how can the slave be coerced to serve in a state or territory, not only without the authority of law, but against its express provisions? What gives the master the right to control the will of his slave? The local law, which exists in some form. But where there is no such law, can the master control the will of the slave by force? Where no slavery exists, the presumption, without regard to color, is in favor of freedom. Under such a jurisdiction, may the colored man be levied on as the property of his master by a creditor? On the decease of the master, does the slave descend to his heirs as property? Can the master sell him? Any one or all of these acts may be done to the slave, where he is legally held to service. But where the law does not confer this power, it cannot be exercised. . . .

By virtue of what law is it that a master may take his slave into free territory, and exact from him the duties of a slave? The law of the territory does not sanction it. No authority can be claimed under the Constitution of the United States, or any law of Congress. Will it be said that the slave is taken as property, the same as other property which the master may own? To this I answer that colored persons are made property by the law of the state, and no such power has been given to Congress. Does the master carry with him the law of the state from which he removes into the territory? And does that enable him to coerce his slave in the territory? Let us test this theory. If this may be done by a master from one slave state, it may be done by a master from every other slave state. This right is supposed to be connected with the person of the master, by virtue of the local law. Is it transferable? May it be negotiated, as a promissory note or bill of exchange? If it be assigned to a man from a free state, may he coerce the slave by virtue of it? What shall this thing be denominated? Is it personal or real property? Or is it an indefinable fragment of sovereignty, which every person carries with him from his late domicile? One thing is certain—that its origin has been very recent, and it is unknown to the laws of any civilized country. . . .

In this case, a majority of the Court have said that a slave may be taken by his master into a territory of the United States, the same as a horse, or any other kind of property. It is true, this was said by the Court, as also many other things, which are of no authority. Nothing that has been said by them, which has not a direct bearing on the jurisdiction of the Court, against which they decided, can be considered as authority. I shall certainly not regard it as such. The question of jurisdiction, being before the Court, was decided by them authoritatively, but nothing beyond that question. A slave is not a mere chattel. He bears the impress of his Maker, and is amenable to the laws of God and man; and he is destined to an endless existence. . . .

The first slave case decided by the Supreme Court of Missouri, contained in the reports, was *Winny v. Whitesides* . . . at October term, 1824. It appeared that, more than twenty-five years before, the defendant, with her husband, had removed from Carolina to Illinois, and brought with them the plaintiff; that they continued to reside in Illinois three or four years, retaining the plaintiff as a slave; after which, they removed to Missouri, taking her with them.

The court held, that if a slave be detained in Illinois until he be entitled to freedom, the right of the owner does not revive when he finds the Negro in a slave state; that when a slave is taken to Illinois by his owner, who takes up his residence there, the slave is entitled to freedom.

Rachel v. Walker . . . (June term, 1836) is a case involving, in every particular, the principles of the case before us. Rachel sued for her freedom; and it appeared that she had been bought as a slave in Missouri, by Stockton, an officer of the army, taken to Fort Snelling, where he was stationed, and she was retained there as a slave a year; and then Stockton removed to Prairie du Chien, taking Rachel with him as a slave, where he continued to hold her three years, and then he took her to the state of Missouri, and sold her as a slave.

"Fort Snelling was admitted to be on the west side of the Mississippi River, and north of the state of Missouri, in the territory of the United States. That Prairie du Chien was in the Michigan Territory, on the east side of the Mississippi River. Walker, the defendant, held Rachel under Stockton."

The court said, in this case:

"The officer lived in Missouri Territory, at the time he bought the slave; he sent to a slaveholding country and procured her; this was his voluntary act, done without any other reason than that of his convenience; and he and those claiming under him must be holden to abide the consequences of introducing slavery both in Missouri Territory and Michigan, contrary to law; and on that ground Rachel was declared to be entitled to freedom."

In answer to the argument that, as an officer of the army, the master had a right to take his slave into free territory, the court said no authority of law or the government compelled him to keep the plaintiff there as a slave.

"Shall it be said, that because an officer of the army owns slaves in Virginia, that when, as officer and soldier, he is required to take the command of a fort in the nonslaveholding states or territories, he thereby has a right to take with him as many slaves as will suit his interests or convenience? It surely cannot be law. If this be true, the court say, then it is also true that the convenience or supposed convenience of the officer repeals, as to him and others who have the same character, the ordinance and the act of 1821, admitting Missouri into the Union, and also the prohibition of the several laws and constitutions of the nonslaveholding states." . . .

The case of *Dred Scott v. Emerson* . . . (March term, 1852) will now be stated. This case involved the identical question before us, Emerson having, since the hearing, sold the plaintiff to Sandford, the defendant.

Two of the judges ruled the case, the chief justice dissenting. It cannot be improper to state the grounds of the opinion of the court, and of the dissent.

The court says: "Cases of this kind are not strangers in our court. Persons have been frequently here adjudged to be entitled to their freedom, on the ground that their masters held them in slavery in territories or states in which that institution is prohibited. From the first case decided in our court, it might be inferred that this result was brought about by a presumed assent of the master, from the fact of having voluntarily taken his slave to a place where the relation of master and slave did not exist. But subsequent cases base the right to 'exact the forfeiture of emancipation,' as they term it, on the ground, it would seem, that it was the duty of the courts of this state to carry into effect the Constitution and laws of other states and territories, regardless of the rights, the policy, or the institutions, of the people of this state." . . .

Chief Justice Gamble dissented from the other two judges. He says:

"In every slaveholding state in the Union, the subject of emancipation is regulated by statute; and the forms are prescribed in which it shall be effected. Whenever the forms required by the laws of the state in which the master and slave are resident are complied with, the emancipation is complete, and the slave is free. If the right of the person thus emancipated is subsequently drawn in question in another state, it will be ascertained and determined by the law of the state in which the slave and his former master resided; and when it appears that such law has been complied with, the right to freedom will be fully sustained in the courts of all the slaveholding states, although the act of emancipation may not be in the form required by law in which the court sits.

"In all such cases, courts continually administer the law of the country where the right was acquired; and when that law becomes known to the court, it is just as much a matter of course to decide the rights of the parties according to its requirements, as it is to settle the title of real estate situated in our state by its own laws."

This appears to me a most satisfactory answer to the argument of the court. The chief justice continues:

"The perfect equality of the different states lies at the foundation of the Union. As the institution of slavery in the states is one over which the Constitution of the United States gives no power to the general government, it is left to be adopted or rejected by the several states, as they think best; nor can any one state, or number of states, claim the right to interfere with any other state upon the question of admitting or excluding this institution.

"A citizen of Missouri, who removed with his slave to Illinois, has no right to complain that the fundamental law of that state to which he removes, and in which he makes his residence, dissolves the relation between him and his slave. It is as much his own voluntary act, as if he had executed a deed of emancipation. No one can pretend ignorance of this constitutional provision, and," he says, "the decisions which have heretofore been made in this state, and in many other slaveholding states, give effect to this and other similar provisions, on the ground that the master, by making the free state the residence of his slave, has submitted his right to the operation of the law of such state; and this," he says, "is the same in law as a regular deed of emancipation."

When Dred Scott, his wife and children, were removed from Fort Snelling to Missouri, in 1838, they were free, as the law was then settled, and continued for fourteen years afterwards, up to 1852, when the above decision was made. Prior to this, for nearly thirty years, as Chief Justice Gamble declares, the residence of a master with his slave in the state of Illinois, or in the territory north of Missouri, where slavery was prohibited by the act called the Missouri Compromise, would manumit the slave as effectually as if he had executed a deed of emancipation; and that an officer of the army who takes his slave into that state or territory, and holds him there as a slave, liberates him the same as any other citizen—and down to the above time it was settled by numerous and uniform decisions; and that on the return of the slave to Missouri, his former condition of slavery did not attach. Such was the settled law of Missouri until the decision of Scott and Emerson. . . .

There is no pretense that the case of *Dred Scott v. Emerson* turned upon the construction of a Missouri statute; nor was there any established rule of property which could have rightfully influenced the decision. On the contrary, the decision overruled the settled law for near thirty years.

This is said by my brethren to be a Missouri question; but there is nothing which gives it this character, except that it involves the right to persons claimed as slaves who reside in Missouri, and the decision was made by the Supreme Court of that state. It involves a right claimed under an act of Congress and the constitution of Illinois, and which cannot be decided without the consideration and construction of those laws. But the Supreme Court of Missouri held, in this case, that it will not regard either of those laws, without which there was no case before it; and Dred Scott, having been a slave, remains a slave. In this respect it is admitted this is a Missouri question—a case which has but one side, if the act of Congress and the Constitution of Illinois are not recognized.

And does such a case constitute a rule of decision for this Court—a case to be followed by this Court? The course of decision so long and so uniformly maintained established a comity of law between Missouri and the free states and territories where slavery was prohibited, which must be somewhat regarded in this case. Rights sanctioned for twenty-eight years ought not and cannot be repudiated, with any semblance of justice, by one or two decisions, influenced, as declared, by a determination to counteract the excitement against slavery in the free states. . . .

We [are now] to consider whether the status of slavery attached to the plaintiff and wife, on their return to Missouri. . . .

The slave states have generally adopted the rule that . . . [when] the master . . . [resided] with his slave in a state or territory where slavery is prohibited, the slave was entitled to his freedom everywhere. This was the settled doctrine of the Supreme Court of Missouri. It has been so held in Mississippi, in Virginia, in Louisiana, formerly in Kentucky, in Maryland, and in other states.

The law, where a contract is made and is to be executed, governs it. This does not depend upon comity, but upon the law of the contract. And if, in the language of the Supreme Court of Missouri, the master, by taking his slave to Illinois, and employing him there as a slave, emancipates him as effectually as by a deed of emancipation, is it possible that such an act is not matter for adjudication in any slave state where the master may take him? Does not the master assent to the law, when he places himself under it in a free state?

The states of Missouri and Illinois are bounded by a common line. The one prohibits slavery, the other admits it. This has been done by the exercise of that sovereign power which appertains to each. We are bound to respect the institutions of each, as emanating from the voluntary action of the people. Have the people of either any right to disturb the relations of the other? Each state rests upon the basis of its own sovereignty, protected by the Constitution. Our Union has been the foundation of our prosperity and national glory. Shall we not cherish and maintain it? This can only be done by respecting the legal rights of each state.

If a citizen of a free state shall entice or enable a slave to escape from the service of his master, the law holds him responsible, not only for the loss of the slave, but he is liable to be indicted and fined for the misdemeanor. And I am bound here to say, that I have never found a jury in the four states which constitute my circuit, which have not sustained this law, where the evidence required them to sustain it. And it is proper that I should also say, that more cases have arisen in my circuit, by reason of its extent and locality, than in all other parts of the Union. This has been done to vindicate the sovereign rights of the Southern states, and protect the legal interests of our brethren of the South.

Let these facts be contrasted with the case now before the court. Illinois has declared in the most solemn and impressive form that there shall be neither slavery nor involuntary servitude in that state, and that any slave brought into it, with a view of becoming a resident, shall be emancipated. And effect has been given to this provision of the Constitution by the decision of the Supreme Court of that state. With a full knowledge of these facts, a slave is brought from Missouri to Rock Island, in the state of Illinois, and is retained there as a slave for two years, and then taken to Fort Snelling, where slavery is prohibited by the Missouri Compromise act, and there he is detained two years longer in a state of slavery. Harriet, his wife, was also kept at the same place four years as a slave, having been purchased in Missouri. They were then removed to the state of Missouri, and sold as slaves, and in the action before us they are not only claimed as slaves, but a majority of my brethren have held that on their being returned to Missouri the status of slavery attached to them.

I am not able to reconcile this result with the respect due to the state of Illinois. Having the same rights of sovereignty as the state of Missouri in adopting a Constitution, I can perceive no reason why the institutions of Illinois should not receive the same consideration as those of Missouri. Allowing to my brethren the same right of judgment that I exercise myself, I must be permitted to say that it seems to me the principle laid down will enable the people of a slave state to introduce slavery into a free state, for a longer or shorter time, as may suit their convenience; and by returning the slave to the state whence he was brought, by force or otherwise, the status of slavery attaches, and protects the rights of the master, and defies the sovereignty of the free state. There is no evidence before us that Dred Scott and his family returned to Missouri voluntarily. The contrary is inferable from the agreed case: "In the year 1838, Dr. Emerson removed the plaintiff and said Harriet, and their daughter Eliza, from Fort Snelling to the state of Missouri, where they have ever since resided." This is the agreed case; and can it be inferred from this that Scott and family returned to Missouri voluntarily? He was removed; which shows that he was passive, as a slave, having exercised no volition on the subject. He did not resist the master by absconding or force. . . . It would be a mockery of law and an outrage on his rights to coerce his return, and then claim that it was voluntary, and on that ground that his former status of slavery attached.

If the decision be placed on this ground, it is a fact for a jury to decide whether the return was voluntary, or else the fact should be distinctly admitted. A presumption against the plaintiff in this respect, I say with confidence, is not authorized from the facts admitted. . . .

I now come to inquire . . . whether the decisions of the Supreme Court of Missouri, on the question before us, are binding on this court. . . .

For twenty-eight years, the decisions of the Supreme Court of Missouri were consistent on all the points made in this case. But this consistent course was suddenly terminated, whether by some new light suddenly springing up, or an excited public opinion, or both, it is not necessary to say. In the case of *Scott v. Emerson*, in 1852, they were overturned and repudiated.

This, then, is the very case in which seven of my brethren declared they would not follow the last decision. On this authority I may well repose. I can desire no other or better basis.

But there is another ground which I deem conclusive, and which I will restate.

The Supreme Court of Missouri refused to notice the act of Congress or the Constitution of Illinois, under which Dred Scott, and his wife and children claimed that they are entitled to freedom.

This being rejected by the Missouri court, there was no case before it, or least it was a case with only one side. And this is the case which, in the opinion of this Court, we are bound to follow. The Missouri court disregards the express provisions of an act of Congress and the Constitution of a sovereign state, both of which laws for twenty-eight years it had not only regarded, but carried into effect.

If a state court may do this, on a question involving the liberty of a human being, what protection do the laws afford? So far from this being a Missouri question, it is a question, as it would seem, within the twenty-fifth section of the Judiciary Act, where a right to freedom being set up under the act of Congress, and the decision being against such right, it may be brought for revision before this Court, from the Supreme Court of Missouri.

I think the judgment of the Court below should be reversed.

JOHN BROWN

— ★ —

A Holy War Against Slavery

Interrogation After His Capture at Harper's Ferry, October 19, 1859

John Brown (1800–1859) was a fanatical abolitionist who was regarded as a martyr and legendary folk hero after his death by hanging. Brown fought for the education and freedom of blacks throughout his life before settling into a pattern of terrorism against proslavery adherents in Kansas and Missouri. In 1857 he began preparations to free the slaves by armed force. On October 16, 1859, Brown and a band of eighteen men seized the U.S. Arsenal at Harper's Ferry, Virginia (now West Virginia). The next day the local militia surrounding the arsenal was augmented by a force of U.S. marines led by Colonel Robert E. Lee. After ten of his men were killed, Brown surrendered. He was subsequently tried for treason and murder and was executed on December 2, 1859. A day after his capture, while he lay seriously wounded in the office of the armory at Harper's Ferry, Brown was questioned by a number of prominent political and military figures.

SENATOR MASON. Can you tell us who furnished money for your expedition?

JOHN BROWN. I furnished most of it myself; I cannot implicate others. It is by my own folly that I have been taken. I could easily have saved myself from it, had I exercised my own better judgment rather than yielded to my feelings.

MASON. You mean if you had escaped immediately?

BROWN. No. I had the means to make myself secure without any escape; but I allowed myself to be surrounded by a force by being too tardy. I should have gone away; but I had

94

thirty-odd prisoners, whose wives and daughters were in tears for their safety, and I felt for them. Besides, I wanted to allay the fears of those who believed we came here to burn and kill. For this reason I allowed the train to cross the bridge, and gave them full liberty to pass on. I did it only to spare the feelings of those passengers and their families, and to allay the apprehensions that you had got here in your vicinity a band of men who had no regard for life and property, nor any feelings of humanity.

MASON. But you killed some people passing along the streets quietly.

BROWN. Well, sir, if there was anything of that kind done, it was without my knowledge. Your own citizens who were my prisoners will tell you that every possible means was taken to prevent it. I did not allow my men to fire when there was danger of killing those we regarded as innocent persons, if I could help it. They will tell you that we allowed ourselves to be fired at repeatedly, and did not return it.

A BYSTANDER. That is not so. You killed an unarmed man at the corner of the house over there at the water tank, and another besides.

BROWN. See here, my friend; it is useless to dispute or contradict the report of your own neighbors who were my prisoners.

MASON. If you would tell us who sent you here—who provided the means—that would be information of some value.

BROWN. I will answer freely and faithfully about what concerns myself—I will answer anything I can with honor—but not about others.

MR. VALLANDIGHAM. Mr. Brown, who sent you here?

BROWN. No man sent me here; it was my own prompting and that of my Maker, or that of the Devil—whichever you please to ascribe it to. I acknowledge no master in human form.

VALLANDIGHAM. Did you get up the expedition yourself?

BROWN. I did.

VALLANDIGHAM. Did you get up this document that is called a constitution?

BROWN. I did. They are a constitution and ordinances of my own contriving and getting up.

VALLANDIGHAM. How long have you been engaged in this business?

BROWN. From the breaking out of the difficulties in Kansas. Four of my sons had gone there to settle, and they induced me to go. I did not go there to settle, but because of the difficulties.

MASON. How many are there engaged with you in this movement?

BROWN. Any questions that I can honorably answer I will—not otherwise. So far as I am myself concerned, I have told everything truthfully. I value my word, sir.

MASON. What was your object in coming?

BROWN. We came to free the slaves, and only that.

A VOLUNTEER. How many men, in all, had you?

BROWN. I came to Virginia with eighteen men only, besides myself.

VOLUNTEER. What in the world did you suppose you could do here in Virginia with that amount of men?

BROWN. Young man, I do not wish to discuss that question here.

VOLUNTEER. You could not do anything.

BROWN. Well, perhaps your ideas and mine on military subjects would differ materially.

MASON. How do you justify your acts?

BROWN. I think, my friend, you are guilty of a great wrong against God and humanity—I say it without wishing to be offensive—and it would be perfectly right for anyone to interfere with you so far as to free those you willfully and wickedly hold in bondage. I do not say this insultingly.

MASON. I understand that.

BROWN. I think I did right, and that others will do right who interfere with you at any time and at all times. I hold that the Golden Rule, "Do unto others as ye would that others should do unto you," applies to all who would help others to gain their liberty. . . .

MASON. Did you consider this a military organization in this constitution? I have not yet read it.

BROWN. I did, in some sense. I wish you would give that paper close attention.

MASON. You consider yourself the commander in chief of these "provisional" military forces?

BROWN. I was chosen, agreeably to the ordinance of a certain document, commander in chief of that force.

MASON. What wages did you offer?

BROWN. None.

STUART. "The wages of sin is death."

BROWN. I would not have made such a remark to you if you had been a prisoner, and wounded, in my hands.

A BYSTANDER. Did you not promise a Negro in Gettysburg twenty dollars a month?

BROWN. I did not.

MASON. Does this talking annoy you?

BROWN. Not in the least.

VALLANDIGHAM. Have you lived long in Ohio?

BROWN. I went there in 1805. I lived in Summit County, which was then Portage County. My native place is Connecticut; my father lived there till 1805.

VALLANDIGHAM. Have you been in Portage County lately?

BROWN. I was there in June last.

VALLANDIGHAM. When in Cleveland, did you attend the Fugitive Slave Law Convention there?

BROWN. No. I was there about the time of the sitting of the court to try the Oberlin rescuers. I spoke there publicly on that subject—on the Fugitive Slave Law and my own rescue. Of course, so far as I had any influence at all, I was supposed to justify the Oberlin people for rescuing the slave, because I have myself forcibly taken slaves from bondage. I was concerned in taking eleven slaves from Missouri to Canada last winter. I think I spoke in Cleveland before the convention. I do not know that I had conversation with any of the Oberlin rescuers. I was sick part of the time I was in Ohio with the ague, in Ashtabula County.

VALLANDIGHAM. Did you see anything of Joshua R. Giddings there?

BROWN. I did meet him.

VALLANDIGHAM. Did you converse with him?

BROWN. I did. I would not tell you, of course, anything that would implicate Mr. Giddings; but I certainly met with him and had conversations with him.

VALLANDIGHAM. About that rescue case?

BROWN. Yes; I heard him express his opinions upon it very freely and frankly.

VALLANDIGHAM. Justifying it?

BROWN. Yes, sir; I do not compromise him, certainly, in saying that.

VALLANDIGHAM. Will you answer this: Did you talk with Giddings about your expedition here?

BROWN. No, I won't answer that; because a denial of it I would not make, and to make any affirmation of it I should be a great dunce.

VALLANDIGHAM. Have you had any correspondence with parties at the North on the subject of this movement?

BROWN. I have had correspondence.

A BYSTANDER. Do you consider this a religious movement?

BROWN. It is, in my opinion, the greatest service man can render to God.

BYSTANDER. Do you consider yourself an instrument in the hands of Providence?

BROWN. I do.

BYSTANDER. Upon what principle do you justify your acts?

BROWN. Upon the Golden Rule. I pity the poor in bondage that have none to help them: that is why I am here; not to gratify any personal animosity, revenge, or vindictive spirit. It is my sympathy with the oppressed and the wronged, that are as good as you and as precious in the sight of God.

BYSTANDER. Certainly. But why take the slaves against their will?

BROWN. I never did.

BYSTANDER. You did in one instance, at least. . . .

VALLANDIGHAM. Who are your advisers in this movement?

BROWN. I cannot answer that. I have numerous sympathizers throughout the entire North.

VALLANDIGHAM. In northern Ohio?

BROWN. No more there than anywhere else; in all the free states.

VALLANDIGHAM. But you are not personally acquainted in southern Ohio?

BROWN. Not very much.

A BYSTANDER. Did you ever live in Washington City?

BROWN. I did not. I want you to understand, gentlemen —and [to the reporter of the *Herald*] you may report that—I want you to understand that I respect the rights of the poorest and weakest of colored people, oppressed by the slave system, just as much as I do those of the most wealthy and powerful. That is the idea that has moved me, and that alone. We expected no reward except the satisfaction of endeavoring to do for those in distress and greatly oppressed as we would be done by. The cry of distress of the oppressed is my reason, and the only thing that prompted me to come here.

BYSTANDER. Why did you do it secretly?

BROWN. Because I thought that necessary to success; no other reason.

BYSTANDER. Have you read Gerrit Smith's last letter?

BROWN. What letter do you mean?

BYSTANDER. The New York *Herald* of yesterday, in speaking of this affair, mentions a letter in this way:

> Apropos of this exciting news, we recollect a very significant passage in one of Gerrit Smith's letters, published a month or two ago, in which he speaks of the folly of attempting to strike the shackles off the slaves by the force of moral suasion or legal

agitation, and predicts that the next movement made in the direction of Negro emancipation would be an insurrection in the South.

BROWN. I have not seen the New York *Herald* for some days past; but I presume, from your remark about the gist of the letter, that I should concur with it. I agree with Mr. Smith that moral suasion is hopeless. I don't think the people of the slave states will ever consider the subject of slavery in its true light till some other argument is resorted to than moral suasion.

VALLANDIGHAM. Did you expect a general rising of the slaves in case of your success?

BROWN. No, sir; nor did I wish it. I expected to gather them up from time to time, and set them free.

VALLANDIGHAM. Did you expect to hold possession here till then?

BROWN. Well, probably I had quite a different idea. I do not know that I ought to reveal my plans. I am here a prisoner and wounded, because I foolishly allowed myself to be so. You overrate your strength in supposing I could have been taken if I had not allowed it. I was too tardy after commencing the open attack—in delaying my movements through Monday night, and up to the time I was attacked by the government troops. It was all occasioned by my desire to spare the feelings of my prisoners and their families and the community at large. I had no knowledge of the shooting of the Negro Heywood.

VALLANDIGHAM. What time did you commence your organization in Canada?

BROWN. That occurred about two years ago; in 1858.

VALLANDIGHAM. Who was the secretary?

BROWN. That I would not tell if I recollected; but I do not recollect. I think the officers were elected in May 1858. I may answer incorrectly, but not intentionally. My head is a little confused by wounds, and my memory obscure on dates, etc. . . .

REPORTER. I do not wish to annoy you; but if you have anything further you would like to say, I will report it.

BROWN. I have nothing to say, only that I claim to be here in carrying out a measure I believe perfectly justifiable, and not to act the part of an incendiary or ruffian, but to aid those suffering great wrong. I wish to say, furthermore, that you had better—all you people at the South—prepare yourselves for a settlement of this question, that must come up for settlement sooner than you are prepared for it. The sooner you are prepared the better. You may dispose of me very easily—I am nearly disposed of now; but this question is still to be settled— this Negro question I mean; the end of that is not yet. These wounds were inflicted upon me—both saber cuts on my head and bayonet stabs in different parts of my body—some minutes after I had ceased fighting and had consented to surrender, for the benefit of others, not for my own. I believe the major would not have been alive; I could have killed him just as easy as a mosquito when he came in, but I supposed he only came in to receive our surrender. There had been loud and long calls of "surrender" from us, as loud as men could yell; but in the confusion and excitement I suppose we were not heard. I do not think the major, or anyone, meant to butcher us after we had surrendered.

AN OFFICER. Why did you not surrender before the attack?

BROWN. I did not think it was my duty or interest to do so. We assured the prisoners that we did not wish to harm them, and they should be set at liberty. I exercised my best judgment, not believing the people would wantonly sacrifice their own fellow citizens, when we offered to let them go on condition of being allowed to change our position about a quarter of a mile. The prisoners agreed by a vote among themselves to pass across the bridge with us. We wanted them only as a sort of guarantee of our own safety—that we should not be fired into. We took them, in the first place, as hostages and to keep them from doing any harm. We did kill some men in defending ourselves, but I saw no one fire except directly in self-defense. Our orders were strict not to harm anyone not in arms against us.

JEFFERSON DAVIS

—— ★ ——

Inaugural Address as President of the Provisional Government of the Confederate States of America

Capitol, Montgomery, Alabama, February 18, 1861

Born in Kentucky, Jefferson Davis (1808–1889) graduated from West Point in 1828 and was a planter in Mississippi from 1835 to 1845. He became a representative from Mississippi in Congress in 1845, but resigned to serve in the Mexican War. He was U.S. senator from Mississippi, 1847–1851 and 1857–1861, and he served as secretary of war under President Franklin Pierce from 1853 to 1857. Davis was a prominent supporter of slavery and states' rights, and the leading advocate of the Southern position. When Kentucky seceded from the Union, Davis resigned from the Senate. Before his popular election to a six-year term as president of the Confederacy in 1861 and his official inauguration on February 22, 1862, he was already serving as provisional president, having been appointed by the Congress of the Confederate States. Davis's address at his first inauguration was delivered on February 18, 1861.

Gentlemen of the Congress of the Confederate States of America, Friends, and Fellow Citizens: Called to the difficult and responsible station of chief magistrate of the Provisional Government which you have instituted, I approach the discharge of the duties assigned to me with humble distrust of my abilities, but with a sustaining confidence in the wisdom of those who are to guide and aid me in the administration of public affairs, and an abiding faith in the virtue and patriotism of the people. Looking forward to the speedy establishment of a permanent government to take the place of this, which by its greater moral and physical power will be better able to combat with many difficulties that arise from the conflicting interests of separate nations, I enter upon the duties of the office to which I have been chosen with the hope that the beginning of our career, as a Confederacy, may not be obstructed by hostile opposition to our enjoyment of the separate existence and independence we have asserted, and which, with the blessing of Providence, we intend to maintain.

Our present political position has been achieved in a manner unprecedented in the history of nations. It illustrates the American idea that governments rest on the consent of the governed, and that it is the right of the people to alter or abolish them at will whenever they become destructive of the ends for which they were established. The declared purpose of the compact of the Union from which we have withdrawn was to "establish justice, insure domestic tranquillity, provide for the common defense, promote the general welfare, and secure the blessings of liberty to ourselves and our posterity"; and when, in the judgment of the sovereign states composing this Confederacy, it has been perverted from the purposes for which it was ordained, and ceased to answer the ends for which it was established, a peaceful appeal to the ballot box declared that, so far as they are concerned, the government created by that compact should cease to exist. In this they merely asserted the right which the Declaration of Independence of July 4, 1776, defined to be "inalienable." Of the time and occasion of its exercise they as sovereigns were the final judges, each for itself. The impartial and enlightened verdict of mankind will vindicate the rectitude of our conduct; and He who knows the hearts of men will judge of the sincerity with which we have labored to preserve the government of our fathers in its spirit.

The right solemnly proclaimed at the birth of the United States, and which has been solemnly affirmed and reaffirmed in the Bills of Rights of the states subsequently admitted into the Union of 1789, undeniably recognizes in the people the power to resume the authority delegated for the purposes of government.

Thus the sovereign states here represented have proceeded to form this Confederacy; and it is by abuse of language that their act has been denominated a revolution. They formed a new alliance, but within each state its government has remained; so that the rights of person and property have not been disturbed. The agent through which they communicated with foreign nations is changed, but this does not necessarily interrupt their international relations. Sustained by the consciousness that the transition from the former Union to the present Confederacy has not proceeded from a disregard on our part of just obligations, or any failure to perform every constitutional duty, moved by no interest or passion to invade the rights of others, anxious to cultivate peace and commerce with all nations, if we may not hope to avoid war, we may at least expect that posterity will acquit us of having needlessly engaged in it. Doubly justified by the absence of wrong on our part, and by wanton aggression on the part of others, there can be no cause to doubt that the courage and patriotism of the people of the Confederate States will be found equal to any measure of defense which their honor and security may require.

An agricultural people, whose chief interest is the export of commodities required in every manufacturing country, our true policy is peace, and the freest trade which our necessities will permit. It is alike our interest and that of all those to whom we would sell, and from whom we would buy, that there should be the fewest practicable restrictions upon the interchange of these commodities. There can, however, be but little rivalry between ours and any manufacturing or navigating community, such as the northeastern states of the American Union. It must follow, therefore, that mutual interest will invite to good will and kind offices on both parts. If, however, passion or lust of dominion should cloud the judgment or inflame the ambition of those states, we must prepare to meet the emergency and maintain, by the final arbitrament of the sword, the position which we have assumed among the nations of the earth.

We have entered upon the career of independence, and it

must be inflexibly pursued. Through many years of controversy with our late associates of the Northern states, we have vainly endeavored to secure tranquillity and obtain respect for the rights to which we were entitled. As a necessity, not a choice, we have resorted to the remedy of separation, and henceforth our energies must be directed to the conduct of our own affairs, and the perpetuity of the Confederacy which we have formed. If a just perception of mutual interest shall permit us peaceably to pursue our separate political career, my most earnest desire will have been fulfilled. But if this be denied to us, and the integrity of our territory and jurisdiction be assailed, it will but remain for us with firm resolve to appeal to arms and invoke the blessing of Providence on a just cause.

As a consequence of our new condition and relations, and with a view to meet anticipated wants, it will be necessary to provide for the speedy and efficient organization of branches of the executive department having special charge of foreign intercourse, finance, military affairs, and the postal service. For purposes of defense, the Confederate States may, under ordinary circumstances, rely mainly upon the militia; but it is deemed advisable, in the present condition of affairs, that there should be a well-instructed and disciplined army, more numerous than would usually be required on a peace establishment. I also suggest that, for the protection of our harbors and commerce on the high seas, a navy adapted to those objects will be required. But this, as well as other subjects appropriate to our necessities, have doubtless engaged the attention of Congress.

With a Constitution differing only from that of our fathers insofar as it is explanatory of their well-known intent, freed from sectional conflicts, which have interfered with the pursuit of the general welfare, it is not unreasonable to expect that states from which we have recently parted may seek to unite their fortunes to ours under the government which we have instituted. For this your Constitution makes adequate provision; but beyond this, if I mistake not the judgment and will of the people, a reunion with the states from which we have separated is neither practicable nor desirable. To increase the power, develop the resources, and promote the happiness of the Confederacy, it is requisite that there should be so much of homogeneity that the welfare of every portion shall be the aim of the whole. When this does not exist, antagonisms are engendered which must and should result in separation.

Actuated solely by the desire to preserve our own rights, and promote our own welfare, the separation by the Confederate States has been marked by no aggression upon others, and followed by no domestic convulsion. Our industrial pursuits have received no check, the cultivation of our fields has progressed as heretofore, and, even should we be involved in war, there would be no considerable diminution in the production of the staples which have constituted our exports, and in which the commercial world has an interest scarcely less than our own. This common interest of the producer and consumer can only be interrupted by exterior force which would obstruct the transmission of our staples to foreign markets—a course of conduct which would be as unjust, as it would be detrimental, to manufacturing and commercial interests abroad.

Should reason guide the action of the government from which we have separated, a policy so detrimental to the civilized world, the Northern states included, could not be dictated by even the strongest desire to inflict injury upon us; but, if the contrary should prove true, a terrible responsibility will rest upon it, and the suffering of millions will bear testimony to the folly and wickedness of our aggressors. In the meantime there will remain to us, besides the ordinary means before suggested, the well-known resources for retaliation upon the commerce of an enemy.

Experience in public stations, of subordinate grade to this which your kindness has conferred, has taught me that toil and care and disappointment are the price of official elevation. You will see many errors to forgive, many deficiencies to tolerate; but you shall not find in me either want of zeal or fidelity to the cause that is to me the highest in hope, and of most enduring affection. Your generosity has bestowed upon me an undeserved distinction, one which I neither sought nor desired. Upon the continuance of that sentiment, and upon your wisdom and patriotism, I rely to direct and support me in the performance of the duties required at my hands.

We have changed the constituent parts, but not the system of government. The Constitution framed by our fathers is that of these Confederate States. In their exposition of it, and in the judicial construction it has received, we have a light which reveals its true meaning.

Thus instructed as to the true meaning and just interpretation of that instrument, and ever remembering that all offices are but trusts held for the people, and that powers delegated are to be strictly construed, I will hope by due diligence in the performance of my duties, though I may disappoint your expectations, yet to retain, when retiring, something of the good will and confidence which welcome my entrance into office.

It is joyous in the midst of perilous times to look around upon a people united in heart, where one purpose of high resolve animates and actuates the whole; where the sacrifices to be made are not weighed in the balance against honor and right and liberty and equality. Obstacles may retard, but they cannot long prevent, the progress of a movement sanctified by its justice and sustained by a virtuous people. Reverently let us invoke the God of our fathers to guide and protect us in our efforts to perpetuate the principles which by his blessing they were able to vindicate, establish, and transmit to their posterity. With the continuance of his favor ever gratefully acknowledged, we may hopefully look forward to success, to peace, and to prosperity.

SOJOURNER TRUTH

———— ★ ————

In Commemoration of the Eighth Anniversary of the Emancipation of the Slaves in the United States

Speech at Tremont Temple,
Boston, Massachusetts, January 1, 1871

Sojourner Truth (1797–1883) was a New York slave who, free from 1827, became an abolitionist, evangelist, storyteller, and women's rights advocate. She worked for her causes and the rights of freed persons from her home in Battle Creek, Michigan, and was held in high esteem by such persons as William Lloyd Garrison, Harriet Beecher Stowe, and Abraham Lincoln, as well as by the leading feminists of the period. She attended the First National Women's Rights Convention in Worcester, Massachusetts, in 1850 and spoke at the Ohio Women's Rights Convention in Akron the following year. In celebration of the eighth anniversary of emancipation, a major meeting was held at Tremont Temple in Boston on January 1, 1871, sponsored by the National Association for the Spread of Temperance and Night Schools Among the Freed People of the South. Sojourner Truth was among the many distinguished speakers.

Well, children, I'm glad to see so many together. If I am eighty-three years old, I only count my age from the time that I was emancipated. Then I began to live. God is fulfilling, and my lost time that I lost being a slave was made up. When I was a slave I hated the white people. My mother said to me when I was to be sold from her, "I want to tell you these things that you will always know that I have told you, for there will be a great many things told you after I start out of this life into the world to come." And I say this to you all, for here is a great many people that when I step out of this existence, that you will know what you heard old Sojoun' Truth tell you.

I was born a slave in the state of New York, Ulster County, among the low Dutch. When I was ten years old, I couldn't speak a word of English, and had no education at all. There's wonder what they has done for me. As I told you, when I was sold my master died, and we was going to have an auction. We was all brought up to be sold. My mother, my father who was very old, my brother younger than myself; and my mother took my hand. They opened a canopy of heaven. And she sat down and I and my brother sat down by her, and she says, "Look up to the moon and stars that shine upon your father and your mother when you're sold far away, "and upon your brothers and sisters that is sold away," for there was a great number of us, and was all sold away before my 'membrance. I asked her who had made the moon and the stars, and she says, "God," and says I, "Where is God?" "Oh!" says she, "child, he sits in the sky, and he hears you when you ask him when you are away from us to make your master and mistress good, and he will do it."

When we were sold, I did what my mother told me. I said, "Oh God, my mother told me if I asked you to make my master and mistress good, you'd do it, and they didn't get good. Why," says I, "God, maybe you can't do it. Kill 'em." I didn't think he could make them good. That was the idea I had. After I made such wishes my conscience burned me. Then I would say, "Oh God, don't be mad. My master made me wicked." And I often thought how people can do such 'bominable wicked things and their conscience not burn them. Now I only made wishes. I used to tell God this: I would say, "Now, God, if I was you, and you was me, and you wanted any help, I'd help you; why don't you help me?" Well, you see I was in want, and I felt that there was no help. I know what it is to be taken in the barn and tied up and the blood drawed out of your back, and I tell you it would make you think about God. Yes, and then I felt, "Oh God, if I was you and you felt like I do, and asked me for help, I would help you—now why won't you help me?"

Truly I don't know but God has helped me. But I got no good master until the last time I was sold, and then I found one and his name was Jesus. Oh, I tell you, didn't I find a good master when I used to feel so bad, when I used to say, "Oh God, how can I live? I'm sorely pressed both within and without"? When God give me that master he healed all the wounds up. My soul rejoiced. I used to hate the white people so, and I tell you when the love come in me I had so much love I didn't know what to love. Then the white people came, and I thought that love was too good for them. Then I said, "Yea, God, I'll love everybody and the white people too." Ever since that, that love has continued and kept me among the white people. Well, 'mancipation came; we all know; can't stop to go through the whole. I go for agitatin'. But I believe there is works belong with agitatin' too. Only think of it! Ain't it wonderful that God gives love enought to the Ethiopians to love you?

Now, here is the question that I am here tonight to say. I been to Washington, and I find out this: that the colored people that is in Washington livin' on the government—that the United States ought to give them land and move them on it. They are livin' on the government, and there is people taking care of them costing you so much, and it don't benefit them at all. It degrades them worse and worse.

Therefore I say that these people—take and put them in the West where you can enrich them. I know the good people in the South can't take care of the Negroes as they ought to, cause the rebels won't let them. How much better will it be to take them colored people and give them land! We've earned land enough for a home, and it would be a benefit for you all and God would bless the whole of you for doin' it. They say let 'em take care of themselves. Why, you've taken that all away from them. Ain't got nothing left. Get these colored people out of Washington off of the government, and get the old people out and build them homes in the West, where they can feed themselves, and they would soon be able to be a people among you.

That is my commission. Now educate them people and put them there; learn them to read one part of the time and learn them to work the other part of the time.

Elizabeth Cady Stanton

——— ★ ———

Women's Right to Suffrage

Memorial to the U.S. Senate Judiciary Committee,
January 10, 1872

After marrying the abolitionist Henry B. Stanton in 1840, Eliza-
beth Cady Stanton (1815–1902) honeymooned in London and
attended the World's Anti-Slavery Convention. There she met
Lucretia Mott, another American abolitionist. Years later, in the
Stantons' home town of Seneca Falls, New York, the two
women organized the first Woman's Rights Convention. For the
rest of the century, Cady Stanton agitated for women's rights
and suffrage. With Susan B. Anthony she formed the National
Woman Suffrage Association in 1869. But in the 1870s and 1880s,
as she developed an antireligious bias and increasingly adopted
more radical positions—for liberalized divorce laws, pregnancy
avoidance, and sexual freedom—she began to find herself out-
side the mainstream of the women's movement, which had
become allied with the Christian-oriented temperance move-
ment. In 1872 she presented the case for full voting rights for
women before the Judiciary Committee of the U.S. Senate.

Gentlemen of the Judiciary Committee: We appear before
you at this time to call your attention to our memorial
asking for a declaratory act that shall protect women in the
exercise of the right of suffrage. Benjamin F. Butler, early in the
session, presented a bill in the House to this effect that may
soon, in the order of legislation, come before you for consideration in the Senate of the United States. As you well know,
women are demanding their rights as citizens today under the
original Constitution, believing that its letter and spirit, fairly
interpreted, guarantee the blessings of liberty to every citizen
under our flag. But more especially do we claim that our title

deed to the elective franchise is clearly given in the Fourteenth and Fifteenth amendments. Therein, for the first time, the Constitution defines the term *citizen* and, in harmony with our best lexicographers, declares a citizen to be a person possessed of the right to vote. In the last year the question of woman's political status has been raised from one of vague generalities to one of constitutional law. . . .

Gentlemen hold seats in Congress today by the votes of women. The legality of the election of Mr. Garfield, of Washington Territory, and Mr. Jones, of Wyoming, involves the question whether or not their constituents are legal voters. Ultimately, this question, involving the fundamental rights of citizens, must be considered in the Senate as well as the House. Women have voted in the general elections in several of the states, and if legislators chosen by women choose senators, their right to their seats cannot be decided until it is first decided whether women are legal voters. Some speedy action on this question is inevitable, to preserve law and order.

In some states women have already voted; in others they are contesting their rights in the courts, and the decisions of judges differ as widely as the capacities of men to see first principles.

Judge Howe, Judge Cartter, and Judge Underwood have given their written opinions in favor of woman's citizenship under the Fourteenth and Fifteenth amendments. Even the majority report of the Judiciary Committee, presented by John A. Bingham, though adverse to the prayer of Victoria Woodhull, admits the citizenship of woman. In the late cases of Sarah Spencer against the Board of Registration, and Sarah E. Webster against the superintendent of election, the judge decided that under the Fourteenth Amendment women are citizens.

We do not ask to vote outside of law, or in open violation of it, nor to avail ourselves of any strained interpretations of constitutional provisions, but in harmony with the federal Constitution, the Declaration of Independence, and our American theory of just government. The women of this country and a handful of foreign citizens in Rhode Island, the only disfranchised classes, ask you today to secure to them a republican form of government to protect them against the oppression of state authorities, who, in violation of your amendments, assume the right not merely to regulate the suffrage but to abridge and deny it to these two classes of citizens. The federal Constitution, in its amendment, clearly defines, for the first time, who are citizens: "All persons born or naturalized in the United States, and subject to the jurisdiction thereof, are citizens of the United States, and of the states wherein they reside."

No one denies that "all persons," in the Fourteenth Amendment, is used without limitation of sex or, in other words, that not men only but women also are citizens. Whether in theory the citizenship of women is generally admitted or not, it certainly is in practice. Women preempt land; women register ships; women obtain passports; women pay the penalty of their own crimes; women pay taxes, sometimes work out the road tax. In some states, even married women can make contracts, sue and be sued, and do business in their own names; in fact, the old Blackstone idea that husband and wife are one, and that one the husband, received its death blow twenty years ago, when the states of New York and Massachusetts passed their first laws securing to married women the property they inherited in their own right.

You may consider me presumptuous, gentlemen, but I claim to be a citizen of the United States, with all the qualifications of a voter. I can read the Constitution, I am possessed of $250, and the last time I looked in the old family Bible I found I was over twenty-one years of age.

"Individual rights," "Individual conscience and judgment" are great American ideas, underlying our whole political and religious life. We are here today to ask a Congress of Republicans for that crowning act that shall secure to fifteen million women the right to protect their persons, property, and opinions by law. The Fourteenth Amendment, having told us who are citizens of the Republic, further declares that "no state shall make or enforce any law which shall abridge the 'privileges or immunities' of 'citizens' of the United States." Some say that "privileges and immunities" do not include the right of suffrage. We answer that any person under government who has no voice in the laws or the rulers has his privileges and immunities abridged at every turn, and when a state denies the right of suffrage, it robs the citizen of his citizenship and of all power to protect his person or property by law.

Disfranchised classes are ever helpless and degraded classes. One can readily judge the political status of a citizen by the tone of the press. Go back a few years, and you find the Irishman the target for all the gibes and jeers of the nation. You could scarce take up a paper without finding some joke about "Pat" and his last bull. But in process of time "Pat" became a political power in the land, and editors and politicians could not afford to make fun of him. Then "Sambo" took his turn. They ridiculed his thick skull, woolly head, shinbone, long heel, etc., but he, too, has become a political power; he sits in the Congress of the United States and in the legislature of Massachusetts, and now politicians and editors cannot afford to make fun of him.

Now who is their target? Woman. They ridicule all alike—the strong-minded for their principles, the weak-minded for their panniers. How long think you the New York *Tribune* would maintain its present scurrilous tone if the votes of women could make Horace Greeley governor of New York? The editor of the *Tribune* knows the value of votes, and if, honorable gentlemen, you will give us a declaratory law, forbidding the states to deny or abridge our rights, there will be no need of arguments to change the tone of his journal; its columns will speedily glow with demands for the protection of woman as well as broadcloth and pig iron. Then we might find out what he knows and cares for our real and relative value in the government.

Without some act of Congress regulating suffrage for women as well as black men, women citizens of the United States who, in Washington, Utah, and Wyoming territories, are voters and jurors, and who, in the state of Kansas, vote on school and license questions, would be denied the exercise of their right to vote in all the states of the Union, and no naturalization papers, education, property, residence, or age could help them. What an anomaly is this in a republic! A woman who in Wyoming enjoys all the rights, privileges, and immunities of a sovereign, by crossing the line into Nebraska, sinks at once to the political degradation of a slave. Humiliated with such injustice, one set of statesmen answer her appeals by sending her for redress to the courts; another advises her to submit her qualifications to the states; but we, with a clearer intuition of the rightful power, come to you who thoughtfully, conscientiously, and understandingly passed that amendment defining the word *citizen,* declaring suffrage a foundation right. How are women "citizens" from Utah, Wyoming, Kansas, moving in other states, to be protected in the rights they have heretofore enjoyed, unless Congress shall pass the bill presented by Mr. Butler, and thus give us a homogeneous law on suffrage from Maine to Louisiana? Remember, these are citizens of the United States as well as of the territories and states wherein they may reside, and their rights as such are of primal consideration. One of your own amendments to the federal Constitution, honorable gentlemen, says that "the right of citizens of the United States to vote shall not be denied or abridged by any state on account of race, color, or previous condition of servitude." We have women of different races and colors, as well as men. It takes more than men to compose peoples and races, and no one denies that all women suffer the disabilities of a present or previous condition of servitude. Clearly the state may regulate but cannot deny the exercise of this right to any citizen.

You did not leave the Negroes to the tender mercies of the courts and states. Why send your mothers, wives, and daughters as suppliants at the feet of the unwashed, unlettered, unthinking masses that carry our elections in the states? Would you compel the women of New York to sue the Tweeds, the Sweeneys, the Connollys for their inalienable rights, or to have the scales of justice balanced for them in the unsteady hand of a Cardozo, a

Barnard, or a McCunn? Nay, nay; the proper tribunal to decide nice questions of human rights and constitutional interpretations, the political status of every citizen under our national flag, is the Congress of the United States. This is your right and duty, clearly set forth in Article I, Section 5, of the Constitution, for how can you decide the competency and qualifications of electors for members of either House without settling the fundamental question on what the right of suffrage is based? All power centers in the people. Our federal Constitution, as well as that of every state, opens with the words "We, the people." However this phrase may have been understood and acted on in the past, women today are awake to the fact that they constitute one-half the American people; that they have the right to demand that the constitution shall secure to them "justice," "domestic tranquillity,'" and the "blessings of liberty." So long as women are not represented in the government they are in a condition of tutelage, perpetual minority, slavery.

You smile at the idea of women being slaves in this country. Benjamin Franklin said long ago that "they who have no voice in making the laws, or in the election of those who administer them, do not enjoy liberty but are absolutely enslaved to those who have votes and to their representatives." I might occupy hours in quoting grand liberal sentiments from the fathers— Madison, Jefferson, Otis, and Adams—in favor of individual representation. . . . But what do lofty utterances and logical arguments avail so long as men, blinded by old prejudices and customs, fail to see their application to the women by their side? Alas! gentlemen, women are your subjects. Your own selfish interests are too closely interwoven for you to feel their degradation, and they are too dependent to reveal themselves to you in their nobler aspirations, their native dignity. Did Southern slaveholders ever understand the humiliations of slavery to a proud man like Frederick Douglass? Did the coarse, low-bred master ever doubt his capacity to govern the Negro better than he could govern himself? Do cowboys, hustlers, pothouse politicians ever doubt their capacity to prescribe woman's sphere better than she could herself? We have yet to learn that, with the wonderful progress in art, science, education, morals, religion, and government we have witnessed in the last century, woman has not been standing still but has been gradually advancing to an equal place with the man by her side, and stands today his peer in the world of thought.

American womanhood has never worn iron shoes, burned on the funeral pile, or skulked behind a mask in a harem, yet, though cradled in liberty, with the same keen sense of justice and equality that man has, she is still bound by law in the swaddling bands of an old barbarism. Though the world has been steadily advancing in political science, and step by step recognizing the rights of new classes, yet we stand today talking of precedents, authorities, laws, and constitutions, as if each generation were not better able to judge of its wants than the one that preceded it. If we are to be governed in all things by the men of the eighteenth century, and the twentieth by the nineteenth, and so on, the world will be always governed by dead men. The exercise of political power by woman is by no means a new idea. It has already been exercised in many countries, and under governments far less liberal in theory than our own. As to this being an innovation on the laws of nature, we may safely trust nature at all times to vindicate herself. . . .

We have declared in favor of a government of the people, for the people, by the people, the whole people. Why not begin the experiment? If suffrage is a natural right, we claim it in common with all citizens; if it is a political right, that the few in power may give or take away, then it is clearly the duty of the ruling powers to extend it in all cases as the best interests of the state require. No thinking man would admit that educated, refined womanhood would not constitute a most desirable element and better represent the whole humanitarian idea than a government of men alone. . . .

Visiting Chicago not long since, I saw great pieces of rock of the most wonderful mineral combination—gold, silver, glass, iron, layer after layer, all welded beautifully together, and that done in the conflagration of a single night which would have taken ages of growth to accomplish in the ordinary rocky formations. Just so revolutions in the moral world suddenly mold ideas, clear, strong, grand, that centuries might have slumbered over in silence; ideas that strike minds ready for them with the quickness and vividness of the lightning's flash. It is in such ways and under such conditions that constitutions and great principles of jurisprudence are written; the letter and spirit are ever on the side of liberty; and highly organized minds, governed by principle, invariably give true interpretations; while others, whose law is expediency, coarse and material in all their conceptions, will interpret law, Bible, constitution, everything, in harmony with the public sentiment of their class and condition. And here is the reason why men differ in their interpretations of law. They differ in their organizations; they see everything from a different standpoint. Could ideas of justice, and liberty, and equality be more grandly and beautifully expressed than in the preamble to our federal Constitution?

It is an insult to those Revolutionary heroes to say that, after seven years' struggle with the despotic ideas of the Old World, in the first hour of victory, with their souls all on fire with newfound freedom, they sat down like so many pettifogging lawyers and drew up a little instrument for the express purpose of robbing women and Negroes of their inalienable rights. Does the preamble look like it? Women did vote in America at the time the Constitution was adopted. If the framers of the Constitution meant they should not, why did they not distinctly say so? The women of the country, having at last roused up to their rights and duties as citizens, have a word to say as to the "intentions" of the fathers. It is not safe to leave the "intentions" of the Pilgrim fathers, or the Heavenly Father, wholly to masculine interpretation, for by Bible and Constitution alike, women have thus far been declared the subjects, the slaves of men.

ANNIE TURNER WITTENMYER

—— ★ ——

The Work of the Woman's Christian Temperance Union

Speech at a Convention of the National Woman's
Christian Temperance Union, c. 1875

---

*The antisaloon Women's Crusade of 1873–1874 in New York
and Ohio revitalized the prohibition movement in America. Vet-
erans of the crusade, including Frances Willard and Annie Wittenmyer (1827–1900), met in Cleveland in November 1874 to
found the Woman's Christian Temperance Union (WCTU).
Wittenmyer was elected president of the national organization
and tirelessly lectured throughout the nation, making the fight
against liquor a religious crusade; by 1876 twenty-three states
had established unions as auxiliaries to the national WCTU.
Frances Willard assumed the group's presidency in 1879, pursuing a more political course and linking the WCTU to the Prohibition party. Wittenmyer, however, saw the movement as
nonpolitical, and in 1890 she helped to organize the Non-Parti-
san Woman's Christian Temperance Union, serving as its president from 1896 to 1898.*

I have been trying to abridge my remarks, to formulate my
creed on the temperance question in a brief sentence. I very
carefully and prayerfully read the *Liquor Dealers' Gazette*
every week, and I have made up my mind that I am in favor,
on general principles, of everything that liquor-dealers are opposed to.

I am in favor of local option. It seems to be a very democratic thing. I can hardly understand how an American man
can be so mean as to sell liquor in the face of law and the express public sentiment of the community. I am in favor of civil

damage laws. I think that when men rob the community and destroy property and life they ought to pay for it, and pay well for it, and if they kill people they ought to be hung for it. I am opposed to license, and in favor of prohibition. I never could understand, though I have given much thought to the subject, and I do not still understand, how the mere putting a thing that is wrong on the statute books makes it right.

Because men, as I have seen them, put their feet upon the back of their desks in legislative halls, and smoke their cigars till the whole ceiling is almost hid with a cloud of tobacco smoke, and vote for license laws, that does not make it right. Then I am in favor of the Crusade. I think that it is well understood that women compose about one-half of the inhabitants of this Republic—that we have an interest, and ought to have a say, in this matter. None have suffered so much as women, and they are suffering still. . . .

I had the privilege a few weeks ago of saying this to the governor of Pennsylvania—and he is a very fine-looking man, I ought to say as I pass along. He knew that a hundred of the first ladies in the state of Pennsylvania were going to visit him. He stood by the mantelpiece in his great parlor, supporting himself, and looking like a bit of statuary. He had braced himself up against the mantelpiece for the shock. Well, it was a shock. I am not going to enter on the course of argument that took twenty-five minutes of the best speaking that I ever did in my life or ever expect to do again. But I said to him this: "If you take from us local option—for we were there to protest against the repeal of the local-option law—we will give you within the next political decade prohibition." I said to him, and I may throw out the hint here, "We hold the balance of power." The boys are just about what their mothers make them, and the men are only boys of larger growth.

The Woman's National Christian Temperance Union . . . is taking hold of the children with a purpose to save the next generation and bring them up to be more temperate, more truthful, and more honorable, if they should happen to be sent to our legislative halls, than the present incumbents.

Well, I can give some reason tonight for the hope that is within me; for I look very hopefully on this national movement of the women.

> Though woman's hands are weak to fight,
> Their voices are strong to pray,
> And with fingers of faith they'll open the gate
> To a brighter, better day.

I can give you some reason, it seems to me, why the Lord has called this mighty force into the field for more active work now than in the past, because it seems to me that this is a movement under divine direction.

The first reason is because God chooses the weak things of the world to confound the mighty. You know we have always been called weak. We did not like it very much; we want to be strong like our brothers, and when they called us the weaker vessels we did not exactly understand it. But the weakest ware that we have on our tables is the finest and most costly. We are looking into those passages of Scripture with enlightened eyes. We did not understand that all the great movements in nature, all the great moving powers, are the silent forces, the little things; and as we come to think about it, it is not the great clumsy instruments that can do the best execution, after all.

Now, these men—and all honor to these temperance workers—have been using the plow. They have been plowing around this tree of evil, while we women (and you know we go right at a thing) come up with the ax in our hands, and lay it at the root of this tree. We intend to cut and slash, woman-fashion, until there is not a root or branch left. We are so weak that we are forced to trust God and to lean upon his almighty arm, from whence cometh our strength. A great many women in this land during the last year have come near enough to Jesus to touch the hem of his garment and feel the mighty outflow of power that comes from divine contact. It seems to me that the women during this last year have followed more closely in the footsteps of the blessed Christ than ever women did since the Marys followed him up Calvary. Women of all denominations are clasping hands around the cross, with one prayer going up to God, as from one heart. The Quakers are singing beautifully. At the Massachusetts State Convention, the other day, the Quaker president started all the tunes. Our Presbyterian ladies are waxing eloquent in the presentation of this subject; and so, forgetting our denominational differences, we join hands and hearts for glorious work in this contest. But there are other reasons.

You know it has been said that woman's work was never done, and we thought that it was an insinuation that we were not very industrious; but we have come to understand it better now. I have been led to ask, Why is it that woman's work is never done? I see that men work about so many hours, and then they quit; they do not work any more, not because all the work of the world has been done up, but because, I suppose, they grow weary. But women never grow weary; they work on and on; they are tireless in their energies. Then, you know, it has been said that when a woman will she will, and when she won't she won't. Well, now, there is deep meaning in these old sayings, and they mean just about this to us now: that women never weary in good works; that if a thing can be done, if it is within the range of human possibilities, they will do it; and they have such will in great moral movements that they cannot be intimidated, or discouraged, or bribed.

In all the contests of last winter, when Congress and our state legislatures were in session, and our women were going up to appeal to the lawmakers—for our blows are not aimed at the drunkards, but at the rum-sellers and the manufacturers, and the lawmakers who shield them—when they have been going up to present their case, I have never yet heard of a bribe being offered. The liquor men are wise.

But there is another reason. They have the moral courage. It is perfectly wonderful to me how these women talk. They talk right out in meeting, and tell about their pastor, about their church, and about the members of the church; and the things that were covered and hid away are being uncovered. They have the moral courage to say what they think. Now, perhaps I cannot better explain this than by telling a little incident. Some of you know what it is to stand in the presence of the enemy's guns—what it is to stand where the shot and the shell come over. That is physical courage. I know all about that kind of courage, for I have come near being shot more than a hundred times, and know the ring of all sorts of destructive missiles. That is one kind of courage. But I have come to know, within the last eighteen months, that there is a higher style of courage than that.

A few months ago some ladies were visiting saloons—and I tell you it takes more courage to go into these saloons, and stand in the presence of the liquor dealers, and protest, in the spirit of the Gospel, against the traffic, than it does to stand up and take the chance of a random shot and shell—they were visiting saloons in Jacksonville, Illinois. They had visited all the saloons but one, and the good, kind brethren advised them not to visit that saloon, as the dealer was a very violent man, and would, perhaps, do violence to them.

"They thought and prayed about it, and one day, when they were in the church praying, there came down upon them the mighty constraining influences of the Divine Spirit, and they rose up as one to go out and visit that saloon. Well, the liquor dealer had been expecting them for several days, and when he saw them coming he threw his door wide open, and stood in the door, with a pistol in his hand. He held it out; they marched right on, and as they approached very near he said, "Ladies, if you undertake to come into my saloon I will shoot the first woman who undertakes it."

Well, they never knew exactly how it was, but a young lady of the company, as if constrained by a divine impulse, sprang up and stood beside him, singing, "Never be afraid to work for Jesus, Never be afraid."

Somehow his arm got weak; the pistol hung by his side; tears came into his eyes; he stepped back, and took a seat in the saloon. They went in and sung and prayed to their hearts' content. That is what I call the highest style of courage; and it is being displayed throughout the length and breadth of the land. . . .

I was speaking in Wheeling not many months ago, and I understood before I commenced speaking that there were a good many liquor dealers in the audience. I was so glad; it always helps me so much. After the meeting was over a gentleman came to me and said:

"Madam, if you go on and have success, you will break up my business."

I said, "I hope I will, if you are a liquor dealer."

"No, I am not a liquor dealer, but I keep the jail, and that is about the same thing."

Our jails would be empty but for this traffic. Not long ago I was in a jail. I am not going to detain you with a description of a jail; but if you want to feel more interest in the temperance cause than ever you did, just visit your police courts and your jails, and you will have something to quicken your interest.

I was in a jail in Ohio. There were, perhaps, twenty men in the outer court, and as many in the inner prison—little dark places with narrow walls, where they were confined in dungeons worse than Barnum keeps his wildest animals in. As I went up to speak to them, I was obliged to thrust my two fingers (I could not get three fingers through) between the iron bars. I wanted to shake hands with them. I found, as I looked into those dark cells, that they were all young men, and learned that everyone (except one) of them was there because of crimes committed under the influence of liquor, and some of them were very young. I pushed my fingers through the iron bars, and pressed my face against them to look in. I felt my two fingers clasped with a tight grasp, and, looking closely, I saw a boy there not seventeen years old. As he held on to my fingertip I said, "You are very young to be here!" and his lip quivered. He had such an innocent face my heart was moved.

I said, "Have you got a mother?"

He said, "No, ma'am; my mother died when I was a baby."

Oh, what a story of heart-hunger, neglect, and temptation that little sentence revealed to me.

I said, "Have you got a father?"

And he answered, "Well, I might just as well have had no father; he did not care for anything but whiskey. I don't know where he is; I expect he is dead."

Oh, what a sad story! And yet it is repeated all over this land. . . .

I just want to say, in conclusion, that the Woman's National Christian Temperance Union has organized in all the Northern states of the Union except four, and it is now arranging for that. All this side of the Missouri River we are organizing, more thoroughly than any set of politicians ever organized, by states and congressional districts, down to little school districts. We are not in politics, we want you to understand; but we are determined, whatever party goes up or goes down, that the rum power shall go down.

John Marshall Harlan

——— ★ ———

Equal and Not Separate

Dissenting Opinion, U.S. Supreme Court,
Plessy v. Ferguson, 1896

The case of Plessy v. Ferguson *concerned the constitutionality of a state law that mandated separate accommodations for black and white passengers on railway trains. It was this Supreme Court decision that placed the government's seal of approval on the concept of "separate but equal" facilities for the races, resulting in continued decades of racial segregation. (The concept was finally legally rejected in the Court's 1954 decision in* Brown v. Board of Education of Topeka.) *John Marshall Harlan (1833–1911), the only dissenting justice in* Plessy, *wrote in eloquent opposition: "Our Constitution is color-blind, and neither knows nor tolerates classes among citizens. . . . The sure guarantee of the peace and security of each race is the clear, distinct, unconditional recognition by our governments, national and state, of every right that inheres in civil freedom, and of the equality before the law of all citizens of the United States without regard to race."*

By the Louisiana statute, the validity of which is here involved, all railway companies (other than street railway companies) carrying passengers in that state are required to have separate but equal accommodations for white and colored persons, "by providing two or more passenger coaches for each passenger train, *or* by dividing the passenger coaches by *partition* so as to secure separate accommodations." Under this statute, no colored person is permitted to occupy a seat in a coach assigned to white persons; nor any white person to occupy a seat in the coach assigned to colored persons. The managers of the railroad are not allowed to exercise any discretion in the premises, but are required to assign each passenger to some coach or compartment set apart for the exclusive use of his race. If a passenger insists upon going into a coach or compartment not set apart for persons of his race, he is subject to be fined, or to be imprisoned in the parish jail. Penalties are prescribed for the refusal or neglect of the officers, directors, conductors, and employees of railroad companies to comply with the provisions of the act.

Only "nurses attending children of the other race" are excepted from the operation of the statute. No exception is made of colored attendants traveling with adults. A white man is not permitted to have his colored servant with him in the same coach, even if his condition of health requires the constant personal assistance of such servant. If a colored maid insists upon riding in the same coach with a white woman whom she has been employed to serve, and who may need her personal attention while traveling, she is subject to be fined or imprisoned for such an exhibition of zeal in the discharge of duty.

While there may be in Louisiana persons of different races who are not citizens of the United States, the words in the act, "white and colored races," necessarily include all citizens of the United States of both races residing in that state. So that we have before us a state enactment that compels, under penalties, the separation of the two races in railroad passenger coaches, and makes it a crime for a citizen of either race to enter a coach that has been assigned to citizens of the other race.

Thus the state regulates the use of a public highway by citizens of the United States solely upon the basis of race.

However apparent the injustice of such legislation may be, we have only to consider whether it is consistent with the Constitution of the United States.

That a railroad is a public highway, and that the corporation which owns or operates it is in the exercise of public functions, is not, at this day, to be disputed. . . .

In respect of civil rights, common to all citizens, the Constitution of the United States does not, I think, permit any public authority to know the race of those entitled to be protected in the enjoyment of such rights. Every true man has pride of race, and under appropriate circumstances, when the rights of others, his equals before the law, are not to be affected, it is his privilege to express such pride and to take such action based upon it as to him seems proper. But I deny that any legislative body or judicial tribunal may have regard to the race of citizens when the civil rights of those citizens are involved. Indeed, such legislation as that here in question is inconsistent, not only with that equality of rights which pertains to citizenship, national and state, but with the personal liberty enjoyed by everyone within the United States.

The Thirteenth Amendment does not permit the withholding or the deprivation of any right necessarily inhering in freedom. It not only struck down the institution of slavery as previously existing in the United States, but it prevents the imposition of any burdens or disabilities that constitute badges of slavery or servitude. It decreed universal civil freedom in this country. This Court has so adjudged. But that amendment having been found inadequate to the protection of the rights of those who had been in slavery, it was followed by the Fourteenth Amendment, which added greatly to the dignity and glory of American citizenship, and to the security of personal liberty, by declaring that "all persons born or naturalized in the United States, and subject to the jurisdiction thereof, are citizens of the United States and of the state wherein they reside," and that "no state shall make or enforce any law which shall abridge the privileges or immunities of citizens of the United States; nor shall any state deprive any person of life, liberty, or property without due process of law, nor deny to any person within its jurisdiction the equal protection of the laws." These two amendments, if enforced according to their true intent and meaning, will protect all the civil rights that pertain to freedom and citizenship. Finally, and to the end that no citizen should be denied, on account of his race, the privilege of participating in the political control of his country, it was declared by the Fifteenth Amendment that "the right of citizens of the United States to vote shall not be denied or abridged by the United States or by any state on account of race, color, or previous condition of servitude."

These notable additions to the fundamental law were welcomed by the friends of liberty throughout the world. They removed the race line from our governmental systems. They had, as this Court has said, a common purpose, namely, to secure "to a race recently emancipated, a race that through many generations have been held in slavery, all the civil rights that the superior race enjoy." They declared, in legal effect, this court has further said, "that the law in the states shall be the same for the black as for the white; that all persons, whether colored or white, shall stand equal before the laws of the states, and, in regard to the colored race, for whose protection the amendment was primarily designed, that no discrimination shall be made against them by law because of their color." We also said: "The words of the amendment, it is true, are prohibitory, but they contain a necessary implication of a positive immunity, or right, most valuable to the colored race—the right to exemption from unfriendly legislation against them distinctively as colored—exemption from legal discriminations, implying inferiority in civil society, lessening the security of their enjoyment of the rights which others enjoy, and discriminations which are steps towards reducing them to the condition of a subject race." It was consequently adjudged that a state law that excluded citizens of the colored race from juries because of their race and however well qualified in other respects to discharge the duties of jurymen was repugnant to the Fourteenth Amendment. . . .

It was said in argument that the statute of Louisiana does not discriminate against either race, but prescribes a rule applicable alike to white and colored citizens. But this argument does not meet the difficulty. Everyone knows that the statute in question had its origin in the purpose, not so much to exclude white persons from railroad cars occupied by blacks, as to exclude colored people from coaches occupied by or assigned to white persons. Railroad corporations of Louisiana did not make discrimination among whites in the matter of accommodation for travelers. The thing to accomplish was, under the guise of giving equal accommodation for whites and blacks, to compel the latter to keep to themselves while traveling in railroad passenger coaches. No one would be so wanting in candor as to assert the contrary. The fundamental objection, therefore, to the statute, is that it interferes with the personal freedom of citizens. . . . If a white man and a black man choose to occupy the same public conveyance on a public highway, it is their right to do so, and no government, proceeding alone on grounds of race, can prevent it without infringing the personal liberty of each.

It is one thing for railroad carriers to furnish, or to be required by law to furnish, equal accommodations for all whom they are under a legal duty to carry. It is quite another thing for government to forbid citizens of the white and black races from traveling in the same public conveyance, and to punish officers of railroad companies for permitting persons of the two races to occupy the same passenger coach. If a state can prescribe as a rule of civil conduct that whites and blacks shall not travel as passengers in the same railroad coach, why may it not so regulate the use of the streets of its cities and towns as to compel white citizens to keep on one side of the street and black citizens to keep on the other? Why may it not, upon like grounds, punish whites and blacks who ride together in street cars or in open vehicles on a public road or street? Why may it not require sheriffs to assign whites to one side of a courtroom and blacks to the other? And why may it not also prohibit the commingling of the two races in the galleries of legislative halls or in public assemblages convened for the political questions of the day? Further, if this statute of Louisiana is consistent with the personal liberty of citizens, why may not the state require the separation in railroad coaches of native and naturalized citizens of the United States, or of Protestants and Roman Catholics?

The answer given at the argument to these questions was that regulations of the kind they suggest would be unreasonable, and could not, therefore, stand before the law. Is it meant that the determination of questions of legislative power depends upon the inquiry whether the statute whose validity is questioned is, in the judgment of the courts, a reasonable one, taking all the circumstances into consideration? A statute may be unreasonable merely because a sound public policy forbade its enactment. But I do not understand that the courts have anything to do with the policy or expediency of legislation. A statute may be valid, and yet upon grounds of public policy may well be characterized as unreasonable. . . . Statutes must always have a reasonable construction. Sometimes they are to be construed strictly; sometimes literally, in order to carry out the legislative will. But however construed, the intent of the legislature is to be respected, if the particular statute in question is valid, although the courts, looking at the public interests, may conceive the statute to be both unreasonable and impolitic. . . .

The white race deems itself to be the dominant race in this country. And so it is, in prestige, in achievements, in education, in wealth, and in power. So, I doubt not that it will continue to be for all time, if it remains true to its great heritage and holds fast to the principles of constitutional liberty. But in view of the Constitution, in the eye of the law, there is in this country no superior, dominant, ruling class of citizens. There is no caste here. Our Constitution is color-blind, and neither knows nor tolerates classes among citizens. In respect of civil rights, all citizens are equal before the law. The humblest is the peer of the most powerful. The law regards man as man, and takes no account of his surroundings or of his color when his civil rights as guaranteed by the supreme law of the land are involved. It is therefore to be regretted that this high tribunal, the final expositor of the fundamental laws of the land, has reached the conclusion that it is competent for a state to regulate the enjoyment by citizens of their civil rights solely upon the basis of race.

In my opinion, the judgment this day rendered will, in time, prove to be quite as pernicious as the decision made by this tribunal in the *Dred Scott* case. It was adjudged in that case that the descendants of Africans who were imported into this country and sold as slaves were not included nor intended to be included under the word "citizens" in the Constitution, and could not claim any of the rights and privileges which that instrument provided for and secured to citizens of the United States. . . . The recent amendments of the Constitution, it was supposed, had eradicated these principles from our institutions. But it seems that we have yet, in some of the states, a dominant race, a superior class of citizens, which assumes to regulate the enjoyment of civil rights, common to all citizens, upon the basis of race. . . . Sixty millions of whites are in no danger from the presence here of eight millions of blacks. The destinies of the two races in this country are indissolubly linked together, and the interests of both require that the common government of all shall not permit the seeds of race hate to be planted under the sanction of law. What can more certainly arouse race hate, what more certainly create and perpetuate a feeling of distrust between these races, than state enactments which in fact proceed on the ground that colored citizens are so inferior and degraded that they cannot be allowed to sit in public coaches occupied by white citizens? That, as all will admit, is the real meaning of such legislation as was enacted in Louisiana.

The sure guarantee of the peace and security of each race is the clear, distinct, unconditional recognition by our governments, national and state, of every right that inheres in civil freedom, and of the equality before the law of all citizens of the United States without regard to race. State enactments, regulating the enjoyment of civil rights, upon the basis of race, and cunningly devised to defeat legitimate results of the war, under the pretense of recognizing equality of rights, can have no other result than to render permanent peace impossible and to keep alive a conflict of races, the continuance of which must do harm to all concerned. This question is not met by the suggestion that social equality cannot exist between the white and black races in this country. That argument, if it can be properly regarded as one, is scarcely worthy of consideration, for social equality no more exists between two races when traveling in a passenger coach or a public highway than when members of the same races sit by each other in a street car or in the jury box, or stand or sit with each other in a political assembly, or when they use in common the streets of a city or town, or when they are in the same room for the purpose of having their names placed on the registry of voters, or when they approach the ballot box in order to exercise the high privilege of voting.

There is a race so different from our own that we do not permit those belonging to it to become citizens of the United States. Persons belonging to it are, with few exceptions, absolutely excluded from our country. I allude to the Chinese race. But by the statute in question a Chinaman can ride in the same passenger coach with white citizens of the United States, while citizens of the black race in Louisiana, many of whom, perhaps, risked their lives for the preservation of the Union, who are entitled by law to participate in the political control of the state and nation, who are not excluded, by law or by reason of their race, from public stations of any kind, and who have all the legal rights that belong to white citizens, are yet declared to be criminals, liable to imprisonment, if they ride in a public coach occupied by citizens of the white race. It is scarcely just to say that a colored citizen should not object to occupying a public coach assigned to his own race. He does not object, nor, perhaps, would he object to separate coaches for his race, if his rights under the law were recognized. But he does object, and he ought never to cease objecting, that citizens of the white and black races can be adjudged criminals because they sit, or claim the right to sit, in the same public coach on a public highway.

The arbitrary separation of citizens, on the basis of race, while they are on a public highway, is a badge of servitude wholly inconsistent with the civil freedom and the equality before the law established by the Constitution. It cannot be justified upon any legal grounds.

If evils will result from the commingling of the two races

upon public highways established for the benefit of all, they will be infinitely less than those that will surely come from state legislation regulating the enjoyment of civil rights upon the basis of race. We boast of the freedom enjoyed by our people above all other peoples. But it is difficult to reconcile that boast with a state of the law which, practically, puts the brand of servitude and degradation upon a large class of our fellow citizens, our equals before the law. The thin disguise of "equal" accommodations for passengers in railroad coaches will not mislead anyone, or atone for the wrong this day done. . . .

I am of opinion that the statute of Louisiana is inconsistent with the personal liberty of citizens, white and black, in that state, and hostile to both the spirit and letter of the Constitution of the United States. If laws of like character should be enacted in the several states of the Union, the effect would be in the highest degree mischievous. Slavery as an institution tolerated by law would, it is true, have disappeared from our country, but there would remain a power in the states, by sinister legislation, to interfere with the full enjoyment of the blessings of freedom; to regulate civil rights, common to all citizens, upon the basis of race; and to place in a condition of legal inferiority a large body of American citizens, now constituting a part of the political community, called the people of the United States, for whom and by whom, through representatives, our government is administered. Such a system is inconsistent with the guarantee given by the Constitution to each state of a republican form of government, and may be stricken down by congressional action, or by the courts in the discharge of their solemn duty to maintain the supreme law of the land, anything in the Constitution or laws of any state to the contrary notwithstanding.

For the reasons stated, I am constrained to withhold my assent from the opinion and judgment of the majority.

CLARENCE DARROW

——— ★ ———

The Argument Against Capital Punishment

From *Resist Not Evil*, 1903

One of America's most renowned lawyers, Clarence Seward Darrow (1857–1938) consistently involved himself in cases concerning labor or social issues. Among those he defended were the socialist Eugene V. Debs (for his involvement in the American Railway Union strike), the McNamara brothers (for a bombing of the Los Angeles Times Building), teenagers Nathan Leopold and Richard Loeb (for the murder of a young boy), and John T. Scopes (for teaching evolution). Darrow was a staunch opponent of capital punishment, and no person he defended ever received the death penalty. In his book Resist Not Evil, *in which he deals in depth with the causes of crimes and the value of punishments, Darrow writes: "Any evil consequences that could flow from a casual killing of a human being by an irresponsible man would be like a drop of water in the sea compared with a public execution by the state."*

The last refuge of the apologist is that punishment is inflicted to prevent crime. No one can speak from experience as to whether punishment prevents what is called crime or not, for the experiment of nonresistance has never yet been fairly or fully tried. To justify killing or penning a human being upon the theory that this prevents crime should call for the strictest proof on the part of those who advocate this course. To take the life or liberty of a fellow man is the most serious responsibility that can devolve upon an individual or community. The theory that punishment is a preventive to unlawful acts does not seriously mean that it is administered to prevent the individual from committing a second or a third unlawful act. If this were the case the death penalty should never be inflicted, as life imprisonment accomplishes the same results. Neither would it be necessary to restrain men in the way that is done in our penal institutions, to deprive them of all pleasure and the income of their labor. All that would then be needed would be to keep men safely locked from the world. But most unlawful acts are committed hastily in the heat of passion or upon what seems adequate provocation, or through sore need. Such acts as these would almost never be repeated. Genuine repentance follows most really vicious acts, but repentance, however genuine, gives no waiver of punishment.

Then, too, many men who commit no act in violation of the law are known to be more likely to commit such acts than others who through some circumstances may have violated a criminal statute. Men of hasty temper, of strong will, of intemperate habits, often with no means of support—all of these are more liable to crime than one who has once overstepped the bounds. But it is obvious that this is not the real reason for punishment; if it were it would be the duty of judge and jury to determine not whether a man had committed a crime but whether he was liable to commit one at some future time—an inquiry which is never made and which it is obvious could not be made.

The safety aimed at through punishment is not meant the safety for the individual, but it is contended that the fact that one person is punished for an act deters others from the commission of similar unlawful acts; it is obvious that there is a large class who are not deterred by these examples, for the inmates of prisons never grow less; in fact, prisons grow and increase in the same proportion as other institutions grow. But here, too, the theories and acts of rulers have been as various and contradictory as in relation to other matters concerning crime and its punishment. If the purpose of punishment is to terrorize the community so that none will dare again to commit these acts, then the more terrible the punishment the surer the result. This was generally admitted not many years ago, but in its treatment of crime the world ever prefers to be illogical and ineffectual rather than too brutal.

If terrorism is the object aimed at, death should again be substituted for the various crimes, great and small, which ever justified taking human life. Death, too, should be administered in the most cruel way. Boiling, the rack, wild beasts, and slow fires should be the methods sought. It should be steadfastly remembered by all squeamish judges and executioners that one vigorous punishment would prevent a thousand crimes. But more than all this, death should be in the most public way. The kettle of boiling oil should be heated with its victim inside, out upon the commons, where all eyes could see and all ears could hear. The scaffold should be erected high on a hill, and the occasion be made a public holiday for miles around. This was once the case even within the last half-century.

These public hangings in Europe and America have drawn great crowds of spectators, sometimes reaching into the tens of thousands, to witness the value that the state places on human life. But finally, even stupid legislators began to realize that these scenes of violence, brutality, and crime bred their like upon those who came to see. Even governments discovered that many acts of violence followed a public hanging. The hatred of the state which calmly took a human life engendered endless hatred as its fruit. And in all countries that claim a semblance of civilization, public hangings are now looked back upon with horror and amazement. Hangings today take place inside the jail in the presence of a few invited guests, a state doctor who watches carefully to see that the victim is not cut down before his heart has ceased to beat, a chaplain who calls on the Creator of life to take back to his bosom the divine spark which man in his cruelty and wrath is seeking to snuff out. Even the state is not so cruel but that it will officially ask the Almighty to look after the soul that it blackens and defiles and does its best to everlastingly destroy. A few friends of the jailer are present to witness the rare performance, and the newspapers too are represented, so that the last detail, including the breakfast bill of fare, may be graphically set before the hungry mob to take the place of the real tragedy that they had the right to witness in the good old days.

Many states today have provided that executions shall be inside the penitentiary walls, that the victim shall be wakened, if perchance he is asleep, in the darkness and dead of night; that he shall be hurried off alone and unobserved and hastily put to death outside the gaze of any curious eye; that this barbarism shall be done, this unholy, brutal deed committed in silence, in darkness, that the heavens and earth alike may cover up the shocking crime, from which a sensitive public conscience stands aghast. The ever-present public press in many cases is allowed to print only the barest details of the bloody scene, so that oblivion may the more quickly and deeply cover this crowning infamy of the state.

The abolition of public hangings may speak something for the sensitiveness, or at least, the squeamishness of the state. But it is evident that all of this is a terrible admission of guilt upon the part of those who uphold this crime. It is possible that one might believe at least in the sincerity of those who argue that punishment prevents crime if these terrible scenes of violence were carried out in open day before the multitude and fully understood and discussed in all their harrowing, shocking details of cruelty and blood. If the sight of punishment terrorizes men from the commission of crime, then, of course, punishment should be as open as the day. Insofar as the state is successful in keeping secret the execution of its victim, in this far does it abandon every claim of prevention and rests its case for punishment on vengeance and cruelty alone. The rulers of this generation, who are ashamed of their deeds, may be wiser and more sensitive than those of the last, but our ancestors, although less refined, were much more logical and infinitely more honest than are we.

The whole question of punishment is not only proven but fully admitted by our rulers in their dealings with the death penalty. It is now everywhere admitted that the brutalizing effects of public executions are beyond dispute. It was only after the completest evidence that the believers in the beneficence of punishment and violence abandoned public executions, for to abandon these was to utterly abandon the principle on which all punishment is based.

It would, of course, be impossible to prove the exact result of a public execution. Somewhere in a quiet rural community, growing out of sudden passion or some unexplained and temporary aberration, a man takes the life of his fellow man. To the shock incident to this fatal act is added a long public trial in the courts where every detail is distorted and magnified and passed from tongue to tongue until even the lisping babe is thoroughly familiar with every circumstance of the case with all its harrowing details iterated and reiterated again and again. There grows up in the public mind a bitter hatred against the unfortunate victim whose antecedents, life, and motives they can in no way understand or judge. It is really believed that no one has the right to look upon this person with any feeling save that of hatred, and the least word of pity or sign of sympathy for the outcast is set down as sickly sentimentalism and the mark of mental and spiritual disease.

Weeks and months, sometimes even years, elapse in the slow and unending process of the courts. The whole tragedy has been well nigh forgot, at least it no longer has any vital effect upon the community. Finally it is announced that on a certain day a public hanging will take place. Once more every detail of the tragedy is recalled to the public mind; once more each man conjures up a monster in the place of the hunted, weak, doomed victim whose act no one either fathoms or seeks to understand. A sightly spot is chosen, perhaps upon the village green. For several days men are kept busy erecting a strange and ominous machine; the old men and women, the middle-aged, the boys and girls, the little children, even the toddling babes, filled with curiosity watch the work and discuss every detail of the weird and fatal trap.

At length the day arrives for the majesty of the law to

vindicate itself. From every point of the compass comes a great throng of both sexes, all conditions and ages, each to witness the most startling event of their lives; children are there, babes in arms, and even the unborn. A rope is tied around a beam, a noose is formed of the other end, a trembling, helpless, frantic, friendless victim is led up the steps, placed on a trap, his hands and feet are bound, a black cap is pulled down to hide his face, the noose is securely fastened around his neck below his ears. The crowd watches breathless with suspense, the signal is given, the trap opens, the man falls through space, he is caught in midair by the rope tightening about his neck, and strangling him to death. His body heaves, his legs and arms move with violent convulsions, he swings a few minutes in midair before the crowd, a ghastly human pendulum moving back and forth, the mortal body of a man created in the image of God whom the state has led out and killed to show the glory and majesty of law!

The advocate of punishment is right in the belief that such a scene will produce a profound impression upon all who see or hear or know. The human being does not live who can witness such a tragedy or even know its details and not receive some impression that the rest of life cannot efface. The impression must be to harden and brutalize the heart and conscience, to destroy the finer sensibilities, to cheapen human life, to breed cruelty and malice that will bear fruit in endless ways and unknown forms. No parent who loved his child and who had any of the human sentiments that should distinguish man from the brute creation, would ever dare to trust that child to witness a scene like this. Every intelligent loving mother carrying an unborn babe would close her eyes and stop her ears and retire to the darkest corner she could find lest the unborn babe marked by the baleful scene should one day stand upon the same trembling trap with a rope about his neck.

The true morality of a community does not depend alone upon the number of men who slay their fellows. These at most are very few. The true morality depends upon every deed of kindness or malice, of love or hatred, of charity or cruelty, and the sum of these determine the real character and worth of a community. Any evil consequences that could flow from a casual killing of a human being by an irresponsible man would be like a drop of water in the sea compared with a public execution by the state.

It would probably not be possible to find a considerable number of men today who would believe that a public hanging could have any but bad results. This must be true because the knowledge of its details tends to harden, embitter, and render cruel the hearts of men. Only in a less degree does the publication of all the details affect the characters and lives of men, but unless they are at least published to the world, then the example is of no effect. The state which would take life without any hope or expectation that the community would in any way be bettered could not rank even among savage tribes. Such cruelty could only be classed as total depravity.

But the effect of other punishment is no whit different save in degree from that of hanging. Cultivated, sensitive people have long since deplored the tendency of newspapers to give full and vivid accounts of crimes and their punishment, and the better and humaner class of citizens shun those journals which most magnify these details. All of this has a tendency to familiarize man with violence and force, to weaken human sensibilities, to accustom man to cruelty, to blood, to scenes of suffering and pain. What right-thinking parent would place this literature before his child and familiarize his mind with violence practiced either by the individual or the state? And yet if punishment is a deterrent, the widest publicity should be given to the story of every crime and the punishment inflicted by the state.

That men even unconsciously feel that punishment is wrong is shown by their attitude toward certain classes of society. A hangman would not be tolerated in a self-respecting body of men or women, and this has been the case for many years, in fact since men made a trade of butchering their fellow man. A professional hangman is really as much despised as any other professional murderer. A detective, jailer, policeman, constable, and sheriff are not generally regarded as being subjects of envy by their fellows. Still none of these are as much responsible for their acts as the real rulers who make and execute the law. The time will come when the public prosecutor and the judge who sentences his brother to death or imprisonment will be classed with the other officers who lay violent and cruel hands upon their fellows. . . .

All communities and states are in reality ashamed of jails and penal institutions of whatever kind. Instinctively they seem to understand that these are a reflection on the state. More and more the best judgment and best conscience of men are turned toward the improvement of prisons, the introduction of sanitary appliances, the bettering of jail conditions, the modification of punishment, the treatment of convicts as men. All of this directly disproves the theory that the terrible example of punishment tends to prevent crime. All these improvements of prison conditions show that society is unconsciously ashamed of its treatment of so-called criminals; that the excuse of prevention of crime is really known to be humbug and hypocrisy, and that the real motive that causes the punishment of crime is malice and hatred and nothing else. The tendency to abrogate capital punishment, to improve prisons, to modify sentences, to pardon convicts is all in one direction. It can lead to but one inevitable result, the abolition of all judgment of man by man, the complete destruction of all prisons and the treatment of all men as if each human being was the child of the one loving Father and a part and parcel of the same infinite and mysterious life.

W.E.B. Du Bois

★

Of the Sons of Master and Man

From *The Souls of Black Folk*, 1903

William Edward Burghardt Du Bois (1868–1963) was one of the founders of the National Association for the Advancement of Colored People (NAACP); as director of publications from 1910 to 1932, he edited the organization's magazine, Crisis. *Throughout his career, Du Bois combined scholarship and teaching with social activism. He was a professor of Greek and Latin, economics, history, and sociology, and in 1944 he became the first African American to be elected a member of the National Institute of Arts and Letters. He helped organize the first Pan-African Congress in Paris in 1919 and was involved with the founding conference of the United Nations in 1945. During the 1950s, charges of communist association tainted Du Bois's reputation. He settled in Ghana in 1961, and pursued his project of the* Encyclopedia Africana. *When it was published in 1903, Du Bois's most influential work,* The Souls of Black Folk, *stood in stark contrast to the conservative self-improvement approach of such black leaders as Booker T. Washington. In the book Du Bois expresses a pride in the unique character of African Americans and argues for the necessity of settling the problem of racial prejudice: "The Negro cannot stand the present reactionary tendencies and unreasoning drawing of the color-line indefinitely without discouragement and retrogression. . . . Only by a union of intelligence and sympathy across the color-line in this critical period of the Republic shall justice and right triumph."*

The world-old phenomenon of the contact of diverse races of men is to have new exemplification during the new century. Indeed, the characteristic of our age is the contact of European civilization with the world's undeveloped peoples. Whatever we may say of the results of such contact in the past, it certainly forms a chapter in human action not pleasant to look back upon. War, murder, slavery, extermination, and debauchery—this has again and again been the result of carrying civilization and the blessed gospel to the isles of the sea and the heathen without the law. Nor does it altogether satisfy the conscience of the modern world to be told complacently that all this has been right and proper, the fated triumph of strength over weakness, of righteousness over evil, of superiors over inferiors. It would certainly be soothing if one could readily believe all this; and yet there are too many ugly facts for everything to be thus easily explained away. We feel and know that there are many delicate differences in race psychology, numberless changes that our crude social measurements are not yet able to follow minutely, which explain much of history and social development. At the same time, too, we know that these considerations have never adequately explained or excused the triumph of brute force and cunning over weakness and innocence.

It is, then, the strife of all honorable men of the twentieth century to see that in the future competition of races the survival of the fittest shall mean the triumph of the good, the beautiful, and the true; that we may be able to preserve for future civilization all that is really fine and noble and strong, and not continue to put a premium on greed and impudence and cruelty. To bring this hope to fruition, we are compelled daily to turn more and more to a conscientious study of the phenomena of race-contact—to a study frank and fair, and not falsified and colored by our wishes or our fears. And we have in the South as fine a field for such a study as the world affords—a field, to be sure, which the average American scientist deems somewhat beneath his dignity, and which the average man who is not a scientist knows all about, but nevertheless a line of study which, by reason of the enormous race complications with which God seems about to punish this nation, must increasingly claim our sober attention, study, and thought. We must ask, What are the actual relations of whites and blacks in the South? And we must be answered not by apology or fault-finding but by a plain, unvarnished tale.

In the civilized life of today the contact of men and their relations to each other fall in a few main lines of action and communication: there is, first, the physical proximity of homes and dwelling-places, the way in which neighborhoods group themselves, and the contiguity of neighborhoods. Second, and in our age chiefest, there are the economic relations—the methods by which individuals cooperate for earning a living, for the mutual satisfaction of wants, for the production of wealth. Next, there are the political relations, the cooperation in social control, in group government, in laying and paying the burden of taxation. In the fourth place, there are the less tangible but highly important forms of intellectual contact and commerce, the interchange of ideas through conversation and conference, through periodicals and libraries; and, above all, the gradual formation for each community of that curious *tertium quid* which we call public opinion. Closely allied with this come the various forms of social contact in everyday life, in travel, in theaters, in house gatherings, in marrying and giving in marriage. Finally, there are the varying forms of religious enterprise, of moral teaching, and benevolent endeavor. These are the principal ways in which men living in the same communities are brought into contact with each other. It is my present task, therefore, to indicate, from my point of view, how the black race in the South meet and mingle with the whites in these matters of everyday life.

First, as to physical dwelling. It is usually possible to draw in nearly every Southern community a physical color-line on the map, on the one side of which whites dwell and on the other Negroes. The winding and intricacy of the geographical color-line varies, of course, in different communities. I know some towns where a straight line drawn through the middle of the main street separates nine-tenths of the whites from nine-tenths of the blacks. In other towns the older settlement of whites has been encircled by a broad band of blacks; in still other cases little settlements or nuclei of blacks have sprung up amid surrounding whites. Usually in cities each street has its distinctive color, and only now and then do the colors meet in close proximity. Even in the country something of this segregation is manifest in the smaller areas, and of course in the larger phenomena of the Black Belt.

All this segregation by color is largely independent of that natural clustering by social grades common to all communities. A Negro slum may be in dangerous proximity to a white residence quarter, while it is quite common to find a white slum planted in the heart of a respectable Negro district. One thing, however, seldom occurs: the best of the whites and the best of the Negroes almost never live in anything like close proximity. It thus happens that in nearly every Southern town and city, both whites and blacks see commonly the worst of each other. This is a vast change from the situation in the past, when, through the close contact of master and house-servant in the patriarchal big house, one found the best of both races in close contact and sympathy, while at the same time the squalor and dull round of toil among the fieldhands was removed from the sight and hearing of the family. One can easily see how a person who saw slavery thus from his father's parlors, and sees freedom on the streets of a great city, fails to grasp or comprehend the whole of the new picture. On the other hand, the settled belief of the mass of the Negroes that the Southern white people do not have the black man's best interests at heart has been intensified in later years by this continual daily contact of the better class of blacks with the worst representatives of the white race.

Coming now to the economic relations of the races, we are on ground made familiar by study, much discussion, and no little philanthropic effort. And yet with all this there are many essential elements in the cooperation of Negroes and whites for work and wealth that are too readily overlooked or not thoroughly understood. The average American can easily conceive of a rich land awaiting development and filled with black laborers. To him the Southern problem is simply that of making efficient workingmen out of this material, by giving them the requisite technical skill and the help of invested capital. The problem, however, is by no means as simple as this, from the obvious fact that these workingmen have been trained for centuries as slaves. They exhibit, therefore, all the advantages and defects of such training; they are willing and good-natured, but not self-reliant, provident, or careful. If now the economic development of the South is to be pushed to the verge of exploitation, as seems probable, then we have a mass of workingmen thrown into relentless competition with the workingmen of the world, but handicapped by a training the very opposite to that of the modern self-reliant democratic laborer.

What the black laborer needs is careful personal guidance, group leadership of men with hearts in their bosoms, to train them to foresight, carefulness, and honesty. Nor does it require any fine-spun theories of racial differences to prove the necessity of such group training after the brains of the race have been knocked out by 250 years of assiduous education in submission, carelessness, and stealing. After emancipation, it was the plain duty of someone to assume this group leadership and training of the Negro laborer. I will not stop here to inquire whose duty it was—whether that of the white ex-master who had profited by unpaid toil, or the Northern philanthropist whose persistence brought on the crisis, or the national government whose edict freed the bondmen; I will not stop to ask whose duty it was, but I insist it was the duty of someone to see that these workingmen were not left alone and unguided, without capital, without land, without skill, without economic organization, without even the bald protection of law, order, and decency—left in a great land, not to settle down to slow and careful internal development, but destined to be thrown almost immediately into relentless and sharp competition with the best of modern workingmen under an economic system where every participant is fighting for himself, and too often utterly regardless of the rights or welfare of his neighbor.

For we must never forget that the economic system of the South today which has succeeded the old regime is not the same system as that of the old industrial North, of England, or of

France, with their trade unions, their restrictive laws, their written and unwritten commercial customs, and their long experience. It is, rather, a copy of that England of the early nineteenth century before the factory acts—the England that wrung pity from thinkers and fired the wrath of Carlyle. The rod of empire that passed from the hands of Southern gentlemen in 1865, partly by force, partly by their own petulance, has never returned to them. Rather it has passed to those men who have come to take charge of the industrial exploitation of the New South—the sons of poor whites fired with a new thirst for wealth and power, thrifty and avaricious Yankees, shrewd and unscrupulous Jews. Into the hands of these men the Southern laborers, white and black, have fallen; and this to their sorrow. For the laborers as such there is in these new captains of industry neither love nor hate, neither sympathy nor romance; it is a cold question of dollars and dividends. Under such a system all labor is bound to suffer. Even the white laborers are not yet intelligent, thrifty, and well trained enough to maintain themselves against the powerful inroads of organized capital. The results among them, even, are long hours of toil, low wages, child labor, and lack of protection against usury and cheating. But among the black laborers all this is aggravated, first, by a race prejudice which varies from a doubt and distrust among the best element of whites to a frenzied hatred among the worst; and, second, it is aggravated, as I have said before, by the wretched economic heritage of the freedmen from slavery. With this training it is difficult for the freedman to learn to grasp the opportunities already opened to him, and the new opportunities are seldom given him, but go by favor to the whites.

Left by the best elements of the South with little protection or oversight, he has been made in law and custom the victim of the worst and most unscrupulous men in each community. The crop-lien system which is depopulating the fields of the South is not simply the result of shiftlessness on the part of Negroes, but is also the result of cunningly devised laws as to mortgages, liens, and misdemeanors, which can be made by conscienceless men to entrap and snare the unwary until escape is impossible, further toil a farce, and protest a crime. I have seen, in the Black Belt of Georgia, an ignorant, honest Negro buy and pay for a farm in installments three separate times, and then in the face of law and decency the enterprising Russian Jew who sold it to him pocketed money and deed and left the black man landless, to labor on his own land at thirty cents a day. I have seen a black farmer fall in debt to a white storekeeper, and that storekeeper go to his farm and strip it of every single marketable article—mules, ploughs, stored crops, tools, furniture, bedding, clocks, looking-glass—and all this without a warrant, without process of law, without a sheriff or officer, in the face of the law for homestead exemptions, and without rendering to a single responsible person any account or reckoning. And such proceedings can happen, and will happen, in any community where a class of ignorant toilers are placed by custom and race-prejudice beyond the pale of sympathy and race-brotherhood. So long as the best elements of a community do not feel in duty bound to protect and train and care for the weaker members of their group, they leave them to be preyed upon by these swindlers and rascals.

This unfortunate economic situation does not mean the hindrance of all advance in the black South, or the absence of a class of black landlords and mechanics who, in spite of disadvantages, are accumulating property and making good citizens. But it does mean that this class is not nearly so large as a fairer economic system might easily make it, that those who survive in the competition are handicapped so as to accomplish much less than they deserve to, and that, above all, the *personnel* of the successful class is left to chance and accident, and not to any intelligent culling or reasonable methods of selection. As a remedy for this, there is but one possible procedure. We must accept some of the race prejudice in the South as a fact—deplorable in its intensity, unfortunate in results, and dangerous for the future, but nevertheless a hard fact which only time can efface. We cannot hope, then, in this generation, or for several generations, that the mass of the whites can be brought to assume that close, sympathetic, and self-sacrificing leadership of the blacks which their present situation so eloquently demands. Such leadership, such social teaching and example, must come from the blacks themselves. For some time men doubted as to whether the Negro could develop such leaders; but today no one seriously disputes the capability of individual Negroes to assimilate the culture and common sense of modern civilization, and to pass it on, to some extent at least, to their fellows. If this is true, then here is the path out of the economic situation, and here is the imperative demand for trained Negro leaders of character and intelligence—men of skill, men of light and leading, college-bred men, black captains of industry, and missionaries of culture; men who thoroughly comprehend and know modern civilization, and can take hold of Negro communities and raise and train them by force of precept and example, deep sympathy, and the inspiration of common blood and ideals. But if such men are to be effective they must have some power—they must be backed by the best public opinion of these communities, and able to wield for their objects and aims such weapons as the experience of the world has taught are indispensable to human progress.

Of such weapons the greatest, perhaps, in the modern world is the power of the ballot; and this brings me to a consideration of the third form of contact between whites and blacks in the South—political activity.

In the attitude of the American mind toward Negro suffrage can be traced with unusual accuracy the prevalent conceptions of government. In the fifties we were near enough the echoes of the French Revolution to believe pretty thoroughly in universal suffrage. We argued, as we thought then rather logically, that no social class was so good, so true, and so disinterested as to be trusted wholly with the political destiny of its neighbors; that in every state the best arbiters of their own welfare are the persons directly affected; consequently that it is only by arming every hand with a ballot—with the right to have a voice in the policy of the state—that the greatest good to the greatest number could be attained. To be sure, there were objections to these arguments, but we thought we had answered them tersely and convincingly; if someone complained of the ignorance of voters, we answered, "Educate them." If another complained of their venality, we replied, "Disfranchise them or put them in jail." And, finally, to the men who feared demagogues and the natural perversity of some human beings we insisted that time and bitter experience would teach the most hardheaded. It was at this time that the question of Negro suffrage in the South was raised. Here was a defenseless people suddenly made free. How were they to be protected from those who did not believe in their freedom and were determined to thwart it? Not by force, said the North; not by government guardianship, said the South; then by the ballot, the sole and legitimate defense of a free people, said the Common Sense of the Nation. No one thought, at the time, that the ex-slaves could use the ballot intelligently or very effectively; but they did think that the possession of so great power by a great class in the nation would compel their fellows to educate this class to its intelligent use.

Meantime, new thoughts came to the nation: the inevitable period of moral retrogression and political trickery that ever follows in the wake of war overtook us. So flagrant became the political scandals that reputable men began to leave politics alone, and politics consequently became disreputable. Men began to pride themselves on having nothing to do with their own government, and to agree tacitly with those who regarded public office as a private perquisite. In this state of mind it became easy to wink at the suppression of the Negro vote in the South, and to advise self-respecting Negroes to leave politics entirely alone. The decent and reputable citizens of the North who neglected their own civic duties grew hilarious over the exaggerated importance with which the Negro regarded the franchise. Thus it easily happened that more and more the better class of Negroes followed the advice from abroad and the pressure from home, and took no further interest in politics, leaving to the careless and the venal of their race the exercise of their rights as voters. The black vote that still remained was not trained and educated, but further debauched by open and unblushing bribery, or force and fraud—until the Negro voter was thoroughly inoculated with the idea that politics was a method of private gain by disreputable means.

And finally, now, today, when we are awakening to the fact that the perpetuity of republican institutions on this continent depends on the purification of the ballot, the civic training of voters, and the raising of voting to the plane of a solemn duty which a patriotic citizen neglects to his peril and to the peril of his children's children—in this day, when we are striving for a renaissance of civic virtue, what are we going to say to the black voter of the South? Are we going to tell him still that politics is a disreputable and useless form of human activity? Are we going to induce the best class of Negroes to take less and less interest in government, and to give up their right to take such an interest, without a protest? I am not saying a word against all legitimate efforts to purge the ballot of ignorance, pauperism, and crime. But few have pretended that the present movement for disfranchisement in the South is for such a purpose; it has been plainly and frankly declared in nearly every case that the object of the disfranchising laws is the elimination of the black man from politics.

Now, is this a minor matter which has no influence on the main question of the industrial and intellectual development of the Negro? Can we establish a mass of black laborers and artisans and landholders in the South who, by law and public opinion, have absolutely no voice in shaping the laws under which they live and work? Can the modern organization of industry, assuming as it does free democratic government and the power and ability of the laboring classes to compel respect for their welfare—can this system be carried out in the South when half its laboring force is voiceless in the public councils and powerless in its own defense? Today the black man of the South has almost nothing to say as to how much he shall be taxed, or how those taxes shall be expended; as to who shall execute the laws, and how they shall do it; as to who shall make the laws, and how they shall be made. It is pitiable that frantic efforts must be made at critical times to get lawmakers in some states even to listen to the respectful presentation of the black man's side of a current controversy. Daily the Negro is coming more and more to look upon law and justice, not as protecting safeguards, but as sources of humiliation and oppression. The laws are made by men who have little interest in him; they are executed by men who have absolutely no motive for treating the black people with courtesy or consideration; and, finally, the accused lawbreaker is tried, not by his peers, but too often by men who would rather punish ten innocent Negroes than let one guilty one escape.

I should be the last one to deny the patent weaknesses and shortcomings of the Negro people; I should be the last to withhold sympathy from the white South in its efforts to solve its intricate social problems. I freely acknowledge that it is possible, and sometimes best, that a partially undeveloped people should be ruled by the best of their stronger and better neighbors for their own good, until such time as they can start and fight the world's battles alone. I have already pointed out how sorely in need of such economic and spiritual guidance the emancipated Negro was, and I am quite willing to admit that if the representatives of the best white Southern public opinion were the ruling and guiding powers in the South today the conditions indicated would be fairly well fulfilled. But the point I have insisted upon, and now emphasize again, is that the best opinion of the South today is not the ruling opinion—that to leave the Negro helpless and without a ballot today is to leave him, not to the guidance of the best, but rather to the exploitation and debauchment of the worst. . . .

Moreover, the political status of the Negro in the South is closely connected with the question of Negro crime. There can be no doubt that crime among Negroes has sensibly increased in the last thirty years, and that there has appeared in the slums of great cities a distinct criminal class among the blacks. In explaining this unfortunate development, we must note two things: (1) that the inevitable result of emancipation was to increase crime and criminals, and (2) that the police system of the South was primarily designed to control slaves. As to the first point, we must not forget that under a strict slave system there can scarcely be such a thing as crime. But when these variously constituted human particles are suddenly thrown broadcast on the sea of life, some swim, some sink, and some hang suspended, to be forced up or down by the chance currents of a busy hurrying world. So great an economic and social evolution as swept the South in '63 meant a weeding out among the Negroes of the incompetents and vicious, the beginning of a differentiation of social grades. Now a rising group of people are not lifted bodily from the ground like an inert solid mass, but rather stretch upward like a living plant with its roots still clinging in the mould. The appearance, therefore, of the Negro criminal was a phenomenon to be awaited; and while it causes anxiety, it should not occasion surprise. . . .

But the chief problem in any community cursed with crime is not the punishment of the criminals, but the preventing of the young from being trained to crime. And here again the peculiar conditions of the South have prevented proper precautions. I have seen twelve-year-old boys working in chains on the public streets of Atlanta, directly in front of the schools, in company with old and hardened criminals; and this indiscriminate mingling of men and women and children makes the chain-gangs perfect schools of crime and debauchery. The struggle for reformatories, which has gone on in Virginia, Georgia, and other states, is the one encouraging sign of the awakening of some communities to the suicidal results of this policy.

It is the public schools, however, which can be made, outside the homes, the greatest means of training decent self-respecting citizens. We have been so hotly engaged recently in discussing trade schools and the higher education that the pitiable plight of the public-school system in the South has almost dropped from view. Of every five dollars spent for public education in the State of Georgia, the white schools get four dollars and the Negro one dollar; and even then the white public-school system, save in the cities, is bad and cries for reform. If this is true of the whites, what of the blacks? I am becoming more and more convinced, as I look upon the system of common-school training in the South, that the national government must soon step in and aid popular education in some way. . . .

I have thus far sought to make clear the physical, economic, and political relations of the Negroes and whites in the South, as I have conceived them, including, for the reasons set forth, crime and education. But after all that has been said on these more tangible matters of human contact, there still remains a part essential to a proper description of the South which it is difficult to describe or fix in terms easily understood by strangers. It is, in fine, the atmosphere of the land, the thought and feeling, the thousand and one little actions which go to make up life. . . .

Before and directly after the war, when all the best of the Negroes were domestic servants in the best of the white families, there were bonds of intimacy, affection, and sometimes blood relationship, between the races. They lived in the same home, shared in the family life, often attended the same church, and talked and conversed with each other. But the increasing civilization of the Negro since then has naturally meant the development of higher classes: there are increasing numbers of ministers, teachers, physicians, merchants, mechanics, and independent farmers, who by nature and training are the aristocracy and leaders of the blacks. Between them, however, and the best element of the whites, there is little or no intellectual commerce. They go to separate churches, they live in separate sections, they are strictly separated in all public gatherings, they travel separately, and they are beginning to read different papers and books. To most libraries, lectures, concerts, and museums, Negroes are either not admitted at all, or on terms peculiarly galling to the pride of the very classes who might otherwise be attracted. The daily paper chronicles the doings of the black world from afar with no great regard for accuracy; and so on, throughout the category of means for intellectual communication—schools, conferences, efforts for social betterment, and the like—it is usually true that the very representatives of the two races, who for mutual benefit and the welfare of the land ought to be in complete understanding and sympathy, are so far strangers that one side thinks all whites are narrow and prejudiced, and the other thinks educated Negroes dangerous and insolent. Moreover, in a land where the tyranny of public opinion and the intolerance of criticism is for obvious historical reasons so strong as in the South, such a situation is extremely difficult to correct. The white man, as well as the Negro, is bound and barred by the color-line, and many a scheme of friendliness and philanthropy, of broad-minded sympathy and generous fellowship between the two has dropped stillborn because some busybody has forced the color-question to the front and brought the tremendous force of unwritten law against the innovators. . . .

It is not enough for the Negroes to declare that color-prejudice is the sole cause of their social condition, nor for the white South to reply that their social condition is the main cause of prejudice. They both act as reciprocal cause and effect, and a change in neither alone will bring the desired effect. Both must change, or neither can improve to any great extent. The Negro cannot stand the present reactionary tendencies and unreasoning drawing of the color-line indefinitely without discouragement and retrogression. And the condition of the Negro is ever the excuse for further discrimination. Only by a union of intelligence and sympathy across the color-line in this critical period of the Republic shall justice and right triumph—

> That mind and soul according well,
> May make one music as before,
> But vaster.

Theodore Roosevelt

——— ★ ———

The Importance of Forest Preservation

Speech at a Meeting of the Society of
American Foresters,
Washington, D.C., March 26, 1903

Theodore Roosevelt (1858–1919) served nearly two terms as the twenty-sixth president of the United States, but he had the heart of an energetic and zealous reformer and the soul of a populist. He was the only president ever to run as a third-party candidate: in the 1912 election, his Progressive, or Bull Moose, party, ran second in popular and electoral votes, another unique achievement for a nonmainstream candidate and party. Roosevelt's presidency was marked by reforms and initiatives in the areas of food-purity regulations, labor relations, corporate regulation, and, especially, forest preservation, reserving hundreds of millions of acres as public land for forest and wildlife preserves and national parks. Roosevelt also won the 1906 Nobel Peace Prize for his mediation of the Russo-Japanese War and after his presidency continued to support such highly progressive concepts as graduated income taxes, greater federal regulation of business, and the recall of judges.

Mr. Pinchot, Mr. Secretary, and Gentlemen: I have felt that this evening the meeting was of such a character as not merely to warrant but in a sense require that I should break through my custom of not coming out to make speeches of this sort. For I believe there are few bodies of men who have it in their power to do a greater service to the country than those engaged in the scientific study and practical application of improved methods of forestry for the preservation of our woods in the United States. I am glad to see here this evening not only the officials, including the head, of the Department of Agriculture, but those, like Governor Richards, most concerned in carrying out the policy of the Department of the Interior.

First and foremost, you can never afford to forget for one moment what is the object of the forest policy. Primarily that object is not to preserve forests because they are beautiful—-though that is good in itself; not to preserve them because they are refuges for the wild creatures of the wilderness—though that too is good in itself; but the primary object of the forest policy, as of the land policy, of the United States, is the making of prosperous homes, is part of the traditional policy of home-making of our country. Every other consideration comes as secondary. The whole effort of the government in dealing with the forests must be directed to this end, keeping in view the fact that it is not only necessary to start the homes as prosperous, but to keep them so. That is the way the forests have need to be kept. You can start a prosperous home by destroying the forest, but you do not keep it. You will be able to make that policy permanently the policy of the country only insofar as you are able to make the people at large, and then all the people concretely, interested in the results in the different localities, appreciative of what it means; give them a full recognition of its value, and make them earnest and zealous adherents of it. Keep that in mind too. In a government such as ours it is out of the question to impose a policy like this upon the people from without. A permanent policy can come only from the intelligent conviction of the people themselves that it is wise and useful—nay, indispensable. We shall decide in the long run whether we will or will not preserve the forests of the Rocky Mountains accordingly as we are or are not able to make the people of the states around the mountains, in their neighborhood, hearty believers in the policy of forest preservation. This is the only way in which this policy can be made a permanent success. In other words, you must convince the people of the truth—and it is the truth—that the success of home-makers depends in the long run upon the wisdom with which the nation takes care of its forests.

That seems a strong statement. It is none too strong. There

are small sections of this country where what is done with the woodlands makes no difference; but over the great extent of the country the ultimate well-being of the home-maker will depend in very large part upon the intelligent use made of the forests. In other words, you yourselves must keep this practical object before your mind. You must remember that the forest which contributes nothing to the wealth, progress, or safety of the country is of no interest to the government, and it should be of little to the forester. Your attention should be directed not to the preservation of the forests as an end in itself, but as the means for preserving and increasing the prosperity of the nation. Forestry is the preservation of forests by wise use. We shall succeed, not by preventing the use, but by making the forests of use to the settler, the rancher, the miner, the man who lives in the neighborhood, and indirectly the man who may live hundreds of miles off, down the course of some great river which has its rise among the forests.

The forest problem is in many ways the most vital internal problem of the United States. The more closely this statement is examined the more evident its truth becomes. In the arid regions of the West agricultural prosperity depends first of all upon the available water supply. Forest protection alone can maintain the streamflow necessary for irrigation in the West and prevent floods destructive to agriculture and manufactures in the East. The relation between forests and the whole mineral industry is an extremely intimate one, for mines cannot be developed without timber, and usually not without timber close at hand. In many regions of the West ore is more abundant than wood, and where the ore is of low grade, transportation of the necessary mine timbers from a distance is out of the question. The use of the mine is strictly limited to the man who has timber available close at hand. The very existence of lumbering, the fourth great industry of the United States, depends upon the success of your work and our work as a nation in putting practical forestry into effective operation.

As it is with mining and lumbering, so it is in only less

degree with transportation, manufacture, and commerce in general. The relation of all these industries to the forests is of the most intimate and dependent kind. It is a matter for congratulation that so many of these great interests are waking up to this fact. The railroads, especially, managed as they are by men who are obliged by the very nature of their profession to possess insight into the future, have awakened to a clearer realization of the vast importance of economical use both of timber and of forests. Even the grazing industry, as it is carried out in the great West, which might at first sight appear to have little relation to forestry, is nevertheless closely related to it, because great areas of winter range would be entirely useless without the summer range in the mountains, where the forest reserves lie.

The forest resources of our country are already seriously depleted. They can be renewed and maintained only by the cooperation of the forester and the lumberman. The most striking and encouraging fact in the forest situation is that lumbermen are realizing that practical lumbering and practical forestry are allies and not enemies, and that the future of each depends upon the other. The resolutions passed at the last great meeting of the representative lumber interests held here in Washington are strong proof of this fact and the most encouraging feature of the present situation. As long as we could not make the men concerned in the great lumbering industry realize that the foresters were endeavoring to work in their interests and not against them, the headway that could be made was but small. And we will be able to work effectively to bring about immediate results of permanent importance largely in proportion as we are able to convince the men at the head of that great business of the practical wisdom of what the foresters of the United States are seeking to accomplish. In the last analysis, the attitude of the lumbermen toward your work will be the chief factor of the success or failure of that work. In other words, gentlemen, I cannot too often say to you, as indeed it cannot be too often said to any body of men of high ideals and of scientific training who are endeavoring to accomplish work of real worth for the country, you must keep your ideals, and yet seek to realize them in practical ways.

The United States is exhausting its forest supplies far more rapidly than they are being produced. The situation is a grave one, and there is but one remedy. That remedy is the introduction of practical forestry on a large scale, and of course that is impossible without trained men—men trained in the closet and trained by actual field work, under practical conditions. You will have created a new profession; a profession of the highest importance; a profession of the highest usefulness toward the state; and you are in honor-bound to yourselves and to the people to make your profession stand as high as the profession of law, as the profession of medicine, as any other profession most intimately connected with our highest and finest development as a nation. You are engaged in pioneer work in a calling whose opportunities for public service are very great. Treat the calling seriously; remember how much it means for the country as a whole; remember that if you do your work in crude fashion, if you only half learn your profession, you discredit it as well as yourselves. Give yourselves every chance by thorough and generous preparation and by acquiring not only a thorough knowledge, but a wide outlook over all the questions on which you have to touch.

The profession which you have adopted is one which touches the Republic on almost every side, political, social, industrial, commercial; and to rise to its level you will need a wide acquaintance with the general life of the nation, and a viewpoint both broad and high. Any profession which makes you deal with your fellow men at large makes it necessary that, if you are to succeed, you should understand what these fellow men are, and not merely what they are thought to be by people who live in the closet and the parlor. You must know who the men are with whom you are acting; how they feel; how far you can go; when you have to stop; when it is necessary to push on; you must know all of these things if you are going to do work of the highest value.

I believe that the foresters of the United States will create and apply a more effective system of forestry than we have yet seen. If you don't gentlemen, I will feel that you have fallen behind your brethren of other callings; and I don't believe you will fall behind them. Nowhere else is the development of a country more closely bound up with the creation and execution of a judicious forest policy. This is of course especially true of the West; but it is true of the East also. Fortunately in the West we have been able relative to the growth of the country to begin at an earlier day—so that we have been able to provide great forest reserves in the Rocky Mountains, instead of waiting and attempting to get Congress to pay a very large sum for their creation, as we are now endeavoring to do in the southern Appalachians. In the administration of the national forest reserves, the introduction of conservative lumbering on the timber tract of the lumberman and the woodlot of the farmer, in the practical solution of forest problems which affect every industry and every activity of the nation, the members of this society have an unexampled field before them.

You have heavy responsibilities—every man that does any work that is worth doing has a heavy responsibility—for upon the quality of your work the development of forestry in the United States and the protection of the industries which depend upon it will largely rest. You have made a good beginning, and I congratulate you upon it. Not only is a sound national forest policy coming rapidly into being, but the lumbermen of the country are proving their interest in forestry by practicing it.

Twenty years ago a meeting such as this tonight would have been impossible, and the desires we hear expressed would have been treated as having no possible relation to practical life. I think, Mr. Secretary, that since you first came into Congress here there has been a complete revolution in the attitude of public men toward this question. We have reached a point where American foresters, trained in American forest schools, are attacking American forest problems with success. That is the way to meet the larger work you have before you. It is a work of peculiar difficulty, because precedents are lacking. It will demand training, steadiness, devotion, and above all esprit de corps, fealty to the body of which you are members, zeal to keep the practice as well as the ideals of that body high. The more harmoniously you work with each other, the better your work will be.

And above all a condition precedent upon your usefulness to the body politic as a whole is the way in which you are able both to instill your own ideals into the mass of your fellowmen with whom you come in contact, and at the same time to show your ability to work in practical fashion with them; to convince them that as a business matter it will pay for them to cooperate with you; to convince the public of that, and then also so to convince the people of the localities, of the neighborhoods in which you work, and especially the lumbermen and all others who make their life trades dealing with the forests.

Jane Addams

— ★ —

Immigrants and Their Children

From *Twenty Years at Hull-House*, 1910

In 1889 Jane Addams (1860–1935) established Hull-House in a
lower-class immigrant neighborhood in Chicago as a settlement
devoted to social work among the poor. Addams and her associates at Hull-House provided local services and programs and
sponsored legislative initiatives to improve the working, living,
and educational environments of the poor. Particular emphasis
was placed on the abolition of child labor, ensuring safe factory
conditions, the support of unions, and encouraging compulsory
school attendance. Addams enthusiatically supported the re-
form-oriented candidacy of Theodore Roosevelt and his Progressive party in the 1912 presidential election. During and after
World War I, she devoted herself to the cause of world peace,
serving as president of the Women's International League for
Peace and Freedom from 1919 until her death in 1935. In her
1910 autobiography, Addams recounts the work at Hull-House
and vividly describes the daily lives of immigrants and their
children in Chicago.

From our very first months at Hull-House we found it much
easier to deal with the first generation of crowded city life
than with the second or third, because it is more natural and cast
in a simpler mold. The Italian and Bohemian peasants who live
in Chicago still put on their bright holiday clothes on a Sunday
and go to visit their cousins. They tramp along with at least a
suggestion of having once walked over plowed fields and
breathed country air. The second generation of city poor too
often have no holiday clothes and consider their relations a "bad
lot." I have heard a drunken man in a maudlin stage babble of
his good country mother and imagine he was driving the cows

home, and I knew that his little son who laughed loud at him
would be drunk earlier in life and would have no such pastroal
interlude to his ravings. Hospitality still survives among foreigners, although it is buried under false pride among the poorest
Americans.

One thing seemed clear in regard to entertaining immigrants; to preserve and keep whatever of value their past life
contained and to bring them in contact with a better type of
Americans. For several years, every Saturday evening the entire
families of our Italian neighbors were our guests. These evenings were very popular during our first winters at Hull-House.
Many educated Italians helped us, and the house became known
as a place where Italians were welcome and where national
holidays were observed. They come to us with their petty law-
suits, sad relics of the vendetta, with their incorrigible boys,
with their hospital cases, with their aspirations for American
clothes, and with their needs for an interpreter.

An editor of an Italian paper made a genuine connection
between us and the Italian colony, not only with the Neapoli-
tans and the Sicilians of the immediate neighborhood, but with
the educated *connazionali* throughout the city, until he went
south to start an agricultural colony in Alabama, in the establishment of which Hull-House heartily cooperated. Possibly the
South Italians more than any other immigrants represent the
pathetic stupidity of agricultural people crowded into city tene-
ments, and we were much gratified when thirty peasant families
were induced to move upon the land which they knew so well
how to cultivate. The starting of this colony, however, was a
very expensive affair in spite of the fact that the colonists purchased the land at two dollars an acre; they needed much more
than raw land, and although it was possible to collect the small
sums necessary to sustain them during the hard time of the first
two years, we were fully convinced that undertakings of this
sort could be conducted properly only by colonization societies
such as England has established, or, better still, by enlarging the
functions of the federal Department of Immigration.

An evening similar in purpose to the one devoted to the Italians was organized for the Germans, in our first year. Owing to the superior education of our Teutonic guests and the clever leading of a cultivated German woman, these evenings reflected something of that cozy social intercourse which is found in its perfection in the fatherland. Our guests sang a great deal in the tender minor of the German folksong or in the rousing spirit of the Rhine, and they slowly but persistently pursued a course in German history and literature, recovering something of that poetry and romance which they had long since resigned with other good things. We found strong family affection between them and their English-speaking children, but their pleasures were not in common, and they seldom went out together. Perhaps the greatest value of the settlement to them was in placing large and pleasant rooms with musical facilities at their disposal, and in reviving their almost forgotten enthusiasms. I have seen sons and daughters stand in complete surprise as their mother's knitting needles softly beat time to the song she was singing, or her worn face turned rosy under the hand-clapping as she made an old-fashioned courtesy at the end of a German poem. It was easy to fancy a growing touch of respect in her children's manner to her, and a rising enthusiasm for German literature and reminiscence on the part of all the family, an effort to bring together the old life and the new, a respect for the older cultivation, and not quite so much assurance that the new was the best.

This tendency upon the part of the older immigrants to lose the amenities of European life without sharing those of America has often been deplored by keen observers from the home countries. When Professor Masurek of Prague gave a course of lectures in the University of Chicago, he was much distressed over the materialism into which the Bohemians of Chicago had fallen. The early immigrants had been so stirred by the opportunity to own real estate, an appeal perhaps to the Slavic land hunger, and their energies had become so completely absorbed in money-making that all other interests had apparently dropped away. And yet I recall a very touching incident in connection with a lecture Professor Masurek gave at Hull-House, in which he had appealed to his countrymen to arouse themselves from this tendency to fall below their home civilization and to forget the great enthusiasm which had united them into the Pan-Slavic movement. A Bohemian widow, who supported herself and her two children by scrubbing, hastily sent her youngest child to purchase, with the twenty-five cents which was to have supplied them with food the next day, a bunch of red roses which she presented to the lecturer in appreciation of his testimony to the reality of the things of the spirit.

An overmastering desire to reveal the humbler immigrant parents to their own children lay at the base of what has come to be called the Hull-House Labor Museum. This was first suggested to my mind one early spring day when I saw an old Italian woman, her distaff against her homesick face, patiently spinning a thread by the simple stick spindle so reminiscent of all southern Europe. I was walking down Polk Street, perturbed in spirit, because it seemed so difficult to come into genuine relations with the Italian women and because they themselves so often lost their hold upon their Americanized children. It seemed to me that Hull-House ought to be able to devise some educational enterprise which should build a bridge between European and American experiences in such wise as to give them both more meaning and a sense of relation. I meditated that perhaps the power to see life as a whole is more needed in the immigrant quarter of a large city than anywhere else, and that the lack of this power is the most fruitful source of misunderstanding between European immigrants and their children, as it is between them and their American neighbors; and why should that chasm between fathers and sons, yawning at the feet of each generation, be made so unnecessarily cruel and impassable to these bewildered immigrants? Suddenly I looked up and saw the old woman with her distaff, sitting in the sun on the steps of a tenement house. She might have served as a model for one of Michelangelo's Fates, but her face brightened as I passed and, holding up her spindle for me to see, she called out that when she had spun a little more yarn, she would knit a pair of stockings for her goddaughter. The occupation of the old woman gave me the clue that was needed. Could we not interest the young people working in the neighboring factories, in these older forms of industry, so that, through their own parents and grandparents, they would find a dramatic representation of the inherited resources of their daily occupation. If these young people could actually see that the complicated machinery of the factory had been evolved from simple tools, they might at least make a beginning toward that education which Dr. Dewey defines as "a continuing reconstruction of experience." They might also lay a foundation for reverence of the past which Goethe declares to be the basis of all sound progress.

My exciting walk on Polk Street was followed by many talks with Dr. Dewey and with one of the teachers in his school who was a resident at Hull-House. Within a month a room was fitted up to which we might invite those of our neighbors who were possessed of old crafts and who were eager to use them.

We found in the immediate neighborhood at least four varieties of these most primitive methods of spinning and three distinct variations of the same spindle in connection with wheels. It was possible to put these seven into historic sequence and order and to connect the whole with the present method of factory spinning. The same thing was done for weaving, and on every Saturday evening a little exhibit was made of these various forms of labor in the textile industry. Within one room a Syrian woman, a Greek, an Italian, a Russian, and an Irish woman enabled even the most casual observer to see that there is no break in orderly evolution if we look at history from the industrial standpoint; that industry develops similarly and peacefully year by year among the workers of each nation, heedless of differences in language, religion, and political experiences.

And then we grew ambitious and arranged lectures upon industrial history. I remember that after an interesting lecture upon the industrial revolution in England and a portrayal of the appalling conditions throughout the weaving districts of the north, which resulted from the hasty gathering of the weavers into the new towns, a Russian tailor in the audience was moved to make a speech. He suggested that whereas time had done much to alleviate the first difficulties in the transition of weaving from hand work to steam power, that in the application of steam to sewing we are still in the first stages, illustrated by the isolated woman who tries to support herself by hand needle-work at home until driven out by starvation, as many of the hand weavers had been. . . .

The textile department is connected directly with the basket weaving, sewing, millinery, embroidery, and dressmaking constantly being taught at Hull-House, and so far as possible with the other educational departments; we have also been able to make a collection of products, of early implements, and of photographs which are full of suggestion. Yet far beyond its direct educational value, we prize it because it so often puts the immigrants into the position of teachers, and we imagine that it affords them a pleasant change from the tutelage in which all Americans, including their own children, are so apt to hold them. . . .

The Labor Museum and the shops pointed out the possibilities which Hull-House has scarcely begun to develop, of demonstrating that culture is an understanding of the long-established occupations and thoughts of men, of the arts with which they have solaced their toil. A yearning to recover for the household arts something of their early sanctity and meaning arose strongly within me one evening when I was attending a Passover feast to which I had been invited by a Jewish family in the neighborhood, where the traditional and religious significance of woman's daily activity was still retained. The kosher food the Jewish mother spread before her family had been prepared according to traditional knowledge and with constant care in the use of utensils; upon her had fallen the responsibility to make all ready according to Mosaic instructions, that the great crisis in a religious history might be fittingly set forth by her husband and son. Aside from the grave religious significance in the ceremony, my mind was filled with shifting pictures of woman's labor with which travel makes one familiar; the Indian women grinding grain outside of their huts as they sing praises to the sun and rain; a file of white-clad Moorish women whom I had once seen waiting their turn at a well in Tangiers; south Italian women kneeling in a row along the stream and beating their wet clothes against the smooth white stones; the milking, the gardening, the marketing in thousands of hamlets, which are such direct expressions of the solicitude and affection at the basis of all family life.

There has been some testimony that the Labor Museum has revealed the charm of woman's primitive activities. I recall a certain Italian girl who came every Saturday evening to a cooking class in the same building in which her mother spun in the Labor Museum exhibit; and yet Angelina always left her mother at the front door while she herself went around to a side door because she did not wish to be too closely identified in the eyes of the rest of the cooking class with an Italian woman who wore a kerchief over her head, uncouth boots, and short petticoats. One evening, however, Angelina saw her mother surrounded by a group of visitors from the School of Education, who much admired the spinning, and she concluded from their conversation that her mother was "the best stick-spindle spinner in America." When she inquired from me as to the truth of this deduction, I took occasion to describe the Italian village in which her mother had lived, something of her free life, and how, because of the opportunity she and the other women of the village had to drop their spindles over the edge of a precipice, they had developed a skill in spinning beyond that of the neighboring towns. I dilated somewhat on the freedom and beauty of that life—how hard it must be to exchange it all for a two-room tenement, and to give up a beautiful homespun kerchief for an ugly department store hat. I intimated it was most unfair to judge her by these things alone, and that while she must depend on her daughter to learn the new ways, she also had a right to expect her daughter to know something of the old ways.

That which I could not convey to the child but upon which my own mind persistently dwelt was that her mother's whole life had been spent in a secluded spot under the rule of traditional and narrowly localized observances, until her very religion clung to local sanctities—to the shrine before which she had always prayed, to the pavement and walls of the low vaulted church—and then suddenly she was torn from it all and literally put out to sea, straight away from the solid habits of her religious and domestic life, and she now walked timidly but with poignant sensibility upon a new and strange shore.

It was easy to see that the thought of her mother with any other background than that of the tenement was new to Angelina and at least two things resulted; she allowed her mother to pull out of the big box under the bed the beautiful homespun garments which had been previously hidden away as uncouth; and she openly came into the Labor Museum by the same door as did her mother, proud at least of the mastery of the craft which had been so much admired. . . .

The Labor Museum continually demanded more space as it was enriched by a fine textile exhibit lent by the Field Museum, and later by carefully selected specimens of basketry from the Philippines. The shops have finally included a group of three or four women, Irish, Italian, Danish, who have become a permanent working force in the textile department which has developed into a self-supporting industry through the sale of its homespun products.

These women and a few men, who come to the museum to utilize their European skill in pottery, metal, and wood, demonstrate that immigrant colonies might yield to our American life something very valuable, if their resources were intelligently studied and developed. I recall an Italian who had decorated the doorposts of his tenement with a beautiful pattern he had previously used in carving the reredos of a Neapolitan church, who was "fired" by his landlord on the ground of destroying property. His feelings were hurt, not so much that he had been put out of his house, as that his work had been so disregarded; and he said that when people traveled in Italy they liked to look at wood carvings but that in America "they only made money out of you."

Sometimes the suppression of the instinct of workmanship is followed by more disastrous results. A Bohemian, whose little girl attended classes at Hull-House, in one of his periodic drunken spells had literally almost choked her to death, and later had committed suicide when in delirium tremens. His poor wife, who stayed a week at Hull-House after the disaster until a new tenement could be arranged for her, one day showed me a gold ring which her husband had made for their betrothal. It exhibited the most exquisite workmanship, and she said that although in the old country he had been a goldsmith, in America he had for twenty years shoveled coal in a furnace room of a large manufacturing plant; that whenever she saw one of his "restless fits," which preceded his drunken periods, "coming on," if she could provide him with a bit of metal and persuade him to stay at home and work at it, he was all right and the time passed without disaster, but that "nothing else would do it." This story threw a flood of light upon the dead man's struggle and on the stupid maladjustment which had broken him down. Why had we never been told? Why had our interest in the remarkable musical ability of his child blinded us to the hidden artistic ability of the father? We had forgotten that a long-established occupation may form the very foundations of the moral life, that the art with which a man has solaced his toil may be the salvation of his uncertain temperament.

There are many examples of touching fidelity to immigrant parents on the part of their grown children; a young man, who day after day, attends ceremonies which no longer express his religious convictions and who makes his vain effort to interest his Russian Jewish father in social problems; a daughter who might earn much more money as a stenographer could she work from Monday morning till Saturday night, but who quietly and docilely makes neckties for low wages because she can thus abstain from work Saturdays to please her father; these young people, . . . through many painful experiences have reached the conclusion that pity, memory, and faithfulness are natural ties with paramount claims.

This faithfulness, however, is sometimes ruthlessly imposed upon by immigrant parents who, eager for money and accustomed to the patriarchal authority of peasant households, hold their children in a stern bondage which requires a surrender of all their wages and concedes no time or money for pleasures.

There are many convincing illustrations that this parental harshness often results in juvenile delinquency. A Polish boy of seventeen came to Hull-House one day to ask a contribution of fifty cents "toward a flowerpiece for the funeral of an old Hull-House club boy." A few questions made it clear that the object was fictitious, whereupon the boy broke down and half-defiantly stated that he wanted to buy two twenty-five-cent tickets, one for his girl and one for himself, to a dance of the Benevolent Social Twos; that he hadn't a penny of his own although he had worked in a brass foundry for three years and had been advanced twice, because he always had to give his pay envelope unopened to his father. "Just look at the clothes he buys me" was his concluding remark.

Perhaps the girls are held even more rigidly. In a recent investigation of two hundred working girls it was found that only 5 percent had the use of their own money and that 62 percent turned in all they earned, literally every penny, to their mothers. It was through this little investigation that we first knew Marcella, a pretty young German girl who helped her widowed mother year after year to care for a large family of younger children. She was content for the most part, although her mother's old-country notions of dress gave her but an infinitesimal amount of her own wages to spend on her clothes, and she was quite sophisticated as to proper dressing because she sold silk in a neighborhood department store. Her mother approved of the young man who was showing her various attentions and agreed that Marcella should accept his invitation to a ball, but would allow her not a penny toward a new gown to replace one impossibly plain and shabby. Marcella spent a sleepless night and wept bitterly, although she well knew that the doctor's bill for the children's scarlet fever was not yet paid. The next day as she was cutting off three yards of shining pink silk, the thought came to her that it would make her a fine new waist to wear to the ball. She wistfully saw it wrapped in paper and carelessly stuffed into the muff of the purchaser, when suddenly the parcel fell upon the floor. No one was looking, and quick as a flash the girl picked it up and pushed it into her blouse. The theft was discovered by the relentless department store detective who, for "the sake of the example," insisted upon taking the case into court. The poor mother wept bitter tears over this downfall of her "frommes Mädchen," and no one had the heart to tell her of her own blindness.

I know a Polish boy whose earnings were all given to his father who gruffly refused all requests for pocket money. One Christmas his little sisters, having been told by their mother that they were too poor to have any Christmas presents, appealed to the big brother as to one who was earning money of his own. Flattered by the implication, but at the same time quite impecunious, the night before Christmas he nonchalantly walked through a neighboring department store and stole a manicure set for one little sister and a string of beads for the other. He was caught at the door by the house detective as one of those children whom each local department store arrests in the weeks before Christmas at the daily rate of eight to twenty. The youngest of these offenders are seldom taken into court but are either sent home with a warning or turned over to the officers of the Juvenile Protective Association. Most of these premature lawbreakers are in search of Americanized clothing and others are only looking for playthings. They are all distracted by the profusion and variety of the display, and their moral sense is confused by the general air of open-handedness. . . .

Many of these children have come to grief through their premature fling into city life, having thrown off parental control as they have impatiently discarded foreign ways. Boys of ten and twelve will refuse to sleep at home, preferring the freedom of an old brewery vault or an empty warehouse to the obedience required by their parents, and for days these boys will live on the milk and bread which they steal from the back porches after the early morning delivery. Such children complain that there is "no fun" at home. One little chap, who was given a vacant lot to cultivate by the City Garden Association, insisted upon raising only popcorn and tried to present the entire crop to Hull-House "to be used for the parties," with the stipulation that he would have "to be invited every single time." Then there are little groups of dissipated young men who pride themselves upon their ability to live without working, and who despise all the honest and sober ways of their immigrant parents. They are at once a menace and a center of demoralization. Certainly the bewildered parents, unable to speak English and ignorant of the city, whose children have disappeared for days or weeks, have often come to Hull-House, evincing that agony which fairly separates the marrow from the bone, as if they had discovered a new type of suffering, devoid of the healing in familiar sorrows. It is as if they did not know how to search for the children without the assistance of the children themselves. Perhaps the most pathetic aspect of such cases is their revelation of the premature dependence of the older and wiser upon the young and foolish, which is in itself often responsible for the situation because it has given the children an undue sense of their own importance and a false security that they can take care of themselves. . . .

It is difficult to write of the relation of the older and most foreign-looking immigrants to the children of other people—the Italians whose fruit-carts are upset simply because they are "dagoes," or the Russian peddlers who are stoned and sometimes badly injured because it has become a code of honor in a gang of boys to thus express their derision. The members of a Protective Association of Jewish Peddlers organized at Hull-House related daily experiences in which old age had been treated with such irreverence, cherished dignity with such disrespect, that a listener caught the passion of Lear in the old texts, as a platitude enunciated by a man who discovers in it his own experience, thrills us as no unfamiliar phrases can possibly do. The Greeks are filled with amazed rage when their very name is flung at them as an opprobrious epithet.

Doubtless these difficulties would be much minimized in America if we faced our own race problem with courage and intelligence, and these very Mediterranean immigrants might give us valuable help. Certainly they are less conscious than the Anglo-Saxon of color distinctions, perhaps because of their traditional familiarity with Carthage and Egypt. They listened with respect and enthusiasm to a scholarly address delivered by Professor Du Bois at Hull-House on a Lincoln's birthday, with apparently no consciousness of that race difference which color seems to accentuate so absurdly, and upon my return from various conferences held in the interest of "the advancement of colored people," I have had many illuminating conversations with my cosmopolitan neighbors.

EMMA GOLDMAN

—— ★ ——

Anarchism: What It Really
Stands For

From *Anarchism and Other Essays*, 1911

*Anarchism has its philosophical and political-action roots in
the nineteenth century with the French writer Pierre Joseph
Proudhon and the Russian revolutionary Michael Bakunin; as
a societal force, anarchism lasted only into the early 1920s. Unlike socialism, with its emphasis on state control, anarchism
promoted the primacy of the individual and rejected all governments; the two political philosophies converged on anticapital-
ism and prounionism. Emma Goldman (1869–1940), born in
Russia, was a leader of the American anarchist movement from
the 1890s until her deportation to her native country in 1920. She
was imprisoned in the United States a number of times for her
activities, published an anarchist periodical,* Mother Earth, *opposed the imperialism of the First World War, supported and
then severely criticized the new Soviet government in the 1920s,
and worked for the Republican side in the Spanish Civil War
(1936–1939).*

The history of human growth and development is at the
same time the history of the terrible struggle of every new
idea heralding the approach of a brighter dawn. In its tenacious
hold on tradition, the old has never hesitated to make use of the
foulest and cruelest means to stay the advent of the new, in
whatever form or period the latter may have asserted itself. Nor
need we retrace our steps into the distant past to realize the
enormity of opposition, difficulties, and hardships placed in the
path of every progressive idea. The rack, the thumbscrew, and
the knout are still with us; so are the convict's garb and the

social wrath, all conspiring against the spirit that is serenely marching on.

Anarchism could not hope to escape the fate of all other ideas of innovation. Indeed, as the most revolutionary and uncompromising innovator, anarchism must needs meet with the combined ignorance and venom of the world it aims to reconstruct.

To deal even remotely with all that is being said and done against anarchism would necessitate the writing of a whole volume. I shall therefore meet only two of the principal objections. In so doing, I shall attempt to elucidate what anarchism really stands for.

The strange phenomenon of the opposition to anarchism is that it brings to light the relation between so-called intelligence and ignorance. And yet this is not so very strange when we consider the relativity of all things. The ignorant mass has in its favor that it makes no pretence of knowledge or tolerance. Acting, as it always does, by mere impulse, its reasons are like those of a child. "Why?" "Because." Yet the opposition of the uneducated to anarchism deserves the same consideration as that of the intelligent man.

What, then, are the objections? First, anarchism is impractical, though a beautiful ideal. Second, anarchism stands for violence and destruction, hence it must be repudiated as vile and dangerous. Both the intelligent man and the ignorant mass judge not from a thorough knowledge of the subject, but either from hearsay or false interpretation.

A practical scheme, says Oscar Wilde, is either one already in existence, or a scheme that could be carried out under the existing conditions; but it is exactly the existing conditions that one objects to, and any scheme that could accept these conditions is wrong and foolish. The true criterion of the practical, therefore, is not whether the latter can keep intact the wrong or foolish; rather is it whether the scheme has vitality enough to leave the stagnant waters of the old, and build, as well as sustain, new life. In the light of this conception, anarchism is indeed practical. More than any other idea, it is helping to do away with the wrong and foolish; more than any other idea, it is building and sustaining new life.

The emotions of the ignorant man are continuously kept at a pitch by the most blood-curdling stories about anarchism—not a thing too outrageous to be employed against this philosophy and its exponents. Therefore anarchism represents to the unthinking what the proverbial bad man does to the child—a black monster bent on swallowing everything; in short, destruction and violence.

Destruction and violence! How is the ordinary man to know that the most violent element in society is ignorance—that its power of destruction is the very thing anarchism is combating? Nor is he aware that anarchism, whose roots, as it were, are part of nature's forces, destroys not healthful tissue but parasitic growths that feed on the life's essence of society. It is merely clearing the soil from weeds and sagebrush, that it may eventually bear healthy fruit.

Someone has said that it requires less mental effort to condemn than to think. The widespread mental indolence, so prevalent in society, proves this to be only too true. Rather than to go to the bottom of any given idea, to examine into its origin and meaning, most people will either condemn it altogether, or rely on some superficial or prejudicial definition of nonessentials.

Anarchism urges man to think, to investigate, to analyze every proposition; but that the brain capacity of the average reader be not taxed too much, I also shall begin with a definition, and then elaborate on the latter.

ANARCHISM. The philosophy of a new social order based on liberty unrestricted by man-made law; the theory that all forms of government rest on violence, and are therefore wrong and harmful, as well as unnecessary.

The new social order rests, of course, on the materialistic basis of life; but while all anarchists agree that the main evil today is an economic one, they maintain that the solution of that evil can be brought about only through the consideration of *every phase* of life—individual, as well as the collective; the internal, as well as the external phases.

A thorough perusal of the history of human development will disclose two elements in bitter conflict with each other, elements that are only now beginning to be understood, not as foreign to each other, but as closely related and truly harmonious, if only placed in proper environment: the individual and social instincts. The individual and society have waged a relentless and bloody battle for ages, each striving for supremacy, because each was blind to the value and importance of the other. The individual and social instincts: the one a most potent factor for individual endeavor, for growth, aspiration, self-realization; the other an equally potent factor for mutual helpfulness and social well-being.

The explanation of the storm raging within the individual, and between him and his surroundings, is not far to seek. The primitive man, unable to understand his being, much less the unity of all life, felt himself absolutely dependent on blind, hidden forces ever ready to mock and taunt him. Out of that attitude grew the religious concepts of man as a mere speck of dust dependent on superior powers on high, who can only be appeased by complete surrender. All the early sagas rest on that idea, which continues to be the leitmotiv of the biblical tales dealing with the relation of man to God, to the state, to society. Again and again the same motif: *Man is nothing, the powers are everything.* Thus Jehovah would only endure man on condition of complete surrender. Man can have all the glories of the earth, but he must not become conscious of himself. The state, society, and moral laws all sing the same refrain: Man can have all the glories of the earth, but he must not become conscious of himself.

Anarchism is the only philosophy which brings to man the consciousness of himself, which maintains that God, the state, and society are nonexistent, that their promises are null and void, since they can be fulfilled only through man's subordination. Anarchism is therefore the teacher of the unity of life; not merely in nature, but in man. There is no conflict between the individual and the social instincts, any more than there is between the heart and the lungs: the one the receptacle of a precious life essence, the other the repository of the element that keeps the essence pure and strong. The individual is the heart of society, conserving the essence of social life; society is the lungs which are distributing the element to keep the life essence—that is, the individual—pure and strong.

"The one thing of value in the world," says Emerson, "is the active soul; this every man contains within him. The soul active sees absolute truth and utters truth and creates." In other words, the individual instinct is the thing of value in the world. It is the true soul that sees and creates the truth alive, out of which is to come a still greater truth, the reborn social soul.

Anarchism is the great liberator of man from the phantoms that have held him captive; it is the arbiter and pacifier of the two forces for individual and social harmony. To accomplish that unity, anarchism has declared war on the pernicious influences which have so far prevented the harmonious blending of individual and social instincts, the individual and society.

Religion, the dominion of the human mind; property, the dominion of human needs; and government, the dominion of human conduct, represent the stronghold of man's enslavement and all the horrors it entails. Religion! How it dominates man's mind, how it humiliates and degrades his soul. God is everything, man is nothing, says religion. But out of that nothing God has created a kingdom so despotic, so tyrannical, so cruel, so terribly exacting that naught but gloom and tears and blood have ruled the world since gods began. Anarchism rouses man to rebellion against this black monster. Break your mental fetters, says anarchism to man, for not until you think and judge for yourself will you get rid of the dominion of darkness, the greatest obstacle to all progress.

Property, the dominion of man's needs, the denial of the

right to satisfy his needs. Time was when property claimed a divine right, when it came to man with the same refrain, even as religion, "Sacrifice! Abnegate! Submit!" The spirit of anarchism has lifted man from his prostrate position. He now stands erect, with his face toward the light. He has learned to see the insatiable, devouring, devastating nature of property, and he is preparing to strike the monster dead.

"Property is robbery," said the great French anarchist Proudhon. Yes, but without risk and danger to the robber. Monopolizing the accumulated efforts of man, property has robbed him of his birthright and has turned him loose a pauper and an outcast. Property has not even the time-worn excuse that man does not create enough to satisfy all needs. The A-B-C student of economics knows that the productivity of labor within the last few decades far exceeds normal demand. But what are normal demands to an abnormal institution? The only demand that property recognizes is its own gluttonous appetite for greater wealth, because wealth means power—the power to subdue, to crush, to exploit, the power to enslave, to outrage, to degrade. America is particularly boastful of her great power, her enormous national wealth. Poor America, of what avail is all her wealth, if the individuals comprising the nation are wretchedly poor? If they live in squalor, in filth, in crime, with hope and joy gone, a homeless, soilless army of human prey.

It is generally conceded that unless the returns of any business venture exceed the cost, bankruptcy is inevitable. But those engaged in the business of producing wealth have not yet learned even this simple lesson. Every year the cost of production in human life is growing larger (fifty thousand killed, one hundred thousand wounded in America last year); the returns to the masses, who help to create wealth, are ever getting smaller. Yet America continues to be blind to the inevitable bankruptcy of our business of production. Nor is this the only crime of the latter. Still more fatal is the crime of turning the producer into a mere particle of a machine, with less will and decision than his master of steel and iron. Man is being robbed not merely of the products of his labor, but of the power of free initiative, of originality, and the interest in, or desire for, the things he is making.

Real wealth consists in things of utility and beauty, in things that help to create strong, beautiful bodies and surroundings inspiring to live in. But if man is doomed to wind cotton around a spool, or dig coal, or build roads for thirty years of his life, there can be no talk of wealth. What he gives to the world is only gray and hideous things, reflecting a dull and hideous existence—too weak to live, too cowardly to die. Strange to say, there are people who extol this deadening method of centralized production as the proudest achievement of our age. They fail utterly to realize that if we are to continue in machine subserviency, our slavery is more complete than was our bondage to the king. They do not want to know that centralization is not only the deathknell of liberty, but also of health and beauty, of art and science, all these being impossible in a clocklike, mechanical atmosphere.

Anarchism cannot but repudiate such a method of production: its goal is the freest possible expression of all the latent powers of the individual. Oscar Wilde defines a perfect personality as "one who develops under perfect conditions, who is not wounded, maimed, or in danger." A perfect personality, then, is only possible in a state of society where man is free to choose the mode of work, the conditions of work, and the freedom to work—one to whom the making of a table, the building of a house, or the tilling of the soil is what the painting is to the artist and the discovery to the scientist: the result of inspiration, of intense longing, and deep interest in work as a creative force. That being the ideal of anarchism its economic arrangements must consist of voluntary productive and distributive associations, gradually developing into free communism, as the best means of producing with the least waste of human energy. Anarchism, however, also recognizes the right of the individual, or numbers of individuals, to arrange at all times for other forms of work, in harmony with their tastes and desires.

Such free display of human energy being possible only under complete individual and social freedom, anarchism directs its forces against the third and greatest foe of all social equality; namely, the state, organized authority, or statutory law—the dominion of human conduct.

Just as religion has fettered the human mind, and as property, or the monopoly of things, has subdued and stifled man's needs, so has the state enslaved his spirit, dictating every phase of conduct. "All government in essence," says Emerson, "is tyranny." It matters not whether it is government by divine right or majority rule. In every instance its aim is the absolute subordination of the individual.

Referring to the American government, the greatest American anarchist, David Thoreau, said: "Government: what is it but a tradition, though a recent one, endeavoring to transmit itself unimpaired to posterity, but each instance losing its integrity? It has not the vitality and force of a single living man. Law never made man a whit more just; and by means of their respect for it, even the well disposed are daily made agents of injustice."

Indeed, the keynote of government is injustice. With the arrogance and self-sufficiency of the king who could do no wrong, governments ordain, judge, condemn, and punish the most insignificant offenses, while maintaining themselves by the greatest of all offenses, the annihilation of individual liberty. Thus Ouida is right when she maintains that "the state only aims at instilling those qualities in its public by which its demands are obeyed, and its exchequer is filled. Its highest attainment is the reduction of mankind to clockwork. In its atmosphere all those finer and more delicate liberties, which require treatment and spacious expansion, inevitably dry up and perish. The state requires a taxpaying machine in which there is no hitch, an exchequer in which there is never a deficit, and a public, monotonous, obedient, colorless, spiritless, moving humbly like a flock of sheep along a straight high road between two walls."

Yet even a flock of sheep would resist the chicanery of the

state, if it were not for the corruptive, tyrannical, and oppressive methods it employs to serve its purposes. Therefore Bakunin repudiates the state as synonymous with the surrender of the liberty of the individual or small minorities—the destruction of social relationship, the curtailment, or complete denial even, of life itself, for its own aggrandizement. The state is the altar of political freedom and, like the religious altar, it is maintained for the purpose of human sacrifice.

In fact, there is hardly a modern thinker who does not agree that government, organized authority, or the state, is necessary *only* to maintain or protect property and monopoly. It has proven efficient in that function only. . . .

The most absurd apology for authority and law is that they serve to diminish crime. Aside from the fact that the state is itself the greatest criminal, breaking every written and natural law, stealing in the form of taxes, killing in the form of war and capital punishment, it has come to an absolute standstill in coping with crime. It has failed utterly to destroy or even minimize the horrible scourge of its own creation.

Crime is naught but misdirected energy. So long as every institution of today, economic, political, social, and moral, conspires to misdirect human energy into wrong channels, so long as most people are out of place doing the things they hate to do, living a life they loathe to live, crime will be inevitable, and all the laws on the statutes can only increase, but never do away with, crime. What does society, as it exists today, know of the process of despair, the poverty, the horrors, the fearful struggle the human soul must pass on its way to crime and degradation? . . .

In destroying government and statutory laws, anarchism proposes to rescue the self-respect and independence of the individual from all restraint and invasion by authority. Only in freedom can man grow to his full stature. Only in freedom will he learn to think and move, and give the very best in him. Only in freedom will he realize the true force of the social bonds which knit men together, and which are the true foundation of a normal social life.

But what about human nature? Can it be changed? And if not, will it endure under anarchism?

Poor human nature, what horrible crimes have been committed in thy name! Every fool, from king to policeman, from the flat-headed parson to the visionless dabbler in science, presumes to speak authoritatively of human nature. The greater the mental charlatan, the more definite his insistence on the wickedness and weaknesses of human nature. Yet, how can anyone speak of it today, with every soul in a prison, with every heart fettered, wounded, and maimed?

John Burroughs has stated that experimental study of animals in captivity is absolutely useless. Their character, their habits, their appetites undergo a complete transformation when torn from their soil in field and forest. With human nature caged in a narrow space, whipped daily into submission, how can we speak of its potentialities?

Freedom, expansion, opportunity, and, above all, peace and repose, alone can teach us the real dominant factors of human nature and all its wonderful possibilities.

Anarchism, then, really stands for the liberation of the human mind from the dominion of religion; the liberation of the human body from the dominion of property; liberation from the shackles and restraint of government. Anarchism stands for a social order based on the free grouping of individuals for the purpose of producing real social wealth—an order that will guarantee to every human being free access to the earth and full enjoyment of the necessities of life, according to individual desires, tastes, and inclinations.

This is not a wild fancy or an aberration of the mind. It is the conclusion arrived at by hosts of intellectual men and women the world over, a conclusion resulting from the close and studious observation of the tendencies of modern society: individual liberty and economic equality, the twin forces for the birth of what is fine and true in man. . . .

Anarchism does not stand for military drill and uniformity; it does, however, stand for the spirit of revolt, in whatever form, against everything that hinders human growth. All anarchists agree in that, as they also agree in their opposition to the political machinery as a means of bringing about the great social change.

"All voting," says Thoreau, "is a sort of gaming, like checkers, or backgammon, a playing with right and wrong; its obligation never exceeds that of expediency. Even voting for the right thing is doing nothing for it. A wise man will not leave the right to the mercy of chance, nor wish it to prevail through the power of the majority." A close examination of the machinery of politics and its achievements will bear out the logic of Thoreau.

What does the history of parliamentarism show? Nothing but failure and defeat, not even a single reform to ameliorate the economic and social stress of the people. Laws have been passed and enactments made for the improvement and protection of labor. Thus it was proven only last year that Illinois, with the most rigid laws for mine protection, had the greatest mine disasters. In states where child labor laws prevail, child exploitation is at its highest, and though with us the workers enjoy full political opportunities, capitalism has reached the most brazen zenith.

Even were the workers able to have their own representatives, for which our good socialist politicians are clamoring, what chances are there for their honesty and good faith? One has but to bear in mind the process of politics to realize that its path of good intentions is full of pitfalls: wire-pulling, intriguing, flattering, lying, cheating; in fact, chicanery of every description, whereby the political aspirant can achieve success. Added to that is a complete demoralization of character and conviction, until nothing is left that would make one hope for anything from such a human derelict. Time and time again the people were foolish enough to trust, believe, and support with their last farthing aspiring politicians, only to find themselves betrayed and cheated. . . .

Anarchism therefore stands for direct action, the open defiance of, and resistance to, all laws and restrictions, economic, social, and moral. But defiance and resistance are illegal. Therein lies the salvation of man. Everything illegal necessitates integrity, self-reliance, and courage. In short, it calls for free, independent spirits, for "men who are men, and who have a bone in their backs which you cannot pass your hand through."

Universal suffrage itself owes its existence to direct action. If not for the spirit of rebellion, of the defiance on the part of the American revolutionary fathers, their posterity would still wear the king's coat. If not for the direct action of a John Brown and his comrades, America would still trade in the flesh of the black man. True, the trade in white flesh is still going on; but that, too, will have to be abolished by direct action. Trade unionism, the economic arena of the modern gladiator, owes its existence to direct action. . . .

Direct action, having proven effective along economic lines, is equally potent in the environment of the individual. There a hundred forces encroach upon his being, and only persistent resistance to them will finally set him free. Direct action against the authority in the shop, direct action against the authority of the law, direct action against the invasive, meddlesome authority of our moral code, is the logical, consistent method of anarchism.

Will it not lead to a revolution? Indeed, it will. No real social change has ever come about without a revolution. People are either not familiar with their history, or they have not yet learned that revolution is but thought carried into action.

Anarchism, the great leaven of thought, is today permeating every phase of human endeavor. Science, art, literature, the drama, the effort for economic betterment, in fact every individual and social opposition to the existing disorder of things, is illumined by the spiritual light of anarchism. It is the philosophy of the sovereignty of the individual. It is the theory of social harmony. It is the great, surging, living truth that is reconstructing the world, and that will usher in the Dawn.

MOTHER JONES

—— ★ ——

The Working Poor on Strike

Testimony Before the U.S. Commission on
Industrial Relations, May 13, 1915

---

*Mother Jones (1830–1930) was born Mary Harris near Cork,
Ireland, and was educated in Toronto, Canada. She taught
school in Monroe, Michigan, and Memphis, Tennessee, and
worked as a dressmaker in Chicago, before marrying George
Jones in 1861. After her husband and four children died in a
yellow fever epidemic six years later, Mary Harris Jones returned to dressmaking in Chicago, only to lose all her posses-
sions in that city's great fire of 1871. She then began an
association with the Knights of Labor and in 1877 became involved with the calamitous nationwide railroad workers' strike
in Pittsburgh. In 1890 she became an organizer for the newly
formed United Mine Workers of America. She adopted a socialist political philosophy—her first article, signed "Mother
Jones," was published in the* International Socialist Review
*—and during the next three decades she lent her support to
labor disputes and miners' strikes wherever they occurred and
fought for child-labor legislation. A national and legendary
figure by the time she died at the age of one hundred, Mother
Jones was a promethean reformer and workers' advocate and an
electrifying orator. Her testimony in 1915 before a presidential
commission investigating the Colorado coal-mine strike of
1913–1914 amounted to a social history of labor strikes during
the previous four decades.*

CHAIRMAN WALSH. What is your name?
MOTHER JONES. Mary Jones.
CHAIRMAN WALSH. Where do you reside?
    MOTHER JONES. Well, I reside wherever there is a good fight
against wrong—all over the country.

CHAIRMAN WALSH. Do you claim a residence in any particular state?

MOTHER JONES. No. Wherever the workers are fighting the robbers I go there.

CHAIRMAN WALSH. Now, it may seem unnecessary, but you are the lady that is known to the country as Mother Jones, are you?

MOTHER JONES. I suppose so, Mr. Walsh.

CHAIRMAN WALSH. I will go right to the cause of the inquiry. You have listened to a great deal of it here, I notice. It is the administration or the lack of administration of law in industrial disputes. So I am going to ask you first, Mrs. Jones, were you in the Pittsburgh railroad strike of 1877?

MOTHER JONES. Yes.

CHAIRMAN WALSH. At what point in the country were you, Mrs. Jones?

MOTHER JONES. At Pittsburgh.

CHAIRMAN WALSH. I would like you to give your experience in that strike, so far as the administration of the law or the conduct of the officials was concerned.

MOTHER JONES. Well, the strike began in Martinsburg, Ohio. It started with the Baltimore & Ohio Railroad employees, and it reached down to Pittsburgh and east to Scranton. I was in New York. I came down. I was a member of the Knights of Labor at that time, and some of the boys met me and asked me to stay over with them, and I did. So the traffic was stopped, and a lawless element that had got into Pittsburgh during the panic of 1873, they had gathered in from the eastern part of the country and, of course, began to revolt and started to rioting. The employees of the railroad and others went to the mayor of the city and asked him if he would not swear them in as deputies to preserve the property and have the law enforced. While this was going on the sheriff of the county telegraphed to the governor, and the governor sent the militia.

Now, at that time I believe the troops went to Pittsburgh, but the fight turned onto the Pennsylvania Railroad; it concentrated on the Pennsylvania Railroad mostly, and some of the militia was quartered in the roundhouse. The businessmen of Pittsburgh, who for years had complained of discrimination by the railroad company against the city, were free in their expression of enmity against the company. Some of them connected with this committed acts of violence and actually participated in the riots that followed. Cars were set on fire and run down the tracks to the roundhouse, which was destroyed, together with over a hundred locomotives belonging to the Pennsylvania Railroad Company.

The feeling at that time of many workers and sympathizers was one of distrust and in many instances amounted to hatred, because the corporations of that day were open and successful in passing antilabor legislation, tramp laws, and other legislation, which caused the workers to feel that they were being discriminated against. The corporations succeeded in the passing of the law which required that in case of a strike the train crew should bring in a locomotive to the starting place before the strike would begin. It was because of that legislation that so many locomotives were housed at Pittsburgh and became the prey to the flames by an outraged populace, and not by the workers and not by strikers. I know most of the strikers; all had done everything they could to keep order. Not but what they felt the sting of the lash, the injustice that was done, but nevertheless they wanted to keep order and be steady because they felt that the railroad company had discriminated against them so much. That is about as much as I remember of that. I haven't the notes. I have them laid away, Mr. Walsh, but I am over all the country, and I don't know where to lay hands on things.

CHAIRMAN WALSH. You made notes of all these strikes at the time?

MOTHER JONES. Mostly. I have made notes of them all.

CHAIRMAN WALSH. Were you in the anthracite strike in Pennsylvania in 1900?

MOTHER JONES. Yes.

CHAIRMAN WALSH. I wish you would give us whatever comment you have on that as to violence and administration of the law and the action of the authorities in it.

MOTHER JONES. I had been down in Arnot, Pennsylvania. We had a strike there for six months, but there were no deputies and no gunmen and no militia brought in there, and there was no violence. That is the home of the secretary of labor.

During the whole six months, it was a nine months' strike, but it was six months after I went there; but the men were orderly and they themselves took care of the property. The superintendent and the officials of that company could come up four miles from Blossburg at any hour of the night they wanted to alone, and they were not afraid and had no reason to be. That strike was settled very peacefully. The Erie Company conceded to the men most of what they asked for, and there was no violence during the whole nine months.

Then I went into Maryland. I was not in Maryland very long until I was sent for to come into the anthracite region.

CHAIRMAN WALSH. When was that, Mrs. Jones, in 1902?

MOTHER JONES. No, in 1900.

CHAIRMAN WALSH. Oh, yes.

MOTHER JONES. And in that—there were only 7,000 men organized out of 160,000, and I addressed the convention the day that I got in from Maryland and they called the strike right afterward. Well, of course, we had to go over all the district— three districts—to rally them together. There was no violence up in either Scranton or around Hazelton, and very little of it down in a town named Shamokin—scarcely any violence there, but the militia was brought in. First the company would guard the mines so that the men could not get out, or that we could not get near them; and if we billed a meeting, why, the company would always attend the meeting and the men could not; it was the force of the company entirely that attended the meeting, and I concluded that these men had suffered long enough.

I want to say, Mr. Walsh, that I do not take any orders from any officials. I belong to a class who have been robbed, ex- ploited, and plundered down through many long centuries, and because I belong to that class I have an instinct to go and help break the chains; and so I concluded some moves had to be made to bring the men all out; and I organized the men and women, the women particularly, and I made raids every night; we marched and pulled out those mines—the men. There was no violence. The sheriff in Hazelton was a very fine man. He understood the law, and he knew he could manage the affair without bringing the military there.

But I went down to Panther Creek. There were five thousand men there that could not be reached, and I knew they had to be got out in order to get more bread for the children that were coming, so one night, without saying anything to anyone, I gathered up two or three thousand women, and naturally the men followed. That is their natural instinct—to know what we were going to do. We started. I had to go into the saloons and tell them to close up and not give any liquor to the boys. I knew the women did not go near the saloons; I was the only one that did. We marched, and about two or three o'clock in the morning we met the militia. There was a poor little sheriff, not to be condemned at all, but he was unable to grasp the thing, and he yelled like a mad dog in the night to send the guns to him, the governor. I did not know it, or I would have telegraphed the governor to keep the guns at home and there would be no trouble. Then we marched fifteen miles over the mountains from Hazelton to Panther Creek, and there we met the militia in the middle of the night. The militia did not know what kind of an army I had with me. He thought it was just a few strikers; he told us to go back. I told him that the American working man never goes backward; we go forward, and we did not go out to go back; and he said he would charge bayonets. Well, he didn't do it anyway; but it took us three hours to go back two miles. I don't like to resist officers and create any trouble, but I saw he was a sort of Sunday-school fellow and there wasn't much to him, and I concluded to just pat him on the back a little, and I pulled out the five thousand men.

CHAIRMAN WALSH. You mean by that that you induced the five thousand men to go out on strike?

MOTHER JONES. Yes. I wanted them to win the fight. I had a large army with me and I wanted them all, and so I had to get these miners out, because they were furnishing the coal. I brought out the five thousand men. We held up the street cars and did not hurt anybody, and the men—oh, once in a while when a boss wanted to jump over us we picked him up and threw him over the fence to his wife, and told her to take care of him. We did not hurt him, but we wanted him out of our way; so that thing continued until ten o'clock in the morning; and we had the five thousand men out and that ended it, and that part of the strike was ended peacefully.

The women had nothing but brooms and mops and they were very hungry, and the militia had ordered breakfast at some hotel and I told the women go in and eat their breakfast and let the state pay for it; and it was our breakfast anyhow. So they did. We ate the breakfast. We had more strength to get back.

Mr. Mitchell, then president of the miners, did not know anything about these moves, but I saw him in the morning, and I told him I was up against the militia, and he was a little nervous. But I never get nervous when I face bayonets. I think they are human beings like all the rest of us, and I go in a fight and I am not afraid of bayonets when it comes to a struggle for our rights. One day I got my army together of little boys. I was training them for the future. And when we got everything straightened out, the mines closed and we went back to Hazelton, and Mr. Mitchell asked me what we had done. I told him nothing in the world—just pulled out the five thousand men and told the militia to take a rest. The militia did not follow us, did not interfere with us otherwise at all. And they treated us with a great deal of courtesy, looking at it from their point of view.

At this time the winter was coming, and I knew that the people would need coal and that the strike would have to come

somewhat to a climax. So in Lattimer—I happened to be in
Tennessee when the twenty-three men happened to be shot in
the back by the sheriff and the deputies. I did not come east right
away, because I had other work to do. I concluded I would have
to take the matter up, and the general manager sent word that
if I came in there I was going to get killed. Well, it does not make
any difference to me when I die, if I am dying for a good cause.
I concluded I would go in there; and the newspaper men—while
I am always friendly to them, I know they have to make their
living just as the balance have—they were in the habit of going
to the barns to get buggies to take them out, and the barn fellow
would tell ahead of time what I was doing. So this night I told
the clerk at the hotel, "Don't notify the newspaper men that I
am going out." In that evening I had got one man from each
mining department; the others did not know that I had seen
anyone but themselves, and I arranged with them to bring their
army and meet me.

I got the women—I got about fifteen hundred women lined
up, and we walked into Lattimer. It was dark, and we knocked
at every door and told them there was no work to do; that they
would have to rest. The general manager didn't know, neither
did the sheriff, so they began telephoning. The manager and the
sheriff came, and he said, "What are you going to do, Mother?"
And I said, "I am going to close up this mine." And he said,
"Are the women going to close it up?" And I said, "Yes, we are
going to close it up."

So the drivers came along to take the mules to the mines,
and I had all of the women centered in front of the company's
store, and we had three thousand men down at the mines that
the company or the sheriff or nobody knew anything about—
they had come in on different roads—and I said, when he
ordered the boys to take the mules to the drivers, that the mules
would not scab, he had just as well leave them at home in the
barns, because the mules remembered that Patrick Henry had
passed a Declaration of Independence and that the mules were
conscious of that, and he had just as well make up his mind that

those mines were going to be closed, and we had no pistols or guns, nothing but just our hands, because I don't believe in those instruments and I don't travel with any organizer who carries them. We closed up the mines. The reporters heard of it later in the morning and they came down, but we had our work done by the time they came, so we went back, went home; that really was the key to the situation; that settled the first anthracite strike.

The militia didn't commit any brutal acts, nor did they undertake to force us in any way. I must give Colonel O'Neal credit for that. He was the colonel of that militia; that was the crack Fourteenth of Pennsylvania, but it was not very crack that day, I assure you. We carried on our work and finished. That was the first anthracite strike in 1900, and at the close the men called a convention and the strike was called off, and I think Mark Hanna had something to do with settling it. Then I was sent into West Virginia—

CHAIRMAN WALSH. That was in 1902?

MOTHER JONES. In 1900. The strike in Pennsylvania, I think, had closed in November; that strike, it didn't last very long, only six or seven weeks was all that it lasted, and the men got some concessions; not all they wanted, but they got some to satisfy them. There was no rioting, no bloodshed. The sheriff at Hazelton, Sheriff Harvey, was a very sensible, clear, level-headed man. He came to me that morning and asked me to take them home, and I said, "No; no one is going to get hurt." And he said, "They want me to call for the militia." And I said, "Don't obey them; there is no need for them," and there was no one hurt that morning.

I went into West Virginia; the organization sent me there. I surveyed the situation there. I was mostly in the Kenowa and Norfolk & Western, in the New River country, and I was also in the Fairmount region. I never in my life was arrested until I was arrested in the Fairmount region under a federal injunction. I was arrested while I was speaking to a large crowd in Clarksburg, and someone sent me word that we were all under arrest, and I said to the audience, composed of a great deal of strikers, "Don't you undertake to surrender; I am under arrest, but you keep up the fight; it is a fight for more bread." . . .

Now, then, I am coming to . . . the strike of 1902 in West Virginia. There is a very sad, sad story to be told about that. They were pretty peaceful boys down there as a rule, and we kept them in line, and there was one mountain, Standford Mountain, and they had issued this injunction, that men could not look at the mines. That injunction was always issued on me, and the boys went one day to take a walk along the highway and came back and went home peacefully and quietly, interfering with nobody nor anything. They had never been in court in their lives, none of those boys; they were law-abiding, good men, living quietly up there in the mountains. The United States deputy marshal came in the next morning with a warrant for thirty-three of them. They were holding a meeting in their hall, quietly, and he read the warrant, and some said, "You can't arrest us; we have broken no law; we have hurt nobody; and you will have to leave the town." I think his brother was a company doctor, and they asked him to come, and he did come down and take him away.

Anyhow, the next night they went up that mountain, and they shot seven men while they slept. There were about a hundred of those gunmen and their deputies and these mine owners and their sons, and they went up that mountain, and while those men slept they shot them; they riddled their little shacks with bullets and wounded twenty-three as they were sleeping. I was going to a meeting the next morning, very early, and I was told what happened, and I went and called a couple of boys and told them that they had had some trouble on Standford Mountain, and let's go up. We went up, and the picture I shall never forget. The mattresses were all seeping with blood, and the bodies were lying there. It was sad, and I shudder at the picture, and the women were screaming, and the babies were running to me to call back their papas. It was a sad, sad picture. I knew those men had violated no law outside of walking on the highway and that supposed injunction. They got a coroner, and he held an inquest over them. A few were arrested, but no one was ever convicted for the crime.

Five or six days after this I went back up that mountain; there was a grave out in the field, and a woman was over it and a little baby, and the little baby, when she saw me she screamed, and she said, "Oh, Mother Jones, come and pick up my papa!" And she was scraping the clay with her little, tender hands, and the wife was watering with her tears. That young man was as law-abiding a young man, I think, as you could find in the country. I don't think he ever thought of such thing, but he was shot while standing up on the mountains.

Now, these men did not realize what they were doing.

I left West Virginia; I was called for to go to Illinois for a meeting there, a memorial meeting over the mutilated bodies of the men that were killed in a battle in Illinois—'97—and I was to speak on that day, and I went. On my way back I stopped off at the office. Secretary Wilson was secretary of the miners and he said, "You will have to go right into Colorado at once. The governor has sent the labor commissioner here and a board member to see the board and convince them there that there should not be a strike called." I went into Colorado; I examined the situation; I went around the camps; and the men and women told me their sad stories. I called a meeting of the men that night, the officers, and I related to them that the metal miners were in revolt at that time, on a strike, and so we discussed the matter until morning. I was sent back to Indianapolis. I reported in Indianapolis that the fever was there, and at fever heat. The men were almost wild to come out, and I discussed it with three or four of the officers. So I was sent back immediately to Colorado, and I went back. The governor sent for me when he heard I was down at Trinidad, and he sent for me, and I came up to Denver.

CHAIRMAN WALSH. That was when, Mrs. Jones, in 1903?

MOTHER JONES. In 1903. That was the first strike. The governor sent for me, and I never go to see those officers alone; I generally take some of our officials with me when I go. I know them pretty well. He said, "Are you going to have a strike in the southern coal fields, Mother Jones?" I said, "I don't know, governor; that is up to you. If you can bring the conflicting parties together, I think we can ward off the strike, and both sides concede." He said, "I don't want a strike." "Neither do I, but we will strike rather than slavery." I said, "I suppose you are very anxious to know, Governor?" And he said, "Yes, I am; why do you think so?" And I said, "I suppose you want to get your militia ready to go out." He said that he had them already in another district in Colorado to open a mine. I was not aware that the state owned the mines. I thought they were private property, belonging to a combination of private individuals, and he said, "So they are, but we have to get the militia after that lawbreaking organization." "Who are you talking about, the Western Federation of Miners?" "Yes." And I said, "It is strange that they have become lawless and lawbreakers since you got in. They have developed this state and have their families here, and I think they would hardly become rioters at once." He said, "I won't discuss it." And I said, "What did you send for me for?" And he said, "I want to know if you are going to have a strike." And I said, "Yes, we are, and you had just as well know it now as any time."

And I went back, and the strike order went out. I went around holding meetings of the men, women, and children. We didn't have as large a tent colony then as afterward. From the miners themselves there was little violence at that time, but the militia was brought in there. . . .

There was no violence, for these miners were as lawabiding as this audience is; there was not a single one of them doing anything, only just striking. They were singing a little down in their tents. I was in the back of an old store, and on Saturday night I learned that they were coming in Sunday morning and going to arrest all of the boys; so I sent for them and I said, "Have you got any guns?" And they said, "Yes." And I said, "You take them up and bury them under the range," because I thought if the boys that had their guns and those men came in suddenly there would be some trouble; and I said, "Boys, you go and bury your guns and you go back; I am going to stay up all night." And they said no; and I said, "Yes. And tomorrow we will talk things over."

At four o'clock in the morning the sheriff and forty-five deputies came up. I heard them whooping, and so I put my head out of the window and said, "What is the matter?" The sheriff was the first one, and he said, "We are going to arrest all these fellows." I said, "What have they done?" He said, "They are striking." I said, "They have a right to strike; this nation was founded on a strike, and they have the right to strike; and we have a right to strike; Washington struck against King George, and we will strike against King Gould." But they took them all; they were not allowed to put on their clothes, and they shook like aspen leaves. They took them up several miles and held them there until night and got a boxcar and took them down to Price.

After they were gone a woman came to me with her babe, weeping bitterly, and said, "You see my Johnnie?" I said, "Yes," and she said, "Let me tell you, Mother, this baby was born at eleven o'clock at night, and I got up in the morning and got breakfast for eleven men to go into the mines." And she was watering the baby with her tears. "Now," she said, "tell me what to do; they have got my John; they have got my house; we rented a little piece of land from the company, and I took in boarders and I put up a little house on it, and I want to give my children a chance; but now they have got my house, they have my health, and they have got my John, and what will I do?"

Now, I want to say to this commission and to this audience that are listening here, on the quivering heart and the aching breast and blasted hopes of this mother, and of thousands like her, Miss Gould and her class carries on her philanthropy in the Scofield mines, where four hundred men were roasted to death; their bones are rotting out there, and their wives and children are carrying on life's struggle as best they can, and, my friends, we can have no civilization until such things are abolished.

That woman with her babe and four children was sad to look at, but she is only one of many thousands I know of in this terrific struggle for industrial freedom. It touches a human chord in most anyone. I brought that up before Mr. Rockefeller when I had the meeting with him. I feel that men in that position do not grasp these things as they are, nor do the people outside, nor do our officials who live in offices, nor do our newspapermen; it takes those who are down with them to see the horrors of this industrial tragedy that is going on in our nation today.

I then resigned from the miners for a while; there was other work I had to do, and I took up the Mexican refugee cases, they were going to shoot and murder the men, and I raised the money to save their lives. And I came back and the boys sent me to Colorado again.

A judge had sent fifteen of them to jail, and they were holding a big protest meeting, and I went there. As I said before, judges are human,

And then I went out West to do some work for the Harriman shopmen; and while I was in Butte, Montana, one day I picked up a paper, and it said the Payne Creek Colliery Company would not settle with the miners again, and renew its contract again. I said, "This means that every sort of organization is to be driven out"; and I said, "I will go into the fight and make it cost that company something before I get through." I telegraphed to San Francisco to cancel the dates with the officers of the shopmen, and took the train and went in. I went down to Payne Creek [in West Virginia] and a little boy came running to me and said, "Mother Jones, did you come to stay?" And I said, "Yes, I came to stay." The child was crying, and said, "Mother, do you know what they have done to me and my mamma?" I said no, and he said, "They beat my mamma up, and they beat my little brothers and sisters, and beat me, and if I live to be a man I am going to kill twenty of them for that."

I went up and held a meeting with them and found out—got inside information; and the gunmen were all around, and some of the military in plain clothes in the meeting we had; and I went down the Kanawha River and held a meeting with the miners already organized.

One night two of the miners came to me at about two o'clock at night, at Montgomery, and they said, "We have been down to Charleston, and no one will go up Cabin Creek; will you come?" I said, "Yes." For nine years no organizer had dared to go up that creek, and if he did, he came out on a stretcher, or a corpse. The boys said, "They will kill you, Mother"; and I said, "It don't make any difference to me when I get killed; there is a duty to be performed, and I am going." I said, "Is it billed?" And they said no, and I said, "I will attend to that," and the railroad men circulated the bills.

I went up on Tuesday, and the governor heard I was going and sent a company of the militia; and those men came down over those mountains, and their toes were out through their shoes; they walked twelve miles, some of them. They stood there and looked up as much as to say, "Have you brought us any message of hope?" I talked to them with the militia there, and the company's representatives, and I said, 'Boys, freedom is not dead," and some poor wretch hollowed, "Where is she?" "She is gently sleeping, and when you call her she will awake." Those men screamed, and they said, "Will you organize us, Mother?" I said yes. They said, "Into what?" I said, "Into the mine workers," and I said, "If you get organized, will you stay organized? I left you all organized ten years ago when I went away," and they said, "We will, Mother." I took them over by the church; I don't go to church; I am waiting outside for the fellows in the church to come out and fight with me, and then I will go in. Outside of the church I stood up on a bench and organized the men, and I said for everyone to take out their mine like everyone else. I went to see my boys and then went to see the sheriff, and I asked the sheriff to let my boys out on the ground every day, and I said that if any of them went away they could arrest me and put me in their place. So the next morning he went up to the jail and let the boys all go out on the ground, and they could stay out until ten o'clock every night; and then I went to see the judge himself and had a talk with him, and finally the boys got out of jail.

I then came back and was sent into Westmoreland County, where the strike was. There is where I came up with the constabulary—the mounted constabulary.

COMMISSIONER LENNON. Was that the strike of about five years ago, Mother Jones?

MOTHER JONES. Yes.

CHAIRMAN WALSH. Of 1910?

MOTHER JONES. Yes. I went into that Westmoreland strike, and I did not have any conflict with the constabulary. The only time I came against them at all was when twelve or thirteen women were arrested one day and carried into a squire's office; and he, poor wretch, you could see he was a narrow creature; and I went with the women, and I told them to take their babes along. I said, "Wherever you go, take the children, they are yours"; and so the women took all their little ones and babes; and when the people gave their evidence about them, which did not amount to anything, the judge said he would fine them $30 apiece. I said to the women, "Tell him you are not going to pay it," and he said, "Then you will get thirty days in jail." I said, "Tell him all right, they will go to jail." And the women asked for someone who could take the babies, and I said, "No, God Almighty gave you the babies, and you keep them until they are taken away from you."

Two of the constabulary went with the women, and the women ran across some scabs on the way and they licked them, and I took care of the babies until they licked the scabs. . . .

Now, I am coming . . . to the Colorado situation. . . . I went to Texas to speak on Labor Day. The general manager invited me as their guest—him and his wife both. I declined to go for this reason: that I never do go to persons in that position. I may have to fight them, and it would not be a very pleasant thing after I had taken their hospitality; and so I declined to go, and

I said to the boys, "I prefer to go to a hotel." And we held a Labor Day meeting there, and I left that day and took the train and came into Trinidad, and when I left the train the boys met me at the depot, and they said, "We are going to have a convention here." I did not know they were going to, because I was on the go all the time. "What for?" I said. The boys were all up in the air; they wanted to strike. "Well, can't you settle it without?" I said. "Well, we are going to try." So they sent propositions after propositions I learned, and the convention came and the strike was called. Now, I don't know whether you gentlemen in Colorado read the statements at that convention, but they were very deplorable and very condemnatory to me. The papers, because they all represented the Colorado Fuel & Iron Company, they had to write as they were dictated to, and they charged my speech up with calling the strike. Well, I don't care for that; I don't care what charges they make against me. So the strike came, and the tent colony was established. The day of the strike came on the twenty-fifth, I think it was, of September 1913.

EUGENE V. DEBS

— ★ —

Socialism and the Great War

Speech at Canton, Ohio, June 16, 1918

Eugene Victor Debs (1855–1926) began his work with organized labor as secretary-treasurer of the Brotherhood of Locomotive Firemen from 1880 to 1893, the year he founded the American Railway Union. As the union's president, he helped organize two strikes against the Great Northern Railway in 1894. One of these, the famous Pullman strike, resulted in the use of federal troops and a jail term for Debs, who was soon converted to political socialism. In 1900, Debs ran for the presidency as the candidate of the Social Democratic party, which he had founded three years earlier. He was the candidate of the Socialist party in four subsequent presidential elections; in 1920 he campaigned from prison, while serving a sentence for his opposition to World War I. His prison term of ten years—the sentence was commuted in 1921—was primarily due to his antiwar, international-socialism speech at Canton, Ohio.

Comrades, Friends, and Fellow Workers: For this very cordial greeting, this very hearty reception, I thank you all with the fullest appreciation of your interest in and your devotion to the cause for which I am to speak to you this afternoon.

To speak for labor, to plead the cause of the men and women and children who toil, to serve the working class has always been to me a high privilege—a duty of love.

I have just returned from a visit over yonder [pointing to the workhouse], where three of our most loyal comrades are paying the penalty for their devotion to the cause of the working class. They have come to realize, as many of us have, that it is extremely dangerous to exercise the constitutional right of free speech in a country fighting to make democracy safe in the world.

I realize that, in speaking to you this afternoon, there are certain limitations placed upon the right of free speech. I must be exceedingly careful, prudent, as to what I say, and even more careful and prudent as to how I say it. I may not be able to say all I think; but I am not going to say anything that I do not think. I would rather a thousand times be a free soul in jail than to be a sycophant and coward in the streets. They may put those boys in jail—and some of the rest of us in jail—but they cannot put the socialist movement in jail. Those prison bars separate their bodies from ours, but their souls are here this afternoon. They are simply paying the penalty that all men have paid in all the ages of history for standing erect, and for seeking to pave the way to better conditions for mankind.

If it had not been for the men and women who, in the past, have had the moral courage to go to jail, we would still be in the jungles.

This assemblage is exceedingly good to look upon. I wish it were possible for me to give you what you are giving me this afternoon. What I say here amounts to but little; what I see here is exceedingly important. You workers in Ohio, enlisted in the greatest cause ever organized in the interest of your class, are making history today in the face of threatening opposition of all kinds—history that is going to be read with profound interest by coming generations.

There is but one thing you have to be concerned about, and that is that you keep foursquare with the principles of the international socialist movement. It is only when you begin to compromise that trouble begins. So far as I am concerned, it does not matter what others may say, or think, or do, as long as I am sure that I am right with myself and the cause. There are so many who seek refuge in the popular side of a great question. As a socialist, I have long since learned how to stand alone. . . .

They tell us that we live in a great free republic; that our institutions are democratic; that we are a free and self-governing people. This is too much, even for a joke. But it is not a subject for levity; it is an exceedingly serious matter.

To whom do the Wall Street junkers in our country marry their daughters? After they have wrung their countless millions from your sweat, your agony, and your life's blood, in a time of war as in a time of peace, they invest these untold millions in the purchase of titles of broken-down aristocrats, such as princes, dukes, counts, and other parasites and no-accounts. Would they be satisfied to wed their daughters to honest workingmen? [Shouts from the crowd: "No!"] To real democrats? Oh, no! They scour the markets of Europe for vampires who are titled and nothing else. And they swap their millions for the titles, so that matrimony with them becomes literally a matter of money.

These are the gentry who are today wrapped up in the American flag, who shout their claim from the housetops that they are the only patriots, and who have their magnifying glasses in hand, scanning the country for evidence of disloyalty, eager to apply the brand of treason to the men who dare to even whisper their opposition to junker rule in the United States. No wonder Sam Johnson declared that "patriotism is the last refuge of the scoundrel." He must have had this Wall Street gentry in mind, or at least their prototypes, for in every age it has been the tyrant, the oppressor, and the exploiter who has wrapped himself in the cloak of patriotism, or religion, or both to deceive and overawe the people.

How stupid and shortsighted the ruling class really is! Cupidity is stone blind. It has no vision. The greedy, profit-seeking exploiter cannot see beyond the end of his nose. He can see a chance for an "opening"; he is cunning enough to know what graft is and where it is, and how it can be secured, but vision he has none—not the slightest. He knows nothing of the great throbbing world that spreads out in all directions. He has no capacity for literature; no appreciation of art; no soul for beauty. That is the penalty the parasites pay for the violation of the laws of life. The Rockefellers are blind. Every move they make in their game of greed but hastens their own doom. Every blow they strike at the socialist movement reacts upon themselves. Every time they strike at us they hit themselves. It never fails. Every time they strangle a socialist paper they add a thousand voices proclaiming the truth of the principles of socialism and the ideals of the socialist movement. They help us in spite of themselves.

Socialism is a growing idea; an expanding philosophy. It is spreading over the entire face of the earth: It is as vain to resist it as it would be to arrest the sunrise on the morrow. It is coming, coming, coming all along the line. Can you not see it? If not, I advise you to consult an oculist. There is certainly something the matter with your vision. It is the mightiest movement in the history of mankind. What a privilege to serve it! I have regretted a thousand times that I can do so little for the movement that has done so much for me. The little that I am, the little that I am hoping to be, I owe to the socialist movement. It has given me my ideas and ideals; my principles and convictions, and I would not exchange one of them for all of Rockefeller's bloodstained dollars. It has taught me how to serve—a lesson to me of priceless value. It has taught me the ecstasy in the handclasp of a comrade. It has enabled me to hold high communion with you and made it possible for me to take my place side by side with you in the great struggle for the better day; to multiply myself over and over again, to thrill with a fresh-born manhood; to feel life truly worthwhile; to open new avenues of vision; to spread out glorious vistas; to know that I am kin to all that throbs; to be class-conscious, and to realize that, regardless of nationality, race, creed, color or sex, every man, every woman who toils, who renders useful service, every member of the working class without an exception, is my comrade, my brother and sister—and that to serve them and their cause is the highest duty of my life.

And in their service I can feel myself expand; I can rise to the stature of a man and claim the right to a place on earth—a place where I can stand and strive to speed the day of industrial freedom and social justice.

Yes, my comrades, my heart is attuned to yours. Aye, all our hearts now throb as one great heart responsive to the battle cry of the social revolution. Here, in this alert and inspiring assemblage our hearts are with the Bolsheviki of Russia. Those heroic men and women, those unconquerable comrades have by their incomparable valor and sacrifice added fresh luster to the fame of the international movement. Those Russian comrades of ours have made greater sacrifices, have suffered more, and have shed more heroic blood than any like number of men and women anywhere on earth; they have laid the foundation of the first real democracy that ever drew the breath of life in this world. And the very first act of the triumphant Russian Revolution was to proclaim a state of peace with all mankind, coupled with a fervent moral appeal, not to kings, not to emperors, rulers or diplomats but to *the people* of all nations. Here we have the very breath of democracy, the quintessence of the dawning freedom. The Russian Revolution proclaimed its glorious triumph in its ringing and inspiring appeal to *the peoples* of all the earth. In a humane and fraternal spirit new Russia, emancipated at last from the curse of the centuries, called upon all nations engaged in the frightful war, the Central Powers as well as the Allies, to send representatives to a conference to lay down terms of peace that should be just and lasting. Here was the supreme opportunity to strike the blow to make the world safe for democracy. Was there any response to that noble appeal that in some day to come will be written in letters of gold in the history of the world? Was there any response whatever to that appeal for universal peace? [From the crowd: "No!"] No, not the slightest attention was paid to it by the Christian nations engaged in the terrible slaughter.

It has been charged that Lenin and Trotsky and the leaders of the revolution were treacherous, that they made a traitorous peace with Germany. Let us consider that proposition briefly. At the time of the revolution, Russia had been three years in the war. Under the czar she had lost more than four million of her ill-clad, poorly equipped, half-starved soldiers, slain outright or disabled on the field of battle. She was absolutely bankrupt. Her soldiers were mainly without arms. This was what was bequeathed to the revolution by the czar and his regime; and for this condition Lenin and Trotsky were not responsible, nor the Bolsheviki. For this appalling state of affairs the czar and his rotten bureaucracy were solely responsible. When the Bolsheviki came into power and went through the archives they found and exposed the secret treaties—the treaties that were made between the czar and the French government, the British government, and the Italian government, proposing, after the victory was achieved, to dismember the German Empire and destroy the Central Powers. These treaties have never been denied nor repudiated. Very little has been said about them in the American press. I have a copy of these treaties, showing that the purpose of the Allies is exactly the purpose of the Central Powers, and that is the conquest and spoliation of the weaker nations that has always been the purpose of war.

Wars throughout history have been waged for conquest and plunder. In the Middle Ages when the feudal lords who inhabited the castles whose towers may still be seen along the Rhine concluded to enlarge their domains, to increase their power, their prestige, and their wealth, they declared war upon one another. But they themselves did not go to war any more than the modern feudal lords, the barons of Wall Street go to war. The feudal barons of the Middle Ages, the economic predecessors of the capitalists of our day, declared all wars. And their miserable serfs fought all the battles. The poor, ignorant serfs had been taught to revere their masters; to believe that when their masters declared war upon one another, it was their patriotic duty to fall upon one another and to cut one another's throats for the profit and glory of the lords and barons who held them in contempt. And that is war in a nutshell. The master class has always declared the wars; the subject class has always fought the battles. The master class has had all to gain and nothing to lose, while the subject class has had nothing to gain and all to lose—especially their lives.

They have always taught and trained you to believe it to be your patriotic duty to go to war and to have yourselves slaughtered at their command. But in all the history of the world you, the people, have never had a voice in declaring war, and strange as it certainly appears, no war by any nation in any age has ever been declared by the people.

And here let me emphasize the fact—and it cannot be repeated too often—that the working class who fight all the battles, the working class who make the supreme sacrifices, the working class who freely shed their blood and furnish the corpses, have never yet had a voice in either declaring war or making peace. It is the ruling class that invariably does both. They alone declare war and they alone make peace. "Yours not to reason why; yours but to do and die." That is their motto and we object on the part of the awakening workers of this nation.

If war is right let it be declared by the people. You who have your lives to lose, you certainly above all others have the right to decide the momentous issue of war or peace. . . .

The heart of the international socialist never beats a retreat.

They are pressing forward, here, there, and everywhere, in all the zones that girdle the globe. Everywhere these awakening workers, these class-conscious proletarians, these hardy sons and daughters of honest toil are proclaiming the glad tidings of the coming emancipation; everywhere their hearts are attuned to the most sacred cause that ever challenged men and women to action in the history of the world. Everywhere they are moving toward democracy and the dawn; marching toward the sunrise, their faces all aglow with the light of the coming day. These are the socialists, the most zealous and enthusiastic crusaders the world has ever known. They are making history that will light up the horizon of coming generations, for their mission is the emancipation of the human race. They have been reviled; they have been ridiculed, persecuted, imprisoned, and have suffered death, but they have been sufficient to themselves and their cause, and their final triumph is but a question of time.

Do you wish to hasten the day of victory? Join the Socialist

party! Don't wait for the morrow. Join now! Enroll your name
without fear and take your place where you belong. You cannot
do your duty by proxy. You have got to do it yourself and do
it squarely and then as you look yourself in the face you will
have no occasion to blush. You will know what it is to be a real
man or woman. You will lose nothing; you will gain everything.
Not only will you lose nothing but you will find something of
infinite value, and that something will be yourself. And that is
your supreme need—to find yourself—to really know yourself
and your purpose in life.

You need at this time especially to know that you are fit for
something better than slavery and cannon fodder. You need to
know that you were not created to work and produce and
impoverish yourself to enrich an idle exploiter. You need to
know that you have a mind to improve, a soul to develop, and
a manhood to sustain.

You need to know that it is your duty to rise above the
animal plane of existence. You need to know that it is for you
to know something about literature and science and art. You
need to know that you are verging on the edge of a great new
world. You need to get in touch with your comrades and fellow
workers and to become conscious of your interests, your powers, and your possibilities as a class. You need to know that you
belong to the great majority of mankind. You need to know that
as long as you are ignorant, as long as you are indifferent, as
long as you are apathetic, unorganized, and content, you will
remain exactly where you are. You will be exploited; you will
be degraded, and you will have to beg for a job. You will get just
enough for your slavish toil to keep you in working order, and
you will be looked down upon with scorn and contempt by the
very parasites that live and luxuriate out of your sweat and
unpaid labor.

If you would be respected you have got to begin by respecting yourself. Stand up squarely and look yourself in the face and
see a man! Do not allow yourself to fall into the predicament of
the poor fellow who, after he had heard a socialist speech

concluded that he too ought to be a socialist. The argument he had heard was unanswerable. "Yes," he said to himself, "all the speaker said was true and I certainly ought to join the party." But after a while he allowed his ardor to cool and he soberly concluded that by joining the party he might anger his boss and lose his job. He then concluded: "I can't take the chance." That night he slept alone. There was something on his conscience and it resulted in a dreadful dream. Men always have such dreams when they betray themselves. A socialist is free to go to bed with a clear conscience. He goes to sleep with his manhood and he awakens and walks forth in the morning with his self-respect. He is unafraid and he can look the whole world in the face, without a tremor and without a blush. But this poor weakling who lacked the courage to do the bidding of his reason and conscience was haunted by a startling dream and at midnight he awoke in terror, bounded from his bed and exclaimed: "My God, there is nobody in this room." He was absolutely right. There was nobody in that room.

How would you like to sleep in a room that had nobody in it? It is an awful thing to be nobody. That is certainly a state of mind to get out of, the sooner the better. . . .

To turn your back on the corrupt Republican party and the still more corrupt Democratic party—the gold-dust lackeys of the ruling class counts for still more after you have stepped out of those popular and corrupt capitalist parties to join a minority party that has an ideal, that stands for a principle, and fights for a cause. This will be the most important change you have ever made and the time will come when you will thank me for having made the suggestion. It was the day of days for me. I remember it well. It was like passing from midnight darkness to the noontide light of day. It came almost like a flash and found me ready. It must have been in such a flash that great, seething, throbbing Russia, prepared by centuries of slavery and tears and martyrdom, was transformed from a dark continent to a land of living light.

There is something splendid, something sustaining and inspiring in the prompting of the heart to be true to yourself and to the best you know, especially in a crucial hour of your life. You are in the crucible today, my socialist comrades! You are going to be tried by fire, to what extent no one knows. If you are weak-fibered and faint-hearted you will be lost to the socialist movement. We will have to bid you goodbye. You are not the stuff of which revolutions are made. We are sorry for you unless you chance to be an "intellectual." The "intellectuals," many of them, are already gone. No loss on our side nor gain on the other. . . .

In the Republican and Democratic parties you of the common herd are not expected to think. That is not only unnecessary but might lead you astray. That is what the "intellectual" leaders are for. They do the thinking and you do the voting. They ride in carriages at the front where the band plays and you tramp in the mud, bringing up the rear with great enthusiasm.

The capitalist system affects to have great regard and reward for intellect, and the capitalists give themselves full credit for having superior brains. When we have ventured to say that the time would come when the working class would rule they have bluntly answered "Never! It requires brains to rule." The workers of course have none. And they certainly try hard to prove it by proudly supporting the political parties of their masters under whose administration they are kept in poverty and servitude.

The government is now operating its railroads for the more effective prosecution of the war. Private ownership has broken down utterly and the government has had to come to the rescue. We have always said that the people ought to own the railroads and operate them for the benefit of the people. We advocated that twenty years ago. But the capitalists and their henchmen emphatically objected. "You have got to have brains to run the railroads," they tauntingly retorted. Well, the other day McAdoo, the governor-general of the railroads under government operation, discharged all the high-salaried presidents and other supernumeraries. In other words, he fired the "brains" bodily and yet all the trains have been coming and going on schedule time. Have you noticed any change for the worse since the "brains" are gone? It is a brainless system now, being operated by "hands." But a good deal more efficiently than it had been operated by so-called "brains" before. And this determines infallibly the quality of their vaunted, high-priced capitalist "brains." It is the kind you can get at a reasonable figure at the market place. They have always given themselves credit for having superior brains and given this as the reason for the supremacy of their class. It is true that they have the brains that indicate the cunning of the fox, the wolf, but as for brains denoting real intelligence and the measure of intellectual capacity they are the most woefully ignorant people on earth. Give me a hundred capitalists just as you find them here in Ohio and let me ask them a dozen simple questions about the history of their own country and I will prove to you that they are as ignorant and unlettered as any you may find in the so-called lower class. They know little of history; they are strangers to science; they are ignorant of sociology and blind to art but they know how to exploit, how to gouge, how to rob, and do it with legal sanction. They always proceed legally for the reason that the class which has the power to rob upon a large scale has also the power to control the government and legalize their robbery. I regret that lack of time prevents me from discussing this phase of the question more at length.

They are continually talking about your patriotic duty. It is not *their* but *your* patriotic duty that they are concerned about. There is a decided difference. Their patriotic duty never takes them to the firing line or chucks them into the trenches.

And now among other things they are urging you to "cultivate" war gardens, while at the same time a government war report just issued shows that practically 52 percent of the arable, tillable soil is held out of use by the landlords, speculators, and profiteers. They themselves do not cultivate the soil. They could not if they would. Nor do they allow others to cultivate it. They keep it idle to enrich themselves, to pocket the millions of dollars of unearned increment. Who is it that makes this land valuable while it is fenced in and kept out of use? It is the people. Who pockets this tremendous accumulation of value? The landlords. And these landlords who toil not and spin not are supreme among American "patriots."

In passing I suggest that we stop a moment to think about the term "landlord." *Landlord!* Lord of the Land! The lord of the land is indeed a superpatriot. This lord who practically owns the earth tells you that we are fighting this war to make the world safe for democracy—he, who shuts out all humanity from his private domain; he who profiteers at the expense of the people who have been slain and mutilated by multiplied thousands, under pretense of being the great American patriot. It is he, this identical patriot who is in fact the archenemy of the people; it is he that you need to wipe from power. It is he who is a far greater menace to your liberty and your well-being than the Prussian junkers on the other side of the Atlantic Ocean.

Fifty-two percent of the land kept out of use, according to their own figures! They tell you that there is an alarming shortage of flour and that you need to produce more. They tell you further that you have got to save wheat so that more can be exported for the soldiers who are fighting on the other side, while half of your tillable soil is held out of use by the landlords and profiteers. What do you think of that?

Again, they tell you there is a coal famine now in the state of Ohio. The state of Indiana, where I live, is largely underlaid with coal. There is practically an inexhaustible supply. The coal is banked beneath our very feet. It is within touch all about us—all we can possibly use and more. And here are the miners, ready to enter the mines. Here is the machinery ready to be put into operation to increase the output to any desired capacity. And three weeks ago a national officer of the United Mine Workers issued and published a statement to the Labor Department of the United States government to the effect that the six hundred thousand coal miners in the United States at this time, when they talk about a coal famine, are not permitted to work more than half time. I have been around over Indiana for many years. I have often been in the coal fields; again and again I have seen the miners idle while at the same time there was a scarcity of coal.

They tell you that you ought to buy your coal right away; that you may freeze next winter if you do not. At the same time they charge you three prices for your coal. Oh, yes, this ought to suit you perfectly if you vote the Republican or Democratic ticket and believe in the private ownership of the coal mines and their operation for private profit.

The coal mines now being privately owned, the operators want a scarcity of coal so they can boost their prices and enrich themselves accordingly. If an abundance of coal were mined there would be lower prices and this would not suit the mine owners. Prices soar and profits increase when there is a scarcity of coal.

It is also apparent that there is collusion between the mine owners and the railroads. The mine owners declare there are no cars while the railroad men insist that there is no coal. And between them they delude, defraud and rob the people. . . .

We socialists say: "Take possession of the mines; call the miner to work and return to him the equivalent of the value of his product." He can then build himself a comfortable home; live in it; enjoy it with his family. He can provide himself and his wife and children with clothes—good clothes—not shoddy; wholesome food in abundance, education for the children, and the chance to live the lives of civilized human beings, while at the same time the people will get coal at just what it costs to mine it.

Of course that would be socialism as far as it goes. But you are not in favor of that program. It is too visionary because it is so simple and practical. So you will have to continue to wait until winter is upon you before you get your coal and then pay three prices for it because you insist upon voting a capitalist ticket and giving your support to the present wage-slave system.

The trouble with you is that you are still in a capitalist state of mind.

Lincoln said: "If you want that thing, that is the thing you want"; and you will get it to your heart's content. But some good day you will wake up and realize that a change is needed and wonder why you did not know it long before. Yes, a change is certainly needed, not merely a change of party but a change of system; a change from slavery to freedom and from despotism to democracy, wide as the world. When this change comes at last, we shall rise from brutehood to brotherhood, and to accomplish it we have to educate and organize the workers industrially and politically, but not along the zigzag craft lines laid down by Gompers, who through all of his career has favored the master class. You never hear the capitalist press speak of him nowadays except in praise and adulation. He has recently come into great prominence as a patriot. You never find him on the unpopular side of a great issue. He is always conservative, satisfied to leave the labor problem to be settled finally at the banqueting board with Elihu Root, Andrew Carnegie, and the rest of the plutocratic civic federationists. When they drink wine and smoke scab cigars together the labor question is settled so far as they are concerned.

And while they are praising Gompers they are denouncing the IWW. There are few men who have the courage to say a word in favor of the IWW. I have. Let me say here that I have great respect for the IWW. Far greater than I have for their infamous detractors. . . .

It is only necessary to label a man "IWW" to have him lynched as they did Praeger, an absolutely innocent man. He was a socialist and bore a German name, and that was his crime. A rumor was started that he was disloyal and he was promptly seized and lynched by the cowardly mob of so-called "patriots."

War makes possible all such crimes and outrages. And war comes in spite of the people. When Wall Street says war the press says war and the pulpit promptly follows with its

"Amen." In every age the pulpit has been on the side of the rulers and not on the side of the people. That is one reason why the preachers so fiercely denounce the IWW. . . .

Now what you workers need is to organize, not along craft lines but along revolutionary industrial lines. All of you workers in a given industry, regardless of your trade or occupation, should belong to one and the same union.

Political action and industrial action must supplement and sustain each other. You will never vote the socialist republic into existence. You will have to lay its foundations in industrial organization. The industrial union is the forerunner of industrial democracy. In the shop where the workers are associated is where industrial democracy has its beginning. Organize according to your industries! Get together in every department of industrial service! United and acting together for the common good your power is invincible.

When you have organized industrially you will soon learn that you can manage as well as operate industry. You will soon realize that you do not need the idle masters and exploiters. They are simply parasites. They do not employ you as you imagine but you employ them to take from you what you produce, and that is how they function in industry. You can certainly dispense with them in that capacity. You do not need them to depend upon for your jobs. You can never be free while you work and live by their sufferance. You must own your own tools and then you will control your own jobs, enjoy the products of your own labor and be free men instead of industrial slaves.

Organize industrially and make your organization complete. Then unite in the Socialist party. Vote as you strike and strike as you vote.

Your union and your party embrace the working class. The Socialist party expresses the interests, hopes, and aspirations of the toilers of all the world.

Get your fellow workers into the industrial union and the

political party to which they rightly belong, especially this year, this historic year in which the forces of labor will assert themselves as they never have before. This is the year that calls for men and women who have courage, the manhood and womanhood to do their duty.

Get into the Socialist party and take your place in its ranks; help to inspire the weak and strengthen the faltering, and do your share to speed the coming of the brighter and better day for us all.

When we unite and act together on the industrial field and when we vote together on election day we shall develop the supreme power of the one class that can and will bring permanent peace to the world. We shall then have the intelligence, the courage, and the power for our great task. In due time industry will be organized on a cooperative basis. We shall conquer the public power. We shall then transfer the title deeds of the railroads, the telegraph lines, the mines, mills, and great industries to the people in their collective capacity; we shall take possession of all these social utilities in the name of the people. We shall then have industrial democracy. We shall be a free nation whose government is of and by and for the people.

And now for all of us to do our duty! The clarion call is ringing in our ears and we cannot falter without being convicted of treason to ourselves and to our great cause.

Do not worry over the charge of treason to your masters, but be concerned about the treason that involves yourselves. Be true to yourself and you cannot be a traitor to any good cause on earth.

Yes, in good time we are going to sweep into power in this nation and throughout the world. We are going to destroy all enslaving and degrading capitalist institutions and re-create them as free and humanizing institutions. The world is daily changing before our eyes. The sun of capitalism is setting; the sun of socialism is rising. It is our duty to build the new nation and the free republic. We need industrial and social builders. We socialists are the builders of the beautiful world that is to be. We are all pledged to do our part. We are inviting—aye, challenging—you this afternoon in the name of your own manhood and womanhood to join us and do your part.

In due time the hour will strike and this great cause triumphant—the greatest in history—will proclaim the emancipation of the working class and the brotherhood of all mankind.

OLIVER WENDELL HOLMES

—— ★ ——

Freedom of Speech and the 1918 Sedition Act

Dissenting Opinion, U.S. Supreme Court,
Abrams v. United States, 1919

*Significant challenges to freedom of speech were produced
by the American government's passage, during World War I, of
the Espionage Act of 1917 and the Sedition Act of 1918.
Many antiwar leaders on the left, including Emma Goldman and
Eugene Debs, were persecuted under the acts. The Supreme
Court decision of 1919 in the case of* Abrams v. United States
*upheld the defendents' convictions for publishing antigovern-
ment leaflets. The dissenting opinion was delivered by Justice
Oliver Wendell Holmes (1841–1935), who inherited much of the
literary talent of his renowned father of the same name. Holmes,
known and respected for his memorable dissents, had a profound effect on the progressive and liberal consciousness of his
time.*

This indictment is founded wholly upon the publication of
two leaflets which I shall describe in a moment. The first
count charges a conspiracy pending the war with Germany to
publish abusive language about the form of government of the
United States, laying the preparation and publishing of the first
leaflet as overt acts. The second count charges a conspiracy
pending the war to publish language intended to bring the form
of government into contempt, laying the preparation and publishing of the two leaflets as overt acts. The third count alleges
a conspiracy to encourage resistance to the United States in the
same war and to attempt to effectuate the purpose by publishing
the same leaflets. The fourth count lays a conspiracy to incite

curtailment of production of things necessary to the prosecution of the war and to attempt to accomplish it by publishing the second leaflets to which I have referred.

The first of these leaflets says that the president's cowardly silence about the intervention in Russia reveals the hypocrisy of the plutocratic gang in Washington. It intimates that "German militarism combined with allied capitalism to crush the Russian revolution," goes on that the tyrants of the world fight each other until they see a common enemy, working class enlightenment, when they combine to crush it; and that now militarism and capitalism combined, though not openly, to crush the Russian Revolution. It says that there is only one enemy of the workers of the world, and that is capitalism; that it is a crime for workers of America, etc., to fight the workers' republic of Russia, and ends: "Awake! Awake, you Workers of the World! Revolutionists." A note adds, "It is absurd to call us pro-German. We hate and despise German militarism more than do you hypocritical tyrants. We have more reasons for denouncing German militarism than has the coward of the White House."

The other leaflet, headed "Workers—Wake Up," with abusive language says that America together with the Allies will march for Russia to help the Czecho-Slovaks in their struggle against the Bolsheviki, and that this time the hypocrites shall not fool the Russian emigrants and friends of Russia in America. It tells the Russian emigrants that they now must spit in the face of the false military propaganda by which their sympathy and help to the prosecution of the war have been called forth and says that with the money they have lent or are going to lend "they will make bullets not only for the Germans but also for the Workers' Soviets of Russia," and further, "Workers in the ammunition factories, you are producing bullets, bayonets, cannon, to murder not only the Germans, but also your dearest, best, who are in Russia and are fighting for freedom." It then appeals to the same Russian emigrants at some length not to consent to the "inquisitionary expedition to Russia" and says that the destruction of the Russian Revolution is "the politics of the march to Russia." The leaflet winds up by saying, "Workers, our reply to this barbaric intervention has to be a general strike!" and after a few words on the spirit of revolution, exhortations not to be afraid, and some usual tall talk, ends: "Woe unto those who will be in the way of progress. Let solidarity live! The Rebels."

No argument seems to me necessary to show that these pronunciamentos in no way attack the form of government of the United States, or that they do not support either of the first two counts. What little I have to say about the third count may be postponed until I have considered the fourth. With regard to that it seems too plain to be denied that the suggestion to workers in the ammunition factories that they are producing bullets to murder their dearest, and the further advocacy of a general strike, both in the second leaflet, do urge curtailment of production of things necessary to the prosecution of the war within the meaning of the Act of May 16, 1918, . . . amending . . . the earlier Act of 1917. But to make the conduct criminal that statute requires that it should be "with intent by such curtailment to cripple or hinder the United States in the prosecution of the war." It seems to me that no such intent is proved.

I am aware of course that the word *intent* as vaguely used in ordinary legal discussion means no more than knowledge at the time of the act that the consequences said to be intended will ensue. Even less than that will satisfy the general principle of civil and criminal liability. A man may have to pay damages, may be sent to prison, at common law might be hanged, if at the time of his act he knew facts from which common experience showed that the consequences would follow, whether he individually could foresee them or not. But, when words are used exactly, a deed is not done with intent to produce a consequence unless that consequence is the aim of the deed. It may be obvious, and obvious to the actor, that the consequence will follow, and he may be liable for it even if he regrets it, but he does not do the act with intent to produce it unless the aim to produce it is the proximate motive of the specific act, although there may be some deeper motive behind.

It seems to me that this statute must be taken to use its words in a strict and accurate sense. They would be absurd in any other. A patriot might think that we were wasting money or planes, or making more cannon of a certain kind than we needed, and might advocate curtailment with success. Yet even if it turned out that the curtailment hindered and was thought by other minds to have been obviously likely to hinder the United States in the prosecution of the war, no one would hold such conduct a crime. I admit that my illustration does not answer all that might be said but it is enough to show what I think and to let me pass to a more important aspect of the case. I refer to the First Amendment to the Constitution that Congress shall make no law abridging the freedom of speech.

I never have seen any reason to doubt that the questions of law that alone were before this Court in the cases of *Schenck*, *Frohwerk* and *Debs*, ... were rightly decided. I do not doubt for a moment that by the same reasoning that would justify punishing persuasion to murder, the United States constitutionally may punish speech that produces or is intended to produce a clear and imminent danger that it will bring about forthwith certain substantive evils that the United States constitutionally may seek to prevent. The power undoubtedly is greater in time of war than in time of peace because war opens dangers that do not exist at other times.

But as against dangers peculiar to war, as against others, the principle of the right to free speech is always the same. It is only the present danger of immediate evil or an intent to bring it about that warrants Congress in setting a limit to the expression of opinion where private rights are not concerned. Congress certainly cannot forbid all effort to change the mind of the country. Now nobody can suppose that the surreptitious publishing of a silly leaflet by an unknown man, without more, would present any immediate danger that its opinions would hinder the success of the government arms or have any appreciable tendency to do so. Publishing those opinions for the very purpose of obstructing, however, might indicate a greater danger and at any rate would have the quality of an attempt. So I assume that the second leaflet if published for the purposes alleged in the fourth count might be punishable. But it seems pretty clear to me that nothing less than that would bring these papers within the scope of this law. An actual intent in the sense that I have explained is necessary to constitute an attempt, where a further act of the same individual is required to complete the substantive crime. . . .

I do not see how anyone can find the intent required by the statute in any of the defendants' words. The second leaflet is the only one that affords even a foundation for the charge, and there, without invoking the hatred of German militarism expressed in the former one, it is evident from the beginning to the end that the only object of the paper is to help Russia and stop American intervention there against the popular government—not to impede the United States in the war that it was carrying on. To say that two phrases taken literally might import a suggestion to conduct that would have interference with the war as an indirect and probably undesired effect seems to me by no means to show an attempt to produce that effect.

I return for a moment to the third count. That charges an intent to provoke resistance to the United States in its war with Germany. Taking the clause in the statute that deals with that in connection with the other elaborate provisions of the act, I think that resistance to the United States means some forcible act of opposition to some proceeding of the United States in pursuance of the war. I think the intent must be the specific intent that I have described and for the reasons that I have given I think that no such intent was proved or existed in fact. I also think that there is no hint at resistance to the United States as I construe the phrase.

In this case sentences of twenty years' imprisonment have been imposed for the publishing of two leaflets that I believe the defendants had as much right to publish as the government has to publish the Constitution of the United States now vainly invoked by them. Even if I am technically wrong and enough can be squeezed from these poor and puny anonymities to turn the color of legal litmus paper—I will add, even if what I think the necessary intent were shown—the most nominal punishment seems to me all that possibly could be inflicted, unless the defendants are to be made to suffer not for what the indictment alleges but for the creed that they avow—a creed that I believe to be the creed of ignorance and immaturity when honestly held, as I see no reason to doubt that it was held here, but which, although made the subject of examination at the trial, no one has a right even to consider in dealing with the charges before the Court.

Persecution for the expression of opinions seems to me perfectly logical. If you have no doubt of your premises or your power and want a certain result with all your heart you naturally express your wishes in law and sweep away all opposition. To allow opposition by speech seems to indicate that you think the speech impotent, as when a man says that he has squared the circle, or that you do not care wholeheartedly for the result, or that you doubt either your power or your premises. But when men have realized that time has upset many fighting faiths, they may come to believe even more than they believe the very foundations of their own conduct that the ultimate good desired is better reached by free trade in ideas—that the best test of truth is the power of the thought to get itself accepted in the competition of the market, and that truth is the only ground upon which their wishes safely can be carried out.

That, at any rate, is the theory of our Constitution. It is an experiment, as all life is an experiment. Every year, if not every day, we have to wager our salvation upon some prophecy based upon imperfect knowledge. While that experiment is part of our system I think that we should be eternally vigilant against attempts to check the expression of opinions that we loathe and believe to be fraught with death, unless they so imminently threaten immediate interference with the lawful and pressing purposes of the law that an immediate check is required to save the country. I wholly disagree with the argument of the government that the First Amendment left the common law as to seditious libel in force. History seems to me against the notion. I had conceived that the United States through many years had shown its repentance for the Sedition Act of 1798, by repaying fines that it imposed. Only the emergency that makes it immediately dangerous to leave the correction of evil counsels to time warrants making any exception to the sweeping command, "Congress shall make no law . . . abridging the freedom of speech." Of course I am speaking only of expressions of opinion and exhortations, which were all that were uttered here, but I regret that I cannot put into more impressive words my belief that in their conviction upon this indictment the defendants were deprived of their rights under the Constitution of the United States.

Nicola Sacco

— ★ —

The Freedom to Fight Against Capitalism

Testimony at the Sacco-Vanzetti Trial,
Norfolk County Superior Court,
Dedham, Massachusetts,
Commonwealth v. Nicola Sacco, 1921

The criminal case of Sacco and Vanzetti, two Italian aliens who were charged with and convicted of the murder of Alessandro Berardelli at South Braintree, Massachusetts, became the most notorious political trial in American history. It was widely believed that the anarchist sympathies of Bartolomeo Vanzetti and Nicola Sacco (1891–1927) were the major factors in their convictions. There was a worldwide outcry, including numerous acts of violence by radicals, in response to the guilty verdict, the years of attempts to persuade Judge Webster Thayer to allow a new trial, and the final sentence of death in 1927. That year, on August 23, Sacco and Vanzetti were executed by electric chair. On the thirty-first day of the Dedham trial, under cross-examination by prosecutor Frederick G. Katzmann, Nicola Sacco gave an impassioned explanation of his view of America, capitalism, and socialism.

KATZMANN. What did you mean when you said yesterday you loved a free country?

SACCO. First thing I came in this country—

KATZMANN. No, pardon me. What did you mean when you said yesterday you loved a free country?

SACCO. Give me a chance to explain.

KATZMANN. I am asking you to explain now.

SACCO. When I was in Italy, a boy, I was a republican, so I always thinking republican has more chance to manage education, develop, to build some day his family, to raise the child and education, if you could. But that was my opinion; so when I came to this country I saw there was not what I was thinking before, but there was all the difference, because I been working in Italy not so hard as I been work in this country. I could live free there just as well. Work in the same condition, but not so hard, about seven or eight hours a day, better food. I mean genuine. Of course, over here is good food, because it is bigger country, to any those who got money to spend, not for the working and laboring class, and in Italy is more opportunity to laborer to eat vegetable, more fresh, and I came in this country. When I been started work here very hard and been work thirteen years, hard worker, I could not been afford much a family the way I did have the idea before. I could not put any money in the bank. I could no push my boy some to go to school and other things. I teach over here men who is with me. The free idea gives any man a chance to profess his own idea, not the supreme idea, not to give any person, not to be like Spain in position, yes, about twenty centuries ago, but to give a chance to print and education, literature, free speech, that I see it was all wrong.

I could see the best men, intelligent, education, they been arrested and sent to prison and died in prison for years and years without getting them out, and Debs, one of the great men in his country, he is in prison, still away in prison, because he is a socialist. He wanted the laboring class to have better conditions and better living, more education, give a push his son if he could have a chance some day, but they put him in prison. Why? Because the capitalist class, they know, they are against that, because the capitalist class, they don't want our child to go to high school or college or Harvard College. There would not be no chance, there would not be no—they don't want the working class educationed; they want the working class to be a low all the times, be underfoot, and not to be up with the head.

So, sometimes, you see, the Rockefellers, Morgans, they give fifty—mean they give five hundred thousand dollars to Harvard College, they give a million dollars for another school. Everybody say, "Well, D. Rockefeller is a great man, the best in the country." I want to ask him who is going to Harvard College? What benefit the working class they will get by those million dollars they give by Rockefeller, D. Rockefellers. They won't get, the poor class, they won't have no chance to go to Harvard College because men who is getting twenty-one dollars a week or thirty dollars a week, I don't care if he gets eighty dollars a week, if he gets a family of five children he can't live and send his child and go to Harvard College if he wants to eat anything nature will give him. If he wants to eat like a cow, and that is the best thing, but I want men to live like men. I like men to get everything that nature will give best, because they belong—we are not the friend of any other place, but we are belong to nations.

So that is why my idea has been changed. So that is why I love people who labor and work and see better conditions every day develop, makes no more war. We no want fight by the gun, and we don't want to destroy young men. The mother been suffering for building the young man. Some day need a little more bread, so when the time the mother get some bread or profit out of that boy, the Rockefellers, Morgans, and some of the peoples, high class, they send to war. Why? What is war? The war is not shoots like Abraham Lincoln's and Abe Jefferson, to fight for the free country, for the better education, to give chance to any other peoples, not the white people but the black and the others, because they believe and know they are mens like the rest, but they are war for the great millionaire. No war for the civilization of men. They are war for business, million dollars come on the side.

What right we have to kill each other? I been work for the Irish, I have been working with the German fellow, with the French, many other peoples. I love them people just as I could love my wife, and my people for that did receive me. Why should I go kill them men? What he done to me? He never done anything, so I don't believe in no war. I want to destroy those guns. All I can say, the government put the literature, give us educations. I remember in Italy, a long time ago, about sixty years ago, I should say, yes, about sixty years ago, the government they could not control very much these two—devilment went on, and robbery, so one of the government in the cabinet he says, "If you want to destroy those devilments, if you want to take off all those criminals, you ought to give a chance to socialist literature, education of people, emancipation. That is why I destroy governments, boys." That is why my idea I love socialists. That is why I like people who want education and living, building, who is good, just as much as they could. That is all.

KATZMANN. And that is why you love the United States of America?

SACCO. Yes.

NORMAN THOMAS

——— ★ ———

Conscientious Objection

From *The Conscientious Objector in America*, 1923

One result of United States participation in World War I was a significant outbreak of pacifism and conscientious objection. Opposition to the conflict and demands for world peace came from progressives and radicals, including Jane Addams, Emma Goldman, Robert La Follette, and Eugene Debs. During the war, Norman Thomas (1884–1968), a New York City Presbyterian minister, embraced socialist politics and became secretary of a Christian pacifist organization, the Fellowship of Reconciliation, and editor of a pacifist periodical, the World Tomorrow. *Thomas's* The Conscientious Objector in America *was published in 1923; the book deals with the reasons for moral and religious pacifism and details the treatment of conscientious objectors during the world war. Norman Thomas ran for president under the banner of the Socialist party in every election from 1928 to 1948.*

A privileged visitor to one of the camps or cantonments in which American soldiers were trained during the Great War would sooner or later have come across a peculiar group of men. Though classified as soldiers and living among soldiers, they wore no uniform and performed no drill. They obviously differed among themselves in education and habit of mind. Some of them belonged to obscure religious sects distinguished by peculiarities of dress or a religious objection to shaving; with these peculiarities often went a remoteness from the great political and social issues which were convulsing the world. Others in the same barracks or guardhouse were uncommonly well informed as to the war and the trend of contemporary thought and feeling.

The young officer who served as guide to the visitor would, nine times out of ten, explain with a rather unpleasant laugh that these men were "conscientious objectors," fools or knaves, he was not sure which, but at any rate cowards and slackers. Occasionally if the official guide happened to have had closer contact with the objectors he would not be so sure about their cowardice, but he would dwell upon their propensity to argue while their country was in peril, and point out how little they agreed as to the extent of their scruples or the reasons for them. "Some of them," he would say, "are willing to take noncombatant service that does not compel them actually to kill the enemy; some refuse all service in uniform as an unsatisfactory compromise but are willing to perform useful civilian service on farms at home or in reconstruction units abroad; a few—the 'absolutists'—will refuse to render any service under conscription either in the army or in any substitute the government may provide." This extreme stand the army, from the youngest shave-tail lieutenant to the commander in chief, found most trying and unreasonable.

And the army from its viewpoint was right. In conscientious objection, especially of the absolutist type, is to be found a challenge to the basic ideas of men and their instinctive obediences on which the philosophy of the modern state and the practice of modern war are built. Despite the differences among conscientious objectors patent to the most superficial observer, they were marked by one common quality, a refusal in time of war to admit the right of the state to dispose of them as it would, irrespective of their own convictions. They were persuaded that participation in a given war—at least to the extent of combatant service—was so at variance with their convictions of right and wrong for themselves and for society that at any cost to themselves they must refuse obedience to the routine military discipline under which an army is formed.

This assertion of the right of the individual to refuse obedience to the state even in the emergency of war or to lay down limits to which his obedience must be confined is the essence of conscientious objection. So revolutionary are its implications that it deserves study even though the number of objectors in the last war was small. Its significance does not depend primarily on the reasoning power of the objectors or their personal ability or their character—important as these matters are—but in its existence as a practical affirmation that under certain circumstances civil disobedience may become a duty for which men will dare to suffer.

In the United States as in other English-speaking countries there was a disposition both in the public mind and in official action to distinguish between objectors to all war and to this particular war, between religious objectors and political, and to extend to religious pacifists a consideration denied to socialists and internationalists. In practice the sheer logic of the situation ultimately broke down these distinctions. It was not even possible to distinguish between "sincere" and "insincere" objectors save by the pragmatic test of the amount of suffering they would endure for their beliefs.

In a thoughtful pamphlet by Professor George Herbert Mead, of the University of Chicago, on the conscientious objector (circulated during the war, curiously enough, by that rampantly militaristic organization, the National Security League) there is this admission: "Whenever and wherever an act runs so counter to a man's moral nature that he cannot carry it out and still keep house with himself, his refusal in the face of any and all authority commands our instant respect. If such men could be certified to the exemption board beyond a doubt, any thinking, self-respecting community would demand their exemption." Professor Mead goes on to argue: "The man then who admits that under some conditions fighting is moral, and that conditions may arise under which the community may call upon him to fight, cannot claim that his objection to the issues of the actual war can be made an excuse for his not registering and responding to the draft. The logic of such conduct would free every man in a defeated party from the duty of obeying the laws which were enacted by the party whose policies he disapproves, when they may have won a victory at the polls."

That is to fall into the familiar error of pressing logic dangerously far in social relations. If I believe that on the whole it is better for me and for society that I should render obedience to laws I do not approve—striving the while to have them changed—shall I be told that because I have yielded obedience in these matters I must therefore give my whole being to the state by submitting to conscription in a war that seems to me the sum of all iniquity?

Every sane person will admit that war at best is a terrible thing. A thoughtful man can invest his life in it and still "keep house with himself" only under the conviction that it is the necessary means to some great end. If he is persuaded—as were the so-called political objectors in the last war—that the end was not holy or the means necessary his moral revulsion against it or against being conscripted for it is just as great as the revulsion of the man who thinks that he would never fight in any conceivable war. Professor Mead concedes too much for his own cause. If the supremacy of a man's moral integrity over the demand of the god-state is ever worthy of respect, it is always worthy of respect whether the objection is to all war or to a given war; whether it seems to a man's fellow citizens reasonable or unreasonable. The consistent apostle of the divinity of the political state can allow no exemptions from conscription as a matter of right. He can admit exemptions only as a matter of grace or of administrative expediency to individuals too few and too obstinate to be worth the trouble of coercing.

In point of fact, all philosophic defenses of conscription are but rationalizations of the fear that without conscription the protection of that sacred entity, the nation, might be impossible. The very men who boasted loudly that the recent war was the people's war revealed their fear by insisting that the people must be conscripted to fight it. From the most remote hamlets of Europe, Asia, and North America the hand of the state dragged men to die in a war which they did not understand. Slayers and slain alike only knew that they who bade them fight told them they fought for freedom and the defense of the fatherland. Not otherwise could the Great War have been waged. The sovereignty of the state and the right of conscription, defended in the name of the supremacy of the common good over the conscience of the individual, were indisputably among the causes of the greatest calamity of modern times.

It is against this doctrine of the divinity of the state even more than against war that conscientious objection is effective. Men, many of whom were innocent of any theories about the state, were quietly challenging it. This challenge raised the question of the limits of state authority. The more articulate objectors answered it variously. Philosophic anarchists, of whom there were few, asserted that the state was an evil per se and had no rightful authority over the individual. Socialists and other radicals who believed in a high degree of social control stressed their conviction that the existing state is the engine of a dominant class and not the expression of the social will of the workers which alone has rightful authority. Other objectors argued that the state is in itself useful but that it has no right to claim an excessive and exclusive power as against other forms of human association or the conscience of the socially minded individual. It was a general conviction among objectors that the state ought to exercise more control over property for the common good and less control over the consciences of men.

To discuss such answers at length would lead us far afield from this history, but this at least is evident: Men's affairs are in sorry plight if it serves society to compel the individual to be true to his fellows by being untrue to himself. In a world where conformity is easy and independent thinking hard, where, demonstrably, heresy has always been the growing point of society; where governments of all sorts are often stupid and cruel, reasonable men are constrained to do some fresh thinking on the duty of civil disobedience. They may—some of them—come to agree with Thoreau:

"There will never be a really free and enlightened state until the state comes to recognize the individual as a higher and independent power, from which all its own power and authority are derived, and treats him accordingly. I please myself with imagining a state at last which can afford to be just to all men, and to treat the individual with respect as a neighbor; which even would not think it inconsistent with its own repose if a few were to live aloof from it, not meddling with it nor embraced by it, who fulfilled all the duties of neighbors and fellow men."

When men begin to do this sort of thinking about the state they will not fail to feel some sort of respect for the conscientious objectors who, in the time when the crowd-mind was lashed by the fury of war, kept the faith that was in them. . . .

The one man who might have been expected to respect conscience and to mold public opinion to a better understanding of conscientious objection was Woodrow Wilson, the president of the United States, and commander in chief of its military forces, prophet of democracy, champion of a war in which he declared "we fought for the right of men everywhere to choose their way of life and obedience." To the tragic record of his failure the treatment of conscientious objectors does not contribute as black a page as the treatment of prisoners under the Espionage Act. Toward Debs and the others he felt and expressed a positive vindictiveness. It was as if they had sinned against the Holy Ghost in disputing his justification of the war. Or possibly it was as if by his harshness toward them he could silence the secret and lingering doubts of his own motives and acts which neither his eloquence or the applause of the militarists could wholly stifle. He who dared to proclaim abroad America's faith in freedom of speech and opinion used none of his great power and greater influence to modify the cruelty of our espionage law or the preposterous rigors of its enforcement.

President Wilson's policy toward conscientious objectors was better than his treatment of Debs by so much as Newton D. Baker was a better man than A. Mitchell Palmer. What initiative if any the president took with reference to objectors we do not know. On a few occasions he discussed specific complaints of cruelty with visitors and afterwards with Mr. Baker. It is possible that the order abolishing manacling was the result of an interview which Mr. Wilson had with Mr. Baker before sailing for the Peace Conference. It is possible, though not probable, that if he had kept his health he might have hastened the release of the objectors, but there is no doubt that the early stages of the War Department's arbitrary postwar policy were approved by him and the fiction that the emergency of war would not end until his treaty had been ratified was dear to his heart. That fiction was the excuse for many sins against civil liberty in America.

But when all this has been said, it is still speculative whether any president or any secretary having willed or accepted war could have greatly liberalized public opinion in its attitude toward objectors. One of the loftiest of the president's speeches was delivered to inaugurate the fourth Liberty Loan drive in September 1918. Yet it was not the beauty of justice which the president preached, but the duty of hate which the billboards proclaimed that was the power in the propaganda behind the loan drive; and it was that spirit which triumphed at Versailles. Under these circumstances one does not look for public appreciation of social heresy. As it was, the public apprehension lest anyone should escape the draft was ironic commentary on the belief that the majority of men fight for glory or ideals. Some men do fight as crusaders, and it pleases others to be told that they do. But if war brought to the average soldier its own rich rewards, the mass of mankind would not have been so concerned lest any one escape the glory to be won at the cannon's mouth. Most men fight only because of a stern sense of duty, or through fear of public opinion, or in some cases under threat of punishment. In any case they seem inclined to take it as a personal injury if another man escapes. Even more is this resentment felt by the stay-at-home who has escaped conscription. That is the characteristic of the crowd-mind.

Newspapers played upon this feeling by the kind of publicity they gave to the problem of conscientious objection. All objectors were "yellow," slackers, pro-German, traitors. With few exceptions the press opened its columns to denunciation and misrepresentation masquerading as news with the same enthusiasm as it closed its columns to accounts of the persecution of objectors. In short, the papers in this matter as in so many others lived up to their sinister role as creators and spokesmen of the mob-mind. One result was that the legislature of a state like Kansas, which had steadily opposed American participation in the war, resolved after the war to memorialize Congress against the admission of any immigrants who might become conscientious objectors. William Penn would have been deported if these Kansans could have had their way.

It might have been expected that after the war was safely won public feeling would have speedily died down. As fear is the basis of cruelty, the common man is inclined to become merciful when danger is passed. American losses were relatively small. Most of the American boys had come back in a blaze of glory. The people of the victorious North had the proud memory that after the Civil War no one had been sentenced to death or even imprisoned for treason. Why, then, was such a people content to maintain a small army of political prisoners?

The reason, one suspects, lay partly in the paradoxical fact that this war which was so generally supported was unpopular. It became more and more unpopular after the signing of the armistice. If Americans had won the ideal ends for which thousands of them fought, they might have been inclined to be generous; but an uneasy and half-unconscious sense that they had won a military victory without achieving any worthy end was to no small degree responsible for the continuing feeling of irritation against those men who dared to refuse service in the war.

MARGARET SANGER

— ★ —

The War Against Birth Control

From the *American Mercury*, June 1924

Margaret Sanger (1879–1966) was a pioneer in the twentieth-century movement to make contraception information available to the public. Proclaiming the gospel of "birth control," she published a pamphlet on the subject in 1914 and was indicted for circulating it by mail. She fled to Europe, where she studied with sex-researcher Havelock Ellis, and returned to the United States when the charges against her were dropped. She served a month's sentence in jail soon after establishing the first American birth control clinic, in Brooklyn, New York, in 1916. During the 1920s, Sanger established and edited the magazine Birth Control Review *and was president of the American Birth Control League, which she founded; the league evolved into Planned Parenthood in 1942. During her lifetime, Sanger's personal leadership, which included campaigning for population control throughout the world, resulted in the reform of American laws regarding contraception and in increased attention to birth control in many countries.*

S trange," exclaims a character in Aldous Huxley's *Antic Hay,* "how long it has taken the ideas of love and procreation to dissociate themselves in the human mind. Even in this so-called twentieth century they are, in the majority of minds, indivisibly wedded."

For ten years I have challenged this union of ideas, and in that turbulent period I have discovered that in this great commonwealth it is still considered "lewd, lascivious, and obscene" to suggest their dissolution. When the diabolic words *birth control* first made their appearance in print, my obscure little journal was forbidden the mails, seven federal indictments were lodged against me, and I was denounced, condemned, and hounded out of the country. Since that time, books on birth control have been suppressed, meetings called to discuss the underlying problem have been illegally broken up, and police officials, city councils, mayors, priests, archbishops, and other self-appointed meddlers have joined in obstructing and overriding all the constitutional guarantees of free speech. Their methods have been of infinite variety, their purposes audacious, and their organization and cohesion admirable.

These ten years of suppression and persecution have taught me many things. Despite the personal inconvenience I have undergone, I can now look with amusement and at times even with tolerance upon the incessant activities of this new caste of thought-controllers. Perhaps I really owe them a debt of gratitude, for I have come to see that they discharge a useful function in our great national pageant, enact a picturesque and perhaps even necessary role in our human-all-too-human comedy. Without the aid of their frenzied opposition the idea of birth control might never have been broadcasted to the remotest outposts of civilization.

It is not my purpose here to argue the cause of birth control. I wish merely to touch upon certain aspects of the psychology of these thought-suppressors—aspects perhaps unfamiliar to many who have never incurred their enmity.

In the first place, let us recognize that in the ordinary acceptance of the term, morality is nothing but the sum total, the net residuum, of social habits, the codification of customs. Decent, conservative, and altogether respectable cannibals find nothing immoral in anthropophagy. The only "immoral" person, in any country, is he who fails to observe the current folkways. Thus nothing can be so absolutely "moral," as Samuel Butler suggested, as complete mental stagnation. To think about something new is as painful to the true conservative as to exercise an atrophied muscle. To doubt the wisdom of tradition is frowned upon. To introduce a new idea is to awaken a violent protest. More than once new inventions and discoveries of great value have been punished as crimes against the public good.

Contrary to a widespread illusion, no sort of conduct among primitive and barbaric tribes is more rigidly regulated than the sexual. Custom controls the sexual impulse as it controls no other, and infraction of the traditional rules is punished by the severest penalties. In contrast with this tyranny of the primitive mores, civilization has brought about the gradual extension of the sphere of individual liberty and of personal choice. It has substituted heterogeneity in behavior and thought for rigid and routine servility to custom.

But during the past half-century in the United States we have been the witnesses of a counter movement. Manifestly, it has been impossible to enforce upon the ebullient and inchoate groups which make up our population any hard and fast set of rules for sexual behavior. It has been perfectly possible, however, to enforce a strict silence concerning sex, and to forbid, under the threat of severe punishment, any frank or open discussion of its problems. This countermovement, therefore, has been not so much an attempt to codify and ritualize sexual conduct among the population at large as an effort to control thought and speech upon the subject.

Fifty-one years have passed since Anthony Comstock, patron saint of our morality mongers, succeeded in having his psychosexual hyperesthesia codified into state and federal statutes. Section 211 of the Penal Code, which legally links contraception with obscenity, is based on his curiously morbid conception of human functions. The only lawful justification of love, he believed, was the procreation of children. Except for this avowed purpose, all intercourse should be made punishable by fine and imprisonment. Unless men and women could prove the virtuous motive of their cohabitation, they should be—and indeed I am informed that in certain sections of the United States they often are—thrown into jail. The Comstockian legislation against contraception was thus aimed at those who held that, independent of prospective parenthood, sexual relations had a legitimate excuse and value of their own.

Comstock, though he is dead, remains the archetype of the successful moral censor. His fanaticism generated a terrific energy. Galvanized into incessant and frenzied activity by the intensity of his obsession, he discovered obscenity everywhere. He came to be a national pontiff of prurience. Congress quailed before his passion. He convinced sheeplike legislators that unless his last-minute measures were enacted into law, American society would be hurled over the cliff into the abyss of eternal damnation. He gained greater and greater authority. He swayed Congress and the state legislatures, he became the moral censor of the post office, and finally he controlled even the port of New York.

Havelock Ellis has told us that anything that sexually excites a prurient mind is obscene to that mind. Obscenity dominated Comstock's mind. "Men think they know," someone has written, "because they feel, and are firmly convinced because they are strongly agitated." There was never any doubt in Anthony's breast and his certainty was always translated into action. He hounded men and women, regardless of their dignity and good intentions. Because, at the age of seventy-five, Moses Harmon published an article discussing matrimonial relations without evasion, he was sentenced to hard labor at Leavenworth. Through the force of his fanatical zeal and the inexhaustible resources of his energy Comstock was able for years to terrorize and anesthetize the American mind. Armed with his newly legal forged weapons, his tyranny became complete. Always he was able to work "within the law."

In one respect the self-appointed guardians of American morality differ today from their heroic ancestor. Speaking on the basis of my own experience and observation, I cannot escape the conclusion that those who have made the birth control movement the object of their particular enmity are totally ignorant of what may be termed the classical tactics of suppression. They are like schoolboys playing with chemicals. Where they have hoped to enforce silence, they have been surprised and shocked by the force and repercussive effect of unexpected detonations. They themselves are often compelled to run to cover. Instead of silencing an idea or a book, they merely dramatize it. Over and over again they have worked miracles of publicity that would have been impossible to a regiment of press agents.

The birth control movement in America has had the good luck to incur the wrath of two distinct schools of censors. At first the Comstockians focused their attention on us. But with the passing of that patriarch any experienced observer must have noted the rapid decline of the Comstockian school. It has now become almost senile. No longer is it actuated by the stupendous frenzy of its founder. The grandiose gestures of the golden age are now things of the past. The neo-Comstocks are making, it is true, occasional spurts of activity, successful mainly because of the feebleness of the literary challenges to Mr. John S. Sumner. But I venture to predict that, in a future not too distant, there will be a gradual disintegration of the whole school. Times are changing. We are no longer in the Victorian era. Despite itself, American society cannot again bring to fruit so perfect a specimen of dynamic psychosexual hyperesthesia as Anthony Comstock presented. And without the impelling force of an overwhelming pathological prurience, no virtuoso of his caliber can arise among us.

Today the chief warfare against birth control is waged by the Roman Catholic clergy and their allies. From the psychological point of view the fact is not without its significance. For at least fifteen hundred years the church has occupied itself with the problem of imposing abstinence upon its priesthood—an intelligent and trained body of men who have been taught to look upon complete asceticism as the highest ideal—and it is not surprising that such a class of professional celibates should be physically sensitive to the implications of the idea of contraception. Taught to look upon all expressions of physical love as sinful, it is but natural that these men should combat a school of thought so diametrically opposed to their own. Thus the opposition of the Roman Catholic church and its representatives, high and low, is logical and to be expected. The philosophy of birth control insists upon the maximum of personal liberty in every sphere of human behavior that is compatible with the maximum of personal responsibility. Rightly or wrongly, it throws back upon the individual full responsibility for his behavior. It requires him to act upon the basis of reason, experience, and prudence. True morality, we claim, is the outgrowth of experience and of the exercise of rational intelligence upon that experience.

The Catholic scheme of ethics, on the contrary, demands strict obedience to the laws and prohibitions that have been codified by authority. That authority declares in no uncertain terms that "all positive methods of this nature [contraception] are immoral and forbidden." In a Christmas pastoral Archbishop (now Cardinal) Patrick J. Hayes ventured so far as to assert that

> even though some little angels in the flesh, through the moral or physical deformities of their parents, may appear to human eyes hideous, misshapen, a blot on civilized society, we must not lose sight of this Christian thought: that under and within such visible malformations lives an immortal soul to be saved and glorified for all eternity among the blessed in heaven.

From exponents of the philosophy represented by this utterance the early advocates of birth control were prepared for the bitterest opposition. As a matter of fact, we welcomed such opposition, hoping only that the battle might be carried on according to the rules of decency and honesty. Neither the theory nor the practice of birth control has ever been thrust upon women unwilling to accept it, least of all upon Catholics. We have conceded to Catholic and all other clergymen the full right to preach their own doctrines, both of theology and of morals. When, however, the Catholic clergy attempt to force their ideas upon non-Catholic sections of the American public and transform them into legislative acts, we believe we are well within our rights as American citizens when we voice our protest.

The unsportsmanlike tactics and strategy of these opponents to birth control may be illustrated by . . . instances of crude and usually unsuccessful attempts at illegal suppression. Hotels have been boycotted by such organizations as the Knights of Columbus because the managers have purveyed luncheons to advocates of birth control. Halls contracted and paid for have been withdrawn at the last minute on account of pressure brought to bear upon their owners. Permits to hold meetings have been refused by mayors or other city officials in cities in which there was a powerful Catholic constituency. Few politicians, though they have sworn to uphold the Constitution, dare jeopardize their future as office holders by incurring the displeasure of clerical authorities who control the thoughts of their adherents.

It is hardly necessary, I hope, to reiterate here that we concede to Catholics and to all other churchmen full freedom to preach their own doctrines, whether theological or moral. But when they attempt, through illegal tactics, to force their opinions and codes upon non-Catholics, they should be and will be challenged.

I do not wish to convey the impression that my ten years of experience have driven me to the conclusion that suppression is an unmixed blessing. It is true that the idea of birth control has been made to thrive by these ill-advised attempts to extirpate it from the American mind. But its vitality is not merely the chance result of such clumsy, clownish antics. If we had not been determined, with all the courage and stamina at our command, constantly, promptly, and unflinchingly to challenge the assumed authority of these self-appointed censors, our movement never would have profited nor advanced.

Looked at from a broad point of view, the disadvantages of opposition have probably outweighed the benefits. If a powerful ecclesiastical organization, armed with the vast authority of tradition, can countenance and even encourage an impudent disregard of the Constitution of the United States, the document which insures to that organization itself the freedom to perpetuate itself and extend its influence, does the fact not set an evil example to any lesser organization or group which sets up shop to interfere in other people's affairs? . . .

Sporadic protests against the program of organized encroachment upon the citizen's constitutional rights; indignation meetings called by radicals, liberals, and intellectuals when some book is banned; anemic, half-hearted denunciations of all censorship; campaigns for free speech, so often inaugurated and so rapidly dropped—such phenomena as these appear to me as one who has been more or less in the trenches for ten years, as not unsuggestive of an awkward squad of schoolboys armed with bean-shooters, advancing against the machine guns and poison gases of a trained army. Nevertheless, as I have tried to show, a little group of women under the direction of one who may be a fanatic have been able to wrest victory from this army. The secret of our success, if I may be permitted for the moment to call it a success, is to be found in the fact that we have never wasted our time and energy whining about our constitutional right to free speech. We have simply spoken out. We have asserted the truth as we have found it. We have spoken openly, honestly, above board, and without equivocation or hypocrisy. We have repeated ourselves, we have reiterated our truisms, we have been, perhaps, at times tiresome and boring, but by following that program—by saying something and standing by what we have said—we have recaptured, for ourselves at least, the right to be heard. In this, I am convinced, we have set an example to others who have ideas to propagate—some of them, perhaps, of infinitely more importance to the American public than birth control. But so far they do not seem to be courageous enough to challenge an authority that invade every field of thought. We have, as a nation, not yet awakened to the realization that eternal vigilance is the price of liberty.

Vituperation of the purity brigade may be an amusing substitute for mah jong and radio concerts for the intellectually detached, and indignant libertarians may derive some satisfaction from making loud-mouthed protests after somebody or something has been suppressed, but such activities contribute exactly nothing toward a cure for our national disease. If the American public is ever to be brought safely out of the mental coma into which it has fallen, something more than persistent criticism of the professional meddler is imperative. An ounce of courage is worth a ton of criticism.

CLARENCE DARROW

——— ★ ———

Teaching Evolution

Opening Statement at the Scopes Evolution Trial,
Rhea County Circuit Court, Dayton, Tennessee,
State of Tennessee v. John Thomas Scopes, 1925

---

*The famous "monkey trial" of John T. Scopes, who was charged
with teaching evolution—prohibited by state law from being
taught in Tennessee's public schools—was a national sensation
in 1925. The proceedings were even broadcast live over the
radio. The legal battle pitted firebrand civil libertarian Clarence
Darrow, defending Scopes, against the respected past presidential candidate William Jennings Bryan, who represented the
state. The presiding judge banned any scientific testimony on
evolution, so discrediting Bryan, who took the stand as a witness
and argued for the supremacy of the Bible's word, was Darrow's
prime defense tactic. Although Scopes was found guilty and
fined one hundred dollars, Bryan was humiliated, his antiscien-
tific religious literalism was seen to be ridiculous, and laws
against teaching evolution were seldom enforced thereafter.*

This case we have to argue is a case at law, and hard as it
is for me to bring my mind to conceive it, almost impossible as it is to put my mind back into the sixteenth century, I am
going to argue it as if it was serious, and as if it was a death
struggle between two civilizations.

We have been informed that the legislature has the right to
prescribe the course of study in the public schools. Within reason, they no doubt have. They could not prescribe a course of
study, I am inclined to think, under your constitution, which
omitted arithmetic and geography and writing. Neither, under
the rest of the constitution, if it shall remain in force in the state,
could they prescribe it if the course of study was only to teach

religion; because several hundred years ago, when our people believed in freedom, and when no men felt so sure of their own sophistry that they were willing to send a man to jail who did not believe them, the people of Tennessee adopted a constitution, and they made it broad and plain, and said that the people of Tennessee should always enjoy religious freedom in its broadest terms. So I assume that no legislature could fix a course of study which violated that. For instance, suppose the legislature should say, "We think the religious privileges and duties of the citizens of Tennessee are much more important than education; we agree with the distinguished governor of the state—if religion must go, or learning must go, why, let learning go." I do not know how much it would have to go, but let it go. "And therefore, we will establish a course in the public schools of teaching that the Christian religion as unfolded in the Bible, is true, and that every other religion, or mode or system of ethics, is false; and to carry that out, no person in the public schools shall be permitted to read or hear anything except Genesis, *Pilgrim's Progress,* Baxter's *Saint Rest,* and *In His Image."* Would that be constitutional? If it is, the constitution is a lie and a snare and the people have forgotten what liberty means.

I remember, long ago, Mr. Bancroft wrote this sentence, which is true: "It is all right to preserve freedom in constitutions, but when the spirit of freedom has fled from the hearts of the people, then its matter is easily sacrificed under law." And so it is, unless there is left enough of the spirit of freedom in the state of Tennessee, and in the United States, there is not a single line of any constitution that can withstand bigotry and ignorance when it seeks to destroy the rights of the individual; and bigotry and ignorance are ever active. Here, we find today, as brazen and as bold an attempt to destroy learning as was ever made in the Middle Ages, and the only difference is we have not provided that they shall be burned at the stake, but there is time for that, Your Honor. We have to approach these things gradually.

Now, let us see what we claim with reference to this law. If this proceeding both in form and substance, can prevail in this court, then, Your Honor, no law—no matter how foolish, wicked, ambiguous, or ancient—but can come back to Tennessee. All the guarantees go for nothing. All of the past has gone, will be forgotten—if this can succeed.

I am going to begin with some of the simpler reasons why it is absolutely absurd to think that this statute, indictment, or any part of the proceedings in this case are legal; and I think the sooner we get rid of it in Tennessee the better for the peace of Tennessee, and the better for the pursuit of knowledge in the world. . . .

The statute should be comprehensible. It should not be written in Chinese anyway. It should be in passing English, so that common human beings would understand what it meant, and so a man would know whether he is liable to go to jail when he is teaching—not so ambiguous as to be a snare or a trap to get someone who does not agree with you. It should be plain, simple, and easy. Does this statute state what you shall teach and what you shall not? Oh, no! Oh, no! Not at all. Does it say you cannot teach the earth is round because Genesis says it is flat? No. Does it say you cannot teach that the earth is millions of ages old, because the account in Genesis makes it less than six thousand years old? Oh, no. It doesn't state that. If it did you could understand it. It says you shan't teach any theory of the origin of man that is contrary to the divine theory contained in the Bible.

Now let us pass up the word "divine"! No legislature is strong enough in any state in the Union to characterize and pick any book as being divine. Let us take it as it is. What is the Bible? Your Honor, I have read it myself. I might read it more or more wisely. Others may understand it better. Others may think they understand it better when they do not. But in a general way I know what it is. I know there are millions of people in the world who look on it as being a divine book, and I have not the slightest objection to it. I know there are millions of people in the world who derive consolation in their times of trouble and solace in times of distress from the Bible. I would be pretty near the last one in the world to do anything or take any action to take it away. I feel just exactly the same toward the religious creed of every human being who lives. If anybody finds anything in this life that brings them consolation and health and happiness I think they ought to have it, whatever they get. I haven't any fault to find with them at all. But what is it?

The Bible is not one book. The Bible is made up of sixty-six books written over a period of about a thousand years, some of them very early and some of them comparatively late. It is a book primarily of religion and morals. It is not a book of science. Never was and was never meant to be. Under it there is nothing prescribed that would tell you how to build a railroad or a steamboat or to make anything that would advance civilization. It is not a textbook or a text on chemistry. It is not big enough to be. It is not a book on geology; they knew nothing about geology. It is not a book on biology; they knew nothing about it. It is not a work on evolution; that is a mystery. It is not a work on astronomy. The man who looked out at the universe and studied the heavens had no thought but that the earth was the center of the universe. But we know better than that. We know that the sun is the center of the solar system. And that there are an infinity of other systems around about us. They thought the sun went around the earth and gave us light and gave us night. We know better. We know the earth turns on its axis to produce days and nights. They thought the earth was created 4,004 years before the Christian Era. We know better. I doubt if there is a person in Tennessee who does not know better. They told it the best they knew. And while suns may change all you may learn of chemistry, geometry, and mathematics, there are no doubt certain primitive, elemental instincts in the organs of man that remain the same. He finds out what he can and yearns to know more and supplements his knowledge with hope and faith.

That is the province of religion and I haven't the slightest fault to find with it. Not the slightest in the world. One has one thought and one another, and instead of fighting each other as in the past, they should support and help each other. Let's see, now. Can Your Honor tell what is given as the origin of man as shown in the Bible? Is there any human being who can tell us? There are two conflicting accounts in the first two chapters. There are scattered all through it various acts and ideas. But to pass that up for the sake of argument, no teacher in any school in the state of Tennessee can know that he is violating a law, but must test every one of its doctrines by the Bible, must he not? You cannot say two times two equals four, or a man is an educated animal if evolution is forbidden. It does not specify what you cannot teach but says you cannot teach anything that conflicts with the Bible.

Then just imagine making it a criminal code that is so uncertain and impossible that every man must be sure that he has read everything in the Bible—and not only read it but understands it—or he might violate the criminal code. Who is the chief mogul that can tell us what the Bible means? He or they should write a book and make it plain and distinct, so we would know. Let us look at it. There are in America at least five hundred different sects or churches, all of which quarrel with each other on the importance and nonimportance of certain things or the construction of certain passages. All along the line they do not agree among themselves and cannot agree among themselves. They never have and probably never will. There is a great division between the Catholics and the Protestants. There is such a disagreement that my client, who is a school-teacher, not only must know the subject he is teaching, but he must know everything about the Bible in reference to evolution. And he must be sure that he expresses this right, or else some fellow will come along here, more ignorant perhaps than he, and say, "You made a bad guess and I think you have committed a crime." No criminal statute can rest that way. There is not a chance for it, for this criminal statute and every criminal statute must be plain and simple. If Mr. Scopes is to be indicted and prosecuted because he taught a wrong theory of the origin of life, why not tell him what he must teach? Why not say that you must teach that man was made of the dust; and still stranger, not directly from the dust, without taking any chances on it, whatever, that Eve was made out of Adam's rib? You will know what I am talking about.

Now my client must be familiar with the whole book, and must know all about all of these warring sects of Christians and know which of them is right and which wrong, in order that he will not commit crime. Nothing was heard of all that until the fundamentalists got into Tennessee. I trust that when they prosecute their wildly made charge upon the intelligence of some other sect they may modify this mistake and state in simple language what was the account contained in the Bible that could not be taught. So, unless other sects have something to do with it, we must know just what we are charged with doing.

This statute, I say, Your Honor, is indefinite and uncertain. No man could obey it, no court could enforce it, and it is bad for indefiniteness and uncertainty. Look at that indictment up there. If that is a good indictment I never saw a bad one. Now, I do not expect, Your Honor, my opinion to go because it is my opinion; because I am like all lawyers who practice law—I have made mistakes in my judgment of law. I will probably make more of them. I insist that you might just as well hand my client a piece of blank paper and then send the sheriff after him to jail him.

The state by constitution is committed to the doctrine of education, committed to schools. It is committed to teaching and I assume when it is committed to teaching it is committed to teaching the truth—ought to be anyhow—plenty of people to do the other. It is committed to teaching literature and science. My friend has suggested that literature and science might conflict. I cannot quite see how, but that is another question. But that indicates the policy of the state of Tennessee, and wherever it is used in construing the unconstitutionality of this act it can only be used as an indication of what the state meant and you could not pronounce a statute void on it. . . .

How many creeds and cults are there this whole world over? No man could enumerate them. At least about five hundred different Christian creeds, all made up of differences, Your Honor, every one of them, and these subdivided into small differences, until they reach every member of every congregation. Because to think is to differ. And then there are any number of creeds older and any number of creeds younger, than the Christian creed, any number of them; the world has had them forever. They have come and they have gone, they have abided their time and have passed away; some of them are here still, some may be here forever, but there has been a multitude, due to the multitude and manifold differences in human beings. And it was meant by the constitutional convention of Tennessee to leave these questions of religion between man and whatever he worshiped, to leave him free.

Has the Mohammedan any right to stay here and cherish his creed? Has the Buddhist a right to live here and cherish his creed? Can the Chinaman who comes here to wash our clothes, can he bring his joss and worship it? Is there any man that holds a religious creed, no matter where he came from, or how old it is or how false it is, is there any man that can be prohibited by any act of the legislature of Tennessee? Impossible?

The constitution of Tennessee, as I understand, was copied from the one that Jefferson wrote, so clear, simple, direct, to encourage the freedom of religious opinion, and said in substance, that no act shall ever be passed to interfere with complete religious liberty. Now is this it or is not this it? What do you say? What does it do? We will say I am a scientist, no, I will take that back; I am a pseudoscientist, because I believe in evolution; pseudoscientist named by somebody who neither knows or cares what science is, except to grab it by the throat and throttle it to death. I am a pseudoscientist, and I believe in evolution. Can a legislative body say, "You cannot read a book or take a lesson, or make a talk on science until you first find out whether you are saying against Genesis"? It can unless that constitutional provision protects me. It can.

Can it say to the astronomer, "You cannot turn your telescope upon the infinite planets and suns and stars that fill space, lest you find that the earth is not the center of the universe and there is not any firmament between us and the heaven"? Can it? It could—except for the work of Thomas Jefferson, which has been woven into every state constitution of the Union, and has stayed there like the flaming sword to protect the rights of man against ignorance and bigotry; and when it is permitted to overwhelm them, then we are taken in a sea of blood and ruin that all the miseries and tortures and carrion of the Middle Ages would be as nothing. They would need to call back these men once more. But are the provisions of the constitutions that they left, are they enough to protect you and me, and everyone else in a land which we thought was free? Now, let us see what it says: "All men have a natural and indefeasible right to worship Almighty God according to the dictates of their own conscience."

That takes care even of the despised modernist, who dares to be intelligent. "That no man can of right be compelled to attend, erect, or support any place of worship, or to maintain any minister against his consent; that no human authority can in any case whatever control or interfere with the rights of conscience in any case whatever"—that does not mean "whatever," that means "barring fundamentalist propaganda." It does not mean "whatever" at all times, sometimes maybe—and that "no preference shall be given by law to any religious establishment or mode of worship." Does it? Could you get any more preference, Your Honor, by law? Let us see.

Here is the state of Tennessee, living peacefully, surrounded by its beautiful mountains, each one of which contains evidence that the earth is millions of years old, people quiet, not all agreeing upon any one subject, and not necessary. If I could not live in peace with people I did not agree with, why, what? I could not live. Here is the state of Tennessee going along in its own business, teaching evolution for years, state boards handing out books on evolution, professors in colleges, teachers in schools, lawyers at the bar, physicians, ministers, a great percentage of the intelligent citizens of the state of Tennessee evolutionists, have not even thought it was necessary to leave their church. They believed that they could appreciate and understand and make their own simple and human doctrine of the Nazarene, to love their neighbor, be kindly with them, not to place a fine on and not try to send to jail some man who did not believe as they believed, and got along all right with it, too, until something happened. They have not thought it necessary to give up their church, because they believed that all that was here was not made on the first six days of creation, but that it had come by a slow process of developments extending over the ages, that one thing grew out of another. There are people who believed that organic life and the plants and the animals and man and the mind of man and the religion of man are the subjects of evolution, and they have not got through, and that the God in which they believed did not finish creation on the first day, but that He is still working to make something better and higher still out of human beings, who are next to God, and that evolution has been working forever and will work forever—they believe it.

And along comes somebody who says, "We have got to believe it as I believe it. It is a crime to know more than I know." And they publish a law to inhibit learning. Now, what is in the way of it? First, what does the law say? This law says that it shall be a criminal offense to teach in the public schools any account of the origin of man that is in conflict with the divine account in the Bible. It makes the Bible the yardstick to measure every man's intellect, to measure every man's intelligence and to measure every man's learning. . . .

Let us look at this act, Your Honor. Here is a law which makes it a crime to teach any theory of the origin of man excepting that contained in the divine account, which we find in the Bible. All right. Now that act applies to what? Teachers in the public schools. Now I have seen somewhere a statement of Mr. Bryan's that the fellow that made the paycheck had a right to regulate the teachers. All right, let us see. I do not question the right of the legislature to fix the courses of study, but the state of Tennessee has no right under the police power of the state to carve out a law which applies to schoolteachers, a law which is a criminal statute and nothing else—which makes no effort to prescribe the school law or course of study. It says that John Smith who teaches evolution is a criminal if he teaches it in the public schools. There is no question about this act; there is no question where it belongs; there is no question of its origin. Nobody would claim that the act could be passed for a minute excepting that teaching evolution was in the nature of a criminal act; that it smacked of policemen and criminals and jails and grand juries; that it was in the nature of something that was criminal and, therefore, the state should forbid it.

It cannot stand a minute in this court on any theory than that it is a criminal act, simply because they say it contravenes the teaching of Moses without telling us what those teachings are. Now, if this is the subject of a criminal act, then it cannot make a criminal out of a teacher in the public schools and leave a man free to teach it in a private school. It cannot make it criminal for a teacher in the public schools to teach evolution, and for the same man to stand among the hustings and teach it. It cannot make it a criminal act for this teacher to teach evolution and permit books upon evolution to be sold in every store in the state of Tennessee and to permit the newspapers from foreign cities to bring into your peaceful community the horrible utterances of evolution. Oh, no, nothing like that. If the state of Tennessee has any force in this day of fundamentalism, in this day when religious bigotry and hatred is being kindled all over our land, see what can be done? . . .

If today you can take a thing like evolution and make it a crime to teach it in the public school, tomorrow you can make it a crime to teach it in the private school, and the next year you can make it a crime to teach it from the hustings or in the church. At the next session you may ban books and the newspapers. Soon you may set Catholic against Protestant and Protestant against Protestant, and try to foist your own religion upon the minds of men. If you can do one you can do the other. Ignorance and fanaticism is ever busy and needs feeding. Always it is feeding and gloating for more. Today it is the public-school teachers, tomorrow the private. The next day the preachers and the lecturers, the magazines, the books, the newspapers. After a while, Your Honor, it is the setting of man against man and creed against creed until, with flying banners and beating drums, we are marching backward to the glorious ages of the sixteenth century when bigots lighted fagots to burn the men who dared to bring any intelligence and enlightenment and culture to the human mind.

JOHN MUNRO WOOLSEY

——— ★ ———

Against Book Censorship:
The Right to Read James Joyce

Opinion of the Court, Second Circuit,
District Court, S.D., New York,
United States v. One Book Called Ulysses, 1933

---

*The Comstock Law of 1873, passed by Congress and named
for the reformer Anthony Comstock, prohibited the use of the
mails for the transmittal of "indecent" matter. The first major
court decision challenging that law was rendered in 1933 by a
federal court in New York, in a case involving the entry into
the United States of James Joyce's great novel* Ulysses. *The
court deemed the book acceptable and not obscene due to its
artistic merit. The opinion by Judge John Munro Woolsey
(1877–1945) reads like a professional book review, stating that
"*Ulysses *is an amazing tour de force. . . . In many places it
seems to me disgusting, but although it contains . . . many
words usually considered dirty, . . . each word of the book
contribute[s] like a bit of mosaic to the detail of the picture
which Joyce is seeking to construct for his readers." Later U.S.
Supreme Court decisions narrowed the scope of prohibitions
against obscene material, notably establishing as the test of obscenity whether a work, taken in its entirety, appeals to the
average person's "prurient interest."*

The motion for a decree dismissing the libel herein is granted,
and consequently, of course, the government's motion for
a decree of forfeiture and destruction is denied. . . .

I have read *Ulysses* once in its entirety and I have read those
passages of which the government particularly complains several times. In fact, for many weeks, my spare time has been

devoted to the consideration of the decision which my duty would require me to make in this matter.

The reputation of *Ulysses* in the literary world, however, warranted me taking such time as was necessary to enable me to satisfy myself as to the intent with which the book was written, for, of course, in any case where a book is claimed to be obscene it must first be determined whether the intent with which it was written was what is called, according to the usual phrase, pornographic,—that is, written for the purpose of exploiting obscenity.

If the conclusion is that the book is pornographic that is the end of the inquiry and forfeiture must follow.

But in *Ulysses,* in spite of its unusual frankness, I do not detect anywhere the leer of the sensualist. I hold, therefore, that it is not pornographic.

In writing *Ulysses,* Joyce sought to make a serious experiment in a new, if not wholly novel, literary genre. He takes persons of the lower middle class living in Dublin in 1904 and seeks not only to describe what they did on a certain day early in June of that year as they went about the city bent on their usual occupation, but also to tell what many of them thought about the while.

Joyce has attempted—it seems to me, with astonishing success—to show how the screen of consciousness with its ever-shifting kaleidoscopic impressions carries, as it were on a plastic palimpsest, not only what is in the focus of each man's observation of the actual things about him, but also in a penumbral zone residua of past impressions, some recent and some drawn up by association from the domain of the subconscious. He shows how each of these impressions affects the life and behavior of the character which he is describing.

What he seeks to get is not unlike the result of a double or, if that is possible, a multiple exposure on a cinema film which would give a clear foreground with a background visible but somewhat blurred and out of focus in varying degrees.

To convey by words an effect which obviously lends itself

more appropriately to a graphic technique, accounts, it seems to me, for much of the obscurity which meets a reader of *Ulysses*. And it also explains another aspect of the book, which I have further to consider, namely, Joyce's sincerity and his honest effort to show exactly how the minds of his characters operate.

If Joyce did not attempt to be honest in developing the technique which he has adopted in *Ulysses*, the result would be psychologically misleading and thus unfaithful to his chosen technique. Such an attitude would be artistically inexcusable.

It is because Joyce has been loyal to his technique and has not funked its necessary implications, but has honestly attempted to tell fully what his characters think about, that he has been the subject of so many attacks and that his purpose has been so often misunderstood and misrepresented. For his attempt sincerely and honestly to realize his objective has required him incidentally to use certain words which are generally considered dirty words and has led at times to what many think is a too poignant preoccupation with sex in the thoughts of his characters.

The words which are criticized as dirty are old Saxon words known to almost all men and, I venture, to many women, and are such words as would be naturally and habitually used, I believe, by the types of folk whose life, physical and mental, Joyce is seeking to describe. In respect of the recurrent emergence of the theme of sex in the minds of his characters, it must always be remembered that his locale was Celtic and his season spring.

Whether or not one enjoys such a technique as Joyce uses is a matter of taste on which disagreement or argument is futile, but to subject that technique to the standards of some other technique seems to me to be little short of absurd.

Accordingly, I hold that *Ulysses* is a sincere and honest book and I think that the criticisms of it are entirely disposed of by its rationale.

Furthermore, *Ulysses* is an amazing *tour de force* when one considers the success which has been in the main achieved with such a difficult objective as Joyce set for himself. As I have stated, *Ulysses* is not an easy book to read. It is brilliant and dull, intelligible and obscure by turns. In many places it seems to me to be disgusting, but although it contains, as I have mentioned above, many words usually considered dirty, I have not found anything that I consider to be dirt for dirt's sake. Each word of the book contributes like a bit of mosaic to the detail of the picture which Joyce is seeking to construct for his readers.

If one does not wish to associate with such folk as Joyce describes, that is one's own choice. In order to avoid indirect contact with them one may not wish to read *Ulysses;* that is quite understandable. But when such a real artist in words, as Joyce undoubtedly is, seeks to draw a true picture of the lower middle class in a European city, ought it to be impossible for the American public legally to see that picture?

To answer this question it is not sufficient merely to find, as I have found above, that Joyce did not write *Ulysses* with what is a commonly called pornographic intent, I must endeavor to apply a more objective standard to his book in order to determine its effect in the result, irrespective of the intent with which it was written.

The statute under which the libel is filed only denounces, in so far as we are here concerned, the importation into the United States from any foreign country of "any obscene book" (Section 305 of the Tariff Act of 1930, Title 19 United States Code, Section 1305). It does not marshal against books the spectrum of condemnatory adjectives found, commonly, in laws dealing with matters of this kind. I am therefore, only required to determine whether *Ulysses* is obscene within the legal definition of that word.

The meaning of the word *obscene* as legally defined by the courts is: tending to stir the sex impulses or to lead to sexually impure and lustful thoughts. . . . Whether a particular book would tend to excite such impulses and thoughts must be tested by the court's opinion as to its effect on a person with average sex instincts. . . .

After I had made my decision in regard to the aspect of *Ulysses,* now under consideration, I checked my impressions with two friends of mine. . . . These literary assessors—as I might properly describe them—were called on separately, and neither knew that I was consulting the other. They are men whose opinion on literature and on life I value most highly. They had both read *Ulysses,* and, of course, were wholly unconnected with this cause.

Without letting either of my assessors know what my decision was, I gave to each of them the legal definition of obscene and asked each whether in his opinion *Ulysses* was obscene within that definition.

I was interested to find that they both agreed with my opinion: that reading *Ulysses* in its entirety, as a book must be read on such a test as this, did not tend to excite sexual impulses or lustful thoughts but that its net effect on them was only that of somewhat tragic and very powerful commentary on the inner lives of men and women.

It is only with the normal person that the law is concerned. Such a test as I have described, therefore, is the only proper test of obscenity in the case of a book like *Ulysses,* which is a sincere and serious attempt to devise a new literary method for the observation and description of mankind.

I am quite aware that owing to some of its scenes *Ulysses* is a rather strong draught to ask some sensitive, though normal, persons to take. But my considered opinion, after long reflection, is that whilst in many places the effect of *Ulysses* on the reader undoubtedly is somewhat emetic, nowhere does it tend to be an aphrodisiac.

Ulysses may, therefore, be admitted into the United States.

HARLAN FISKE STONE

—— ★ ——

School Flag-Salute Ceremonies and Religious Beliefs

Dissenting Opinion, U.S. Supreme Court,
Minersville School District v. Gobitis, 1940

*The clause in the First Amendment of the Constitution that
simply states "Congress shall make no law respecting an establishment of religion, nor prohibiting the free exercise thereof"
has been subject to various interpretations and often contradictory court decisions, especially in the twentieth century. In
1940, the U.S. Supreme Court heard the case of Walter Gobitis,
whose children were expelled from the public schools of Minersville, Pennsylvania, for refusing to salute the American flag. The
Gobitis family were Jehovah's Witnesses and regarded the flag-
saluting ceremony as contrary to the teachings of the Bible. After
Pennsylvania district and circuit courts ruled to allow the
Gobitis children to attend school without saluting the flag, the
Minersville school board appealed to the Supreme Court. The
Court reversed the previous rulings, but Justice Harlan Fiske
Stone (1872–1946), in his dissenting opinion, saw no reason why
the possible inconveniences from "some sensible adjustment of
school discipline" would cause "a problem so momentous or
pressing as to outweigh the freedom from compulsory violation
of religious faith" of the children.*

Two youths, now fifteen and sixteen years of age, are by the
judgment of this Court held liable to expulsion from the
public schools and to denial of all publicly supported educational privileges because of their refusal to yield to the compulsion of a law which commands their participation in a school
ceremony contrary to their religious convictions. They and their
father are citizens and have not exhibited by any action or

statement of opinion, any disloyalty to the government of the United States. They are ready and willing to obey all its laws which do not conflict with what they sincerely believe to be the higher commandments of God. It is not doubted that these convictions are religious, that they are genuine, or that the refusal to yield to the compulsion of the law is in good faith and with all sincerity. It would be a denial of their faith as well as the teachings of most religions to say that children of their age could not have religious convictions.

The law which is thus sustained is unique in the history of Anglo-American legislation. It does more than suppress freedom of speech and more than prohibit the free exercise of religion, which concededly are forbidden by the First Amendment and are violations of the liberty guaranteed by the Fourteenth. For by this law the state seeks to coerce these children to express a sentiment which, as they interpret it, they do not entertain, and which violates their deepest religious convictions. It is not denied that such compulsion is a prohibited infringement of personal liberty, freedom of speech, and religion, guaranteed by the Bill of Rights, except insofar as it may be justified and supported as a proper exercise of the state's power over public education. Since the state, in competition with parents, may through teaching in the public schools indoctrinate the minds of the young, it is said that in aid of its undertaking to inspire loyalty and devotion to constitutional authority and the flag which symbolizes it, it may coerce the pupil to make affirmation contrary to his belief and in violation of his religious faith. And, finally, it is said that since the Minersville School Board and others are of the opinion that the country will be better served by conformity than by the observance of religious liberty which the Constitution prescribes, the courts are not free to pass judgment on the board's choice.

Concededly the constitutional guaranties of personal liberty are not always absolutes. Government has a right to survive, and powers conferred upon it are not necessarily set at naught by the express prohibitions of the Bill of Rights. It may make war and raise armies. . . . It may suppress religious practices dangerous to morals, and presumably those also which are inimical to public safety, health, and good order. . . . But it is a long step, and one which I am unable to take, to the position that government may, as a supposed educational measure and as a means of disciplining the young, compel public affirmations which violate their religious conscience.

The very fact that we have constitutional guaranties of civil liberties and the specificity of their command where freedom of speech and of religion are concerned require some accomodation of the powers which government normally exercises, when no question of civil liberty is involved, to the constitutional demand that those liberties be protected against the action of government itself. The state concededly has power to require and control the education of its citizens, but it cannot by a general law compelling attendance at public schools preclude attendance at a private school adequate in its instruction, where the parent seeks to secure for the child the benefits of religious instruction not provided by the public school. . . .

Where there are competing demands of the interests of government and of liberty under the Constitution, and where the performance of governmental functions is brought into conflict with specific constitutional restrictions, there must, when that is possible, be reasonable accommodation between them so as to preserve the essentials of both and . . . it is the function of courts to determine whether such accommodation is reasonably possible. . . . So here, even if we believe that such compulsions will contribute to national unity, there are other ways to teach loyalty and patriotism which are the sources of national unity, than by compelling the pupil to affirm that which he does not believe and by commanding a form of affirmance which violates his religious convictions. Without recourse to such compulsion the state is free to compel attendance at school and require teaching by instruction and study of all in our history and in the structure and organization of our government, including the guaranties of civil liberty which tend to inspire patriotism and love of country. I cannot say that government here is deprived of any interest or function which it is entitled to maintain at the expense of the protection of civil liberties by requiring it to resort to the alternatives which do not coerce an affirmation of belief.

The guaranties of civil liberty are but guaranties of freedom of the human mind and spirit and of reasonable freedom and opportunity to express them. They presuppose the right of the individual to hold such opinions as he will and to give them reasonably free expression, and his freedom, and that of the state as well, to teach and persuade others by the communication of ideas. The very essence of the liberty which they guaranty is the freedom of the individual from compulsion as to what he shall think and what he shall say, at least where the compulsion is to bear false witness to his religion. If these guaranties are to have any meaning they must, I think, be deemed to withhold from the state any authority to compel belief or the expression of it where that expression violates religious convictions, whatever may be the legislative view of the desirability of such compulsion.

History teaches us that there have been but few infringements of personal liberty by the state which have not been justified, as they are here, in the name of righteousness and the public good, and few which have not been directed, as they are now, at politically helpless minorities. The framers were not unaware that under the system which they created most governmental curtailments of personal liberty would have the support of a legislative judgment that the public interest would be better served by its curtailment than by its constitutional protection. I cannot conceive that in prescribing, as limitations upon the powers of government, the freedom of the mind and spirit secured by the explicit guaranties of freedom of speech and religion, they intended or rightly could have left any latitude for a legislative judgment that the compulsory expression of belief which violates religious convictions would better serve the public interest than their protection. The Constitution may well elicit expressions of loyalty to it and to the government which it created, but it does not command such expressions or otherwise give any indication that compulsory expressions of loyalty play any such part in our scheme of government as to override the constitutional protection of freedom of speech and religion. And while such expressions of loyalty, when voluntarily given, may promote national unity, it is quite another matter to say that their compulsory expression by children in violation of their own and their parents' religious convictions can be regarded as playing so important a part in our national unity as to leave school boards free to exact it despite the constitutional guarantee of freedom of religion. The very terms of the Bill of Rights preclude, it seems to me, any reconciliation of such compulsions with the constitutional guaranties by a legislative declaration that they are more important to the public welfare than the Bill of Rights.

But even if this view be rejected and it is considered that there is some scope for the determination by legislatures whether the citizen shall be compelled to give public expression of such sentiments contrary to his religion, I am not persuaded that we should refrain from passing upon the legislative judgment "as long as the remedial channels of the democratic process remain open and unobstructed." This seems to me no less than the surrender of the constitutional protection of the liberty of small minorities to the popular will. . . .

Here we have such a small minority entertaining in good faith a religious belief, which is such a departure from the usual course of human conduct, that most persons are disposed to regard it with little toleration or concern. In such circumstances careful scrutiny of legislative efforts to secure conformity of belief and opinion by a compulsory affirmation of the desired belief, is especially needful if civil rights are to receive any protection. Tested by this standard, I am not prepared to say that the right of this small and helpless minority, including children having a strong religious conviction, whether they understand its nature or not, to refrain from an expression obnoxious to their religion, is to be overborne by the interest of the state in maintaining discipline in the schools.

The Constitution expresses more than the conviction of the people that democratic processes must be preserved at all costs. It is also an expression of faith and a command that freedom of mind and spirit must be preserved, which government must obey, if it is to adhere to that justice and moderation without which no free government can exist. For this reason it would seem that legislation which operates to repress the religious freedom of small minorities, which is admittedly within the scope of the protection of the Bill of Rights, must at least be subject to the same judicial scrutiny as legislation which we have recently held to infringe the constitutional liberty of religious and racial minorities.

With such scrutiny I cannot say that the inconveniences which may attend some sensible adjustment of school discipline in order that the religious convictions of these children may be spared, presents a problem so momentous or pressing as to outweigh the freedom from compulsory violation of religious faith which has been thought worthy of constitutional protection.

NORMAN THOMAS

— ★ —

McCarthyism and Liberty

From *The Test of Freedom*, 1954

In 1950, Joseph R. McCarthy, a U.S. senator from Wisconsin, began a campaign to expose suspected communists and their sympathizers in the State Department. What started as a right-wing Republican attempt to discredit the policies of the Democratic administration became an ongoing, four-year hunt for communist subversives, from all sectors of American life, through highly publicized Senate hearings. The great American socialist and frequent presidential candidate Norman Thomas used his 1954 book The Test of Freedom *to defend his lifelong commitment to civil liberties, to emphasize his early criticism of the Soviet Communists, and to condemn Senator McCarthy as the "exponent of government by denunciation." McCarthy's charges, based on unsubstantiated accusations and rumors, ruined many careers and fostered a nationwide climate of fear. Finally, the senator's attack on the U.S. Army inspired a special congressional investigation of McCarthy himself, and he was officially censured by the Senate in December 1954.*

It has been the fortune of Senator Joseph McCarthy, from the once progressive state of Wisconsin, to give his name to the complex of attitudes, procedures, and laws with which America most volubly confronts communism within her borders. It would be premature to say that McCarthyism has conquered our courts and our country; there are many heartening evidences to the contrary. It would be contrary to fact to hold the senator solely responsible for McCarthyism. It is an even more serious historical error to credit him with the major measures taken by the federal government against subversion. Nevertheless, he has made himself in the public mind, here and abroad, and only less

273

in official Washington itself, the symbol of militant opposition to insidious disloyalty. In searching out that evil he above all others is the Grand Inquisitor, he above all others the exponent of government by denunciation.

Most of the elements of McCarthyism long antedate the senator's emergence to prominence. The sort of patriotism which is the last refuge of the scoundrel is a perversion of love of country for personal advantage far older than the crusty British Tory, Samuel Johnson, to whom we owe the definition. On a less self-interested plane this kind of patriotism identifies love of country with dislike of foreigners, love of conformity, and exaggerated suspicion of dissent. Specimens of it were to be found in certain resolutions of the American Legion, and in the even more prejudiced utterances of the Daughters of the American Revolution, years before Joe McCarthy terrorized his fellow senators and Republican associates by his identification of patriotism with respect for his fulminations.

Moreover, the Grand Inquisitor has profited by a falsehood which he did not invent and which others propagandize at great cost. That is the lie which identifies communism with democratic socialism and the welfare state, the lie which affirms that liberty is bound up with the right of private owners of the nation's mineral wealth and water power to exploit them for private profit. (Under our present tax laws we taxpayers bear most of the cost of our indoctrination in this falsehood, since great corporations deduct it as an advertising expense before paying their taxes.)

Not even the inquisitorial methods of McCarthyism were originated by the senator. Liberals who passionately denounce them showed no equivalent concern for individual rights when New Dealers controlled the machinery of congressional inquiry. In the investigation of allegedly "un-American" activities Martin Dies set the pattern as chairman of the House Committee, first established in 1938. . . . As for legislation and administrative procedures directed to the discovery and punishment of disloyalty, McCarthy had nothing to do with the passage of the

Smith Act in 1940, and little to do with the McCarran Act of 1950. He had not begun his personal crusade against communism when President Truman instituted loyalty examinations for federal employees in 1947. He contributed nothing to the conviction of Alger Hiss. (But I have run across Americans who believe him responsible for it!)

It is not, however, true that McCarthy has failed to expose a single communist. A relatively small number of his sweeping charges have found legitimate targets. He has exposed some carelessness in loyalty inquiries—but not enough to make his investigatory work important to American security.

Why, then, the term *McCarthyism* and the general acceptance of the senator as symbol of an anticommunism of universal suspicion of dissent? Partly, of course, because of McCarthy's skill as a demagogue; partly because he came along at the right time in a country somewhat disappointed in the consequences of its own attempts at international virtue, shocked by the worldwide impact of communist imperialism, and outraged by communist abuse of its confidence in Stalin as an ally. His publicity techniques made the press and radio unwittingly build him up.

The senator successfully exploited anticommunism as a campaign issue in 1952; he is credited with important help in the campaigns of seven or eight of his colleagues. By the outrageous seniority system he became chairman of a permanent investigating committee in 1953. So his colleagues thought it safer to ignore the very serious questions about his own financial transactions which a Senate subcommittee had raised, questions which the Grand Inquisitor of others contemptuously refused to answer. Such success is unfortunately impressive.

It is significant of the man, of the *ism,* and perhaps of the mind of "the Lonely Crowd" that McCarthy by no means began his public career as conservative or anticommunist. Originally, he was a Democrat. As a Republican in his campaign against Robert M. LaFollette, Jr., for the Republican senatorial nomination back in 1946, before the honeymoon with "our brave Russian ally" had quite faded from memory, McCarthy, at the least, cheerfully accepted support from workers under communist leadership and influence in Wisconsin's open primary. It took him almost two years to discover gold in the hills of anticommunism. In the meantime, his chief interest was in augmenting his own fortune through his relation to the real estate lobby and certain housing interests; consider, for example, his ten-thousand-dollar fee from the Lustron Corporation. He has been the demagogic opportunist, not the bigoted anticommunist fanatic. To the time of my writing, he has never employed his denunciatory power in a full-dress explanation of, and attack on, the imperialistic communism of Moscow and Peking. The objects of his wrath have been General George Marshall, former Secretary of State Dean Acheson, the British leaders Winston Churchill and Clement Attlee, and the Democratic presidential candidate, Adlai Stevenson. (Of Stevenson, McCarthy said that he might make him a "good American with a baseball bat"—or was it a slippery elm club?) He opposed the president, a member of his own party, on the choice of ambassador to Russia. For untoward events in the struggle against imperialistic communism it would appear that there is always some American or Briton to blame, always a simple formula for victory: drive the red rascals out of Washington. Thus he has become the perfect spokesman and leader for tired Americans who want to indulge their fears and hates at cheap price—at the same time to defeat communism and pay lower taxes.

In his role of Grand Inquisitor, Senator McCarthy examined James Wechsler, acknowledged ex-communist but now communism's able foe in his editorial leadership on the New York *Post*. Inquisitor McCarthy doubted Mr. Wechsler's conversion and suggested to him that some Russian commissar had told him to feign his present role the better to serve the cause. The senator should have realized how completely that assumption might be turned against him. Certain it is that by collusion or coincidence he is following the course a philosophic communist might have chosen for him: noisy, indiscriminate criticism of communism with wholesale denunciation of secret communists in government, most of whom he cannot identify. Thus he conditions his followers for a fascist type of anticommunism, makes our Jeffersonian tradition contemptible, destroys the people's faith in their own government, and gives the communists respectability by confusing them with decent dissenters. (I have raised questions of his sixth-column service to the Kremlin in two open letters to the senator, to which he has not replied.)

One of the worst of McCarthy's disservices to his country and to freedom is the general impression that he has created to some extent at home, and to a greater extent abroad, that his spirit controls our judicial and administrative machinery. As a matter of fact, deserving as are some of our laws and loyalty procedures of criticism and repeal or amendment, the worst feature of McCarthyism is the popular fear and suspicion which it expresses and increases. Our jails are not filled with dissenters; speech is still free to heretics who dare claim their freedom. The worst evil in America is local censorship by voluntary vigilantes in libraries and schools, and the cowardice and apathy of the public before this censorship. McCarthy is probably better rather than worse than much prejudiced or frightened and wholly unreflective public opinion.

This sobering conclusion is supported not only by his electoral success but by the responses to civil-liberties questions in a poll conducted by the National Opinion Research Center during May 1953. Similar questions in 1946 had brought disquieting answers, but in seven years intolerance grew worse. Thus in 1953, only 45 percent believed that the Socialist party should be allowed to publish newspapers in this country; 15 percent would allow *no* criticism of "government, Constitution, America"; 55 percent thought it more important "to find out all the communists in the country even if some innocent people are accused" than to protect the innocent.

This situation is in large part due to the apathy or cowardice of liberals who won't speak out. In 1951, I took part in an excellent institute on foreign policy in a midwestern city. Local people attended the meetings but took comparatively little part in discussions. At the conclusion of the conference, I was almost timidly invited to come to an informal discussion club which would talk over the institute. I went on condition that I be taken on time to a late airplane. The informal discussion delighted me by its sense of freedom and its intelligence. But the personable young man who took me to the airport had barely seated me in his car when he said: "Now, Mr. Thomas, I hope you won't think we talk like that outside. I like my job, and the boys in the office might not like that talk." There were enough able and responsible people in that room to have changed the community climate by speaking out.

This is the sort of thing, and worse, that called forth the now famous words of Judge Learned Hand:

> Risk for risk, for myself, I had rather take my chance that some traitors will escape detection than spread abroad a spirit of general suspicion and distrust, which accepts rumor and gossip in place of undismayed and unintimidated inquiry. I believe that that community is already in process of dissolution where each man begins to eye his neighbor as a possible enemy; where nonconformity with the accepted creed, political as well as religious, is a mark of disaffection; where denunciation, without specification or backing, takes the place of evidence; where orthodoxy chokes freedom of dissent; where faith in the eventual supremacy of reason has become so timid that we dare not enter our convictions in the open lists, to win or lose.

That is a description of McCarthyism, although the distinguished judge does not use that term. It is highly significant that Judge Hand is the same man who in a notable decision sustained the Smith Act, under which the communist leaders were convicted in the long trial before Judge Medina in New York. It is evident, therefore, that one can repudiate McCarthyism and still support the constitutionality of stringent anticommunist measures.

MALCOLM X

— ★ —

The Black Muslim Movement

National Educational Television Interview
with Kenneth B. Clark, 1963

In 1963, Kenneth Clark interviewed three leaders of the black civil rights movement on the television program "The Negro and the American Promise," produced for the National Educational Television and Radio Center by Boston's station WGBH-TV. At the time, Malcolm X (1925–1965) was a frequently interviewed and controversial figure and a member of Elijah Muhammad's Black Muslim movement, which preached that white people were devils. Malcolm himself vehemently condemned white racism and advocated black self-defense. He subsequently broke with Muhammad's Nation of Islam, and after a visit to Mecca in Saudi Arabia, he returned to America influenced by the traditional Moslem belief in racial equality. On February 21, 1965, Malcolm was assassinated by a Black Muslim at a New York rally of his Organization of Afro-American Unity. For his televised interviews, Kenneth Clark asked each guest to begin with some personal history.

MALCOLM X. I was born in Omaha, Nebraska, back in 1925, that period when the Ku Klux Klan was quite strong in that area at that time—and grew up in Michigan, partially. Went to school there.

CLARK. What part of Michigan?

MALCOLM X. Lansing. I went to school there—as far as the eighth grade. And left there and then grew up in Boston and in New York.

CLARK. Did you travel with your family from Omaha to Michigan to Boston?

MALCOLM X. Yes. When I was born—shortly after I was

born—the Ku Klux Klan gave my father an ultimatum—or parents an ultimatum—about remaining there, so they left and went to—

CLARK. What was the basis of this ultimatum?

MALCOLM X. My father was a Garveyite, and in those days, you know, it wasn't the thing for a black man to be outspoken or to deviate from the accepted stereotype that was usually considered the right image for Negroes to fulfill or reflect.

CLARK. Of all the words that I have read about you, this is the first time that I've heard that your father was a Garveyite. And, in fact, he *was* an outspoken black nationalist in the 1920s?

MALCOLM X. He was both a Garveyite and a minister, a Baptist minister. In those days you know how it was and how it still is; it has only changed in the method, but the same things still exist: whenever a black man was outspoken, he was considered crazy or dangerous. And the police department and various branches of the law usually were interwoven with that Klan element, so the Klan had the backing of the police, and usually the police had the backing of the Klan, same as today.

CLARK. So in effect your father was required, or he was forced—

MALCOLM X. Yes, they burned the house that we lived in in Omaha, and I think this was in 1925, and we moved to Lansing, Michigan, and we ran into the same experience there. We lived in an integrated neighborhood, by the way, then. And it only proves that whites were as much against integration as they are now, only then they were more openly against it. And today they are shrewd in saying they are for it, but they still make it impossible for you to integrate. So we moved to Michigan and the same thing happened; they burned our home there. And he was—like I say—he was a clergyman, a Christian; and it was Christians who burned the home in both places—people who teach, you know, religious tolerance and brotherhood and all of them.

CLARK. Did you start school in Michigan?

MALCOLM X. Yes.

CLARK. How long did you stay in Michigan?

MALCOLM X. I think I completed the eighth grade while I was still in Michigan.

CLARK. And then where did you go?

MALCOLM X. To Boston.

CLARK. Did you go to high school in Boston?

MALCOLM X. No, I have never gone to high school.

CLARK. You've never gone to high school?

MALCOLM X. The eighth grade was as far as I went.

CLARK. That's phenomenal.

MALCOLM X. Everything I know above the eighth grade, I've learned from Mr. Muhammad. He's been my teacher, and I think he's a better teacher than I would have had had I continued to go to the public schools.

CLARK. How did you meet Mr. Muhammad?

MALCOLM X. I was—when I was in prison, in 1947, I first heard about his teaching; about his religious message. And at that time I was an atheist, myself. I had graduated from Christianity to agnosticism on into atheism.

CLARK. Were the early experiences in Nebraska and Michigan where, as you say, Christians burned the home of your father who was a Christian minister—were these experiences the determinants of your moving away from Christianity?

MALCOLM X. No, no, they weren't, because despite those experiences, I, as I said, lived a thoroughly integrated life. Despite all the experiences I had in coming up—and my father was killed by whites at a later date—I still thought that there were some good white people; at least the ones *I* was associating with, you know, were supposed to be different. There wasn't any experience, to my knowledge, that opened up my eyes, because right up until the time that I went to prison, I was still integrated into the white society and thought that there were some good ones.

CLARK. Was it an integrated prison?

MALCOLM X. It was an integrated prison at the prison level,

but the administrators were all white. You usually find that in any situation that is supposed to be based on integration. At the low level they integrate, but at the administrative or executive level you find whites running it.

CLARK. How long did you stay in prison?

MALCOLM X. About seven years.

CLARK. And you were in prison in Boston. And this is where you got in touch with—

MALCOLM X. My family became Muslims; accepted the religion of Islam, and one of them who had spent pretty much—- had spent quite a bit of time with me on the streets of New York out here in Harlem had been exposed to the religion of Islam. He accepted it, and it made such a profound change in him. He wrote to me and was telling me about it. Well, I had completely eliminated Christianity. After getting into prison and having time to think, I could see the hypocrisy of Christianity. Even before I went to prison, I had already become an atheist and I could see the hypocrisy of Christianity. Most of my associates were white; they were either Jews or Christians, and I saw hypocrisy on both sides. None of them really practiced what they preached.

CLARK. Minister Malcolm—

MALCOLM X. Excuse me, but despite the fact that I had detected this, my own intellectual strength was so weak, or so lacking, till I was not in a position to really see or come to a conclusion concerning this hypocrisy until I had gotten to where I could think a little bit and had learned more about the religion of Islam. Then I could go back and remember all of these experiences and things that I had actually heard—discussions that I had participated in myself with whites. It had made everything that Mr. Muhammad was saying add up.

CLARK. I see.

MALCOLM X. He was the one who drew the line and enabled me to add up everything and say that this is this, and I haven't met anyone since then who was capable of showing me an answer more strong or with more weight than the answer that the Honorable Elijah Muhammad has given.

CLARK. I'd like to go back just a little to your life in prison. What was the basis—how did you—

MALCOLM X. Crime. I wasn't framed. I went to prison for what I did, and the reason that I don't have any hesitation or reluctance whatsoever to point out the fact that I went to prison: I firmly believe that it was the Christian society, as you call it, the Judaic-Christian society, that created all of the factors that send so many so-called Negroes to prison. And when these fellows go to prison there is nothing in the system designed to rehabilitate them. There's nothing in the system designed to reform them. All it does is—it's a breeding ground for more professional type of criminal, especially among Negroes. Since I saw, detected, the reluctance on the part of penologists, prison authorities, to reform men and even detected that—noticed that after a so-called Negro in prison trys to reform and become a better man, the prison authorities are more against *that* man than they were against him when he was completely criminally inclined, so this is again hypocrisy. Not only is the Christian society itself religious hypocrisy, but the court system is hypocrisy, the entire penal system is hypocrisy. Everything is hypocrisy. Mr. Muhammad came along with his religious gospel and introduced the religion of Islam and showed the honesty of Islam, showed the justice in Islam, the freedom in Islam. Why naturally, just comparing the two, Christianity had already eliminated itself, so all I had to do was accept the religion of Islam. I know today what it has done for me as a person.

CLARK. I notice that the Black Muslim movement has put a great deal of time, effort, and energy in seeking recruits within the prisons.

MALCOLM X. This is incorrect.

CLARK. It is incorrect?

MALCOLM X. It is *definitely* incorrect.

CLARK. Eric Lincoln's book—

MALCOLM X. Well, Lincoln is incorrect himself. Lincoln is just a Christian preacher from Atlanta, Georgia, who wanted to make some money, so he wrote a book and called it *The Black Muslims in America*. We're not even Black Muslims. We are black people in a sense that *black* is an adjective. We are black people who are Muslims because we have accepted the religion of Islam, but what Eric Lincoln shrewdly did was capitalize the letter *b*, and made *black* an adjectival noun and then attached it to *Muslim*, and now it is used by the press to make it appear that this is the name of an organization. It has no religious connotation or religious motivation or religious objectives.

CLARK. You do not have a systematic campaign for recruiting or rehabilitating?

MALCOLM X. No, no.

CLARK. What about rehabilitation?

MALCOLM X. The reason that the religion of Islam has spread so rapidly in prison is because the average so-called Negro in prison has had experiences enough to make him realize the hypocrisy of everything in this society, and he also has experienced the fact that the system itself is not designed to rehabilitate him or make him turn away from crime. Then when he hears the religious teaching of the Honorable Elijah Muhammad that restores to him his racial pride, his racial identity, and restores to him also the desire to be a man, to be a human being, he reforms himself. And this spreads so rapidly among the so-called Negroes in prison that, since the sociologist and the psychologists and the penologist and the criminologist have all realized their own inability to rehabilitate the criminal, when Mr. Muhammad comes along and starts rehabilitating the criminal with just the religious gospel, it's a miracle. They look upon it as a sociological phenomenon or psychological phenomena, and it gets great publicity.

CLARK. You do not, therefore, have to actively recruit.

MALCOLM X. The Honorable Elijah Muhammad has no active effort to convert or recruit men in prison any moreso than he does Negroes, period. I think that what you should realize is that in America there are twenty million black people, all of whom are in prison. You don't have to go to Sing Sing to be in prison. If you're born in America with a black skin, you're born in prison, and the masses of black people in America today are beginning to regard our plight or predicament in this society as one of a prison inmate. And when they refer to the president, he's just another warden to whom they turn to open the cell door, but it's no different. It's the same thing, and just as the warden in the prison couldn't rehabilitate those men, the president in this country couldn't rehabilitate or change the thinking of the masses of black people. And as the Honorable Elijah Muhammad has been able to go behind the prison walls—the physical prison walls—and release those men from that which kept them criminals, he likewise on a mass scale throughout this country—he is able to send his religious message into the so-called Negro community and rehabilitate the thinking of our people and made them conquer the habits and the vices and the evils that have held us in the clutches of this white man's society.

CLARK. I think, Minister Malcolm, what you have just said brings me to trying to hear from you directly your ideas concerning the philosophy of the Black Muslim movement. Among the things that have been written about this movement, the things which stand out are the fact that this movement preaches hatred for whites; that it preaches black supremacy; that it, in fact, preaches, or if it does not directly preach, it accepts the inevitability of, violence as a factor in the relationship between the races. Now—

MALCOLM X. That's a strange thing. You know, the Jews here in this city rioted last week against some Nazi, and I was listening to a program last night where the other Jew—where a Jewish commentator was congratulating what the Jews did to this Nazi; complimenting them for it. Now no one mentioned violence in connection with what the Jews did against these Nazis. But these same Jews, who will condone violence on their part or hate someone whom they consider to be an enemy, will join Negro organizations and tell Negroes to be nonviolent; that it is wrong or immoral, unethical, unintelligent for Negroes to reflect some kind of desire to defend themselves from the attacks of whites who are trying to brutalize us. The Muslims who follow the Honorable Elijah Muhammad don't advocate violence, but Mr. Muhammad does teach us that any human being who is intelligent has the right to defend himself. You can't take a black man who is being bitten by dogs and accuse him of advocating violence because he tries to defend himself from the bite of the dog. If you notice, the people who are sicking the dogs on the black people are never accused of violence; they are never accused of hate. Nothing like that is ever used in the context of a discussion when it's about them. It is only when the black man begins to explode and erupt after he has had too much that they say that the black man is violent, and as long as these whites are putting out a doctrine that paves the way to justify their mistreatment of blacks, this is never called hate. It is only when the black man himself begins to spell out the historic deeds of what whites have been doing to him in this country that the shrewd white man with his control over the news media and propaganda makes it appear that the black people today are advocating some kind of hate. Mr. Muhammad teaches us to love each other, and when I say love each other—love our own kind. This is all black people need to be taught in this country because the only ones whom we don't love are our own kind. Most of the Negroes you see running around here talking about "love everybody"—they don't have any love whatsoever for their own kind. When they say, "Love everybody," what they are doing is setting up a situation for us to love white people. This is what their philosophy is. Or when they say, "Suffer peacefully," they mean suffer peacefully at the hands of the white man, because the same nonviolent Negroes are the advocators of nonviolence. If a Negro attacks one of them, they'll fight that Negro all over Harlem. It's only when the white man attacks them that they believe in nonviolence, all of them.

CLARK. Mr. X, is this a criticism of the Reverend Martin Luther King?

MALCOLM X. You don't have to criticize Reverend Martin Luther King. His actions criticize him.

CLARK. What do you mean by this?

MALCOLM X. Any Negro who teaches other Negroes to turn the other cheek is disarming that Negro. Any Negro who teaches Negroes to turn the other cheek in the face of attack is disarming that Negro of his God-given right, of his moral right, of his natural right, of his intelligent right to defend himself. Everything in nature can defend itself, and is right in defending itself except the American Negro. And men like King—their job is to go among Negroes and teach Negroes, "Don't fight back." He doesn't tell them, "Don't fight each other." "Don't fight the white man" is what he's saying in essence, because the followers of Martin Luther King will cut each other from head to foot, but they will not do anything to defend themselves against the attacks of the white man. But King's philosophy falls upon the ears of only a small minority. The majority or masses of black people in this country are more inclined in the direction of the Honorable Elijah Muhammad than Martin Luther King.

CLARK. Is it not a fact though—

MALCOLM X. *White* people follow King. *White* people pay King. *White* people subsidize King. *White* people support King. But the masses of black people don't support Martin Luther King. King is the best weapon that the white man, who wants to brutalize Negroes, has ever gotten in this country, because he is setting up a situation where, when the white man wants to attack Negroes, they can't defend themselves, because King has put this foolish philosophy out—you're not supposed to fight or you're not supposed to defend yourself.

CLARK. But Mr. X, is it not a fact that Reverend King's movement was successful in Montgomery—

MALCOLM X. You can't tell me that you have had success— excuse me, sir.

CLARK. Was it not a success in Birmingham?

MALCOLM X. No, no. What kind of success did they get in Birmingham? A chance to sit at a lunch counter and drink some coffee with a cracker—that's success? A chance to—thousands of little children went to jail; they didn't get out, they were bonded out by King. They had to *pay* their way out of jail. That's not any kind of advancement or success.

CLARK. What *is* advancement from the point of view of the Muslims?

MALCOLM X. Any time dogs have bitten black women, bitten black children—when I say dogs, that is four-legged dogs and two-legged dogs have brutalized thousands of black people—and the one who advocates himself as their leader is satisfied in making a compromise or a deal with the same ones who did this to these people only if they will offer him a job, one job, downtown for one Negro or things of that sort, I don't see where there's any kind of success, sir; it's a sellout. Negroes in Birmingham are in worse condition now than they were then because the line is more tightly drawn. And to say that some moderate—to say that things are better now because a different man, a different white man, a different Southern white man is in office now, who's supposed to be a moderate, is to tell me that you are better off dealing with a fox than you were when you were dealing with a wolf. The ones that they were dealing with previously were wolves, and they didn't hide the fact that they were wolves. The man that they got to deal with now is a fox, but he's no better than the wolf. Only he's better in his ability to lull the Negroes to sleep, and he'll do that as long as they listen to Dr. Martin Luther King.

CLARK. What would be the goals, or what are the goals of the Black Muslim movement? What would the Black Muslim movement insist upon in Birmingham, in Montgomery and in Jackson, Mississippi, et cetera?

MALCOLM X. Well, number one, the Honorable Elijah Muhammad teaches us that the solution will never be brought about by politicians, it will be brought about by God, and that the only way the black man in this country today can receive respect and recognition of other people is to stand on his own feet; get something for himself and do something for himself;

and the solution that God has given the Honorable Elijah Muhammad is the same as the solution that God gave to Moses when the Hebrews in the Bible were in a predicament similar to the predicament of the so-called Negroes here in America today, which is nothing other than a modern house of bondage, or a modern Egypt, or a modern Babylon. And Moses' answer was to separate these slaves from their slave master and show the slaves how to go to a land of their own where they would serve a God of their own and a religion of their own and have a country of their own in which they could feed themselves, clothe themselves, and shelter themselves.

CLARK. In fact then, you're saying that the Black Muslim movement—

MALCOLM X. It's not a Black Muslim movement.

CLARK. All right, then—

MALCOLM X. We are black people who are Muslims because we believe in the religion of Islam.

CLARK. This movement which you so ably represent actually desires separation.

MALCOLM X. Complete separation; not only physical separation but moral separation. This is why the Honorable Elijah Muhammad teaches the black people in this country that we must stop drinking, we must stop smoking, we must stop committing fornication and adultery, we must stop gambling and cheating and using profanity, we must stop showing disrespect for our women, we must reform ourselves as parents so we can set the proper example for our children. Once we reform ourselves of these immoral habits, that makes us more godly, more godlike, more righteous. That means we are qualified then, to be on God's side, and it puts God on our side. God becomes our champion then, and it makes it possible for us to accomplish our own aims.

CLARK. This movement then, is not particularly sympathetic with the integrationist goals of the NAACP, CORE, Martin Luther King, and the student nonviolent movement.

MALCOLM X. Mr. Muhammad teaches us that integration is

only a trick on the part of the white man today to lull Negroes to sleep, to lull them into thinking that the white man is changing and actually trying to keep us here. But America itself, because of the seeds that it has sown in the past against the black man, is getting ready to reap the whirlwind today, reap the harvest. Just as Egypt had to pay for its crime that it committed for enslaving the Hebrews, the Honorable Elijah Muhammad teaches us that America has to pay today for the crime that is committed in enslaving the so-called Negroes.

CLARK. There is one question that has bothered me a great deal about your movement, and it involves just a little incident. Rockwell, who is a self-proclaimed white supremacist and American Nazi, was given an honored front row position at one of your—

MALCOLM X. This is incorrect.

CLARK. Am I wrong?

MALCOLM X. This is a false statement that has been put out by the press. And Jews have used it to spread anti-Muslim propaganda throughout this country. Mr. Muhammad had an open convention to which he invited anyone, black and white. (And this is another reason why we keep white people out of our meetings.) He invited everyone, both black and white, and Rockwell came. Rockwell came the same as any other white person came, and when we took up a collection, we called out the names of everyone who made a donation. Rockwell's name was called out the same as anybody else's, and this was projected to make it look like Rockwell was financing the Muslims. And second, Rockwell came to another similar meeting. At this meeting Mr. Muhammad gave anyone who wanted to oppose him or congratulate him an opportunity to speak. Rockwell spoke; he was not even allowed up on the rostrum; he spoke from a microphone from which other whites spoke at the same meeting. And again the Jewish press, or the Jewish who are a part of the press— Jewish *people* who are part of the press— used this as propaganda to make it look like Rockwell was in cahoots with the Muslims. Rockwell, to us, is no different from any other white man. One of the things that I *will* give Rockwell credit for: he preaches and practices the same thing. And these other whites running around here posing as liberals, patting Negroes on the back—they think the same thing that Rockwell thinks, only they speak a different talk, a different language.

CLARK. Minister Malcolm, you have mentioned the Jews and the Jewish press and Jewish propaganda frequently in this discussion. It has been said frequently that an important part of your movement is anti-Semitism. I have seen you deny this.

MALCOLM X. No. We're a—

CLARK. Would you want to comment on this?

MALCOLM X. No, the followers of Mr. Muhammad aren't antianything but antiwrong, antiexploitation, and antioppression. A lot of the Jews have a guilty conscience when you mention exploitation because they realize that they control 90 percent of the businesses in every Negro community from the Atlantic to the Pacific and that they get more benefit from the Negro's purchasing power than the Negro himself does or than any other white or any other segment of the white community does, so they have a guilt complex on this. And whenever you mention exploitation of Negroes, most Jews think that you're talking about them, and in order to hide what they are guilty of, they accuse you of being anti-Semitic.

CLARK. Do you believe the Jews are more guilty of this exploitation than are—

MALCOLM X. Jews belong to practically every Negro organization Negroes have. Arthur T. Spingarn, the head of the NAACP, is Jewish. Every organization that Negroes—When I say the head of the NAACP, the *president* of the NAACP is Jewish. The same Jews wouldn't let you become the president of the B'nai B'rith or their different organizations.

CLARK. Thank you very much. You have certainly presented important parts of your movement, your point of view. I think we understand more clearly now some of your goals, and I'd like to know if we could talk some other time if you would tell me a little about what you think is the future of the Negro in America other than separation.

MALCOLM X. Yes. As long as they have interviews with the attorney general and take Negroes to pose as leaders, all of whom are married either to white men or white women, you'll always have a race problem. When Baldwin took that crew with him to see Kennedy, he took the wrong crew. And as long as they take the wrong crew to talk to that man, you're not going to get anywhere near any solution to this problem in this country.

MARTIN LUTHER KING, JR.

—— ★ ——

Nonviolent Protest

National Educational Television Interview
with Kenneth B. Clark, 1963

Martin Luther King, Jr. (1929–1968), the great civil rights leader and advocate of nonviolent protest, had been in the forefront of the struggle for African-American equality and integration since the Montgomery, Alabama, bus boycott of 1955–1956. Kenneth Clark's discussion with King for the 1963 educational television series "The Negro and the American Promise" contrasts strongly with Clark's interview with Malcolm X, who advocated segregation of the races and attacked King's "foolish philosophy" that taught blacks "to turn the other cheek in the face of attack." King answered Malcolm's criticisms by stating: "I think of love as something strong and that organizes itself into powerful direct action. . . . The critics . . . confuse nonresistence with nonviolent resistence." King's crowning achievements were the March on Washington of August 28, 1963—when he delivered his famous I Have a Dream speech—and his winning of the 1964 Nobel Peace Prize. By the late 1960s King's steadfast commitment to nonviolence was being increasingly challenged by young militants and "black power" proponents. The advocate of peaceful resistence was assassinated in Memphis, Tennessee, on April 4, 1968.

KING. I was born in the South, in Atlanta, Georgia, and I lived there all of my early years. In fact, I went to the public schools of Atlanta and I went to college in Atlanta. I left after college to attend theological school.

CLARK. What college did you go to?

KING. Morehouse College in Atlanta.

CLARK. Part of the Atlanta University system.

KING. That's right. And I was raised in the home of a minister; my father pastors the Ebenezer Church in Atlanta and has pastored this church for thirty-three years. I am now copastor of the same church with him. And we have—I mean there's a family of three children in the immediate family; I have one brother and one sister.

CLARK. Is your brother a pastor also?

KING. Yes, he is. He's the pastor of the First Baptist Church of Birmingham, Alabama.

CLARK. And you have a sister?

KING. Yes, she's in Atlanta, teaching at Spelman College.

CLARK. Now, about your own immediate family: I remember the last time we were together in Montgomery you had a son who had just been born before the Montgomery disturbances.

KING. Well, that was a daughter. The second child was a son, but our first child was a daughter. Since that time we've had two more, so we have four children now, two sons and two daughters, the most recent one being the daughter that came nine weeks ago.

CLARK. How wonderful. It seems as if you have children at times of major crises.

KING. Yes, that's right, and that brings new life to life.

CLARK. Very good. You went from Morehouse to Boston University to study philosophy, am I correct?

KING. Well, no, I went from Morehouse to Crozer Theological Seminary in Pennsylvania and then I went from Crozer to Boston University.

CLARK. In Boston you studied philosophy and, if I remember correctly, you have a Ph.D. in philosophy.

KING. Well, the actual field is philosophical theology.

CLARK. Now, if we could shift a little from the education within the academic halls to your education in the community. I look at our newspapers and see that you have not only engaged in and led many of these demonstrations but have paid for this by seeing the inside of many jails. I've wondered—how many jails have you been to as a result of your involvement in this direct-action, nonviolent insistence upon the rights of Negroes?

KING. Well, I've been arrested fourteen times since we started out in Montgomery. Some have been in the same jail, that is, I've been in some jails more than once. I haven't calculated the number of different jails. I would say about eight of them were different jails. I remember once within eight days I transferred to three different jails within the state of Georgia. I think I've been to about eight different jails and I've been arrested about fourteen times.

CLARK. Have you attempted to make a study of these jails, for example, the type of jail, the type of individuals you've met in these jails as keepers, say, or wardens? What type of human beings are these or are they different types of human beings?

KING. Well, I have gone through the process of comparing the various jails. I guess this is one of those inevitable things that you find yourself doing to kind of lift yourself from the dull monotony of sameness when you're in jail and I find that they do differ. I've been in some new jails and I've been in some mighty old ones. In the recent jail experience in Birmingham I was in the new jail. The city jail is about a year old, I think, and in Albany, Georgia, last year I was in a very old jail. In Fulton County, Georgia, I was in a very new one.

CLARK. What about the human beings who are the jailers: What about their attitude toward you as a person?

KING. Well, they vary also. I have been in jails where the jailers were exceptionally courteous and they went out of their way to see that everything went all right where I was concerned. On the other hand, I have been in jails where the jailers were extremely harsh and vitriolic in their words and in their manners. I haven't had any experience of physical violence from jailers, but I have had violence of words from them. Even in Birmingham, for the first few days, some of the jailers were extremely harsh in their statements.

CLARK. Have you ever been in an integrated jail? In the South?

KING. No, that's one experience I haven't had yet.

CLARK. Well, maybe after we get through integrating public

accommodations the last thing will be to integrate the jail-houses.

KING. Yes.

CLARK. I am very much interested in the philosophy of nonviolence and particularly I would like to understand more clearly for myself the relationship between the direct-action nonviolence technique which you have used so effectively and your philosophy of, for want of better words I'll use, "love of the oppressor."

KING. All right.

CLARK. Dr. King, what do you see as the relationship between these two things, which could be seen as separate?

KING. Yes, I think so. One is a method of action: nonviolent direct action is a method of acting to rectify a social situation that is unjust and it involves in engaging in a practical technique that nullifies the use of violence or calls for nonviolence at every point. That is, you don't use physical violence against the opponent. Now, the love ethic is another dimension which goes into the realm of accepting nonviolence as a way of life. There are many people who will accept nonviolence as the most practical technique to be used in a social situation, but they would not go to the point of seeing the necessity of accepting nonviolence as a way of life. Now, I accept both. I think that nonviolent resistance is the most potent weapon available to oppressed people in their struggle for freedom and human dignity. It has a way of disarming the opponent. It exposes his moral defenses. It weakens his morale and at the same time it works on his conscience. He just doesn't know how to handle it and I have seen this over and over again in our struggle in the South. Now on the question of love or the love ethic, I think this is so important because hate is injurious to the hater as well as the hated. Many of the psychiatrists are telling us now that many of the strange things that happen in the subconscious and many of the inner conflicts are rooted in hate and so they are now saying "love or perish." Eric Fromm can write a book like *The Art of Loving* and make it very clear that love is the supreme unifying principle of life, and I'm trying to say in this movement that it is necessary to follow the technique of nonviolence as the most potent weapon available to us, but it is necessary also to follow the love ethic which becomes a force of personality integration.

CLARK. But is it not too much to expect that a group of human beings who have been the victims of cruelty and flagrant injustice could actually love those who have been associated with the perpetrators, if not the perpetrators themselves? How could you expect, for example, the Negroes in Birmingham who know Bull Connor to really love him in any meaningful sense?

KING. Well, I think one has to understand the meaning of *love* at this point. I'm certainly not speaking of an affectionate response. I think it is really nonsense to urge oppressed peoples to love their oppressors in an affectionate sense. And I often call on the Greek language to aid me at this point because there are three words in the Greek for "love." One is *eros,* which is sort of an aesthetic or a romantic love. Another is *fileo,* which is sort of an intimate affection between personal friends; this is friendship, it is a reciprocal love and on this level, you love those people that you like. And then the Greek language comes out with the word *agape,* which is understanding, creative, redemptive goodwill for all men. It goes far beyond an affectionate response. Now when I say to you—

CLARK. That form means really understanding.

KING. Yes, that's right. And you come to the point of being able to love the person that does an evil deed in the sense of understanding and you can hate the deed that the person does. And I'm certainly not talking about eros; I'm not talking about friendship. I find it pretty difficult to like people like Bull Connor. I find it difficult to like Senator Eastman, but I think you can love where you can't like the person because life is an affectionate quality.

CLARK. Yes, I have admired your ability to feel this, and I must say to you also that as I read your expounding of the philosophy of love I found myself often feeling personally quite inadequate. Malcolm X, one of the most articulate exponents of the Black Muslim philosophy, has said of your movement and your philosophy that it plays into the hands of the white oppressors, that they are happy to hear you talk about love for the oppressor because this disarms the Negro and fits into the stereotype of the Negro as a meek, turning-the-other-cheek sort of creature. Would you care to comment on Mr. X's beliefs?

KING. Well, I don't think of love, as in this context, as emotional bosh. I don't think of it as a weak force, but I think of love as something strong and that organizes itself into powerful direct action. Now, this is what I try to teach in this struggle in the South: that we are not engaged in a struggle that means we sit down and do nothing; that there is a great deal of difference between nonresistance to evil and nonviolent resistance. Nonresistance leaves you in a state of stagnant passivity and deadly complacency where nonviolent resistance means that you do resist in a very strong and determined manner and I think some of the criticisms of nonviolence or some of the critics fail to realize that we are talking about something very strong and they confuse nonresistance with nonviolent resistance.

CLARK. *He* goes beyond that in some of the things I've heard him say—to say that this is deliberately your philosophy of love of the oppressor which he identifies completely with the nonviolent movement. He says this philosophy and this movement are actually encouraged by whites because it makes them comfortable. It makes them believe that Negroes are meek, supine creatures.

KING. Well, I don't think that's true. If anyone has ever lived with a nonviolent movement in the South, from Montgomery on through the freedom rides and through the sit-in movement and the recent Birmingham movement and seen the reactions of many of the extremists and reactionaries in the white community, he wouldn't say that this movement makes—this philosophy makes them comfortable. I think it arouses a sense of shame within them often—in many instances. I think it does something to touch the conscience and establish a sense of guilt. Now so often people respond to guilt by engaging more in the guilt-evoking act in an attempt to drown the sense of guilt, but this approach certainly doesn't make the white man feel comfortable. I think it does the other thing. It disturbs his conscience and it disturbs this sense of contentment that he's had.

CLARK. James Baldwin raises still another point of the whole nonviolent position, an approach. He does not reject it in the ways that Malcolm X does, but he raises the question of whether it will be possible to contain the Negro people within this framework of nonviolence if we continue to have more of the kinds of demonstrations that we had in Birmingham, wherein police brought dogs to attack human beings. What is your reaction to Mr. Baldwin's anxiety?

KING. Well, I think these brutal methods used by the Birmingham police force and other police forces will naturally arouse the ire of Negroes and I think there is the danger that some will be so aroused that they will retaliate with violence. I think though that we can be sure that the vast majority of Negroes who engage in the demonstrations and who understand the nonviolent philosophy will be able to face dogs and all of the other brutal methods that are used without retaliating with violence because they understand that one of the first principles of nonviolence is the willingness to be the recipient of violence while never inflicting violence upon another. And none of the demonstrators in Birmingham engaged in aggressive or retaliatory violence. It was always someone on the sideline who had never been in the demonstrations and probably not in the mass meetings and had never been in a nonviolent workshop. So I think it will depend on the extent to which we can extend the teaching of the philosophy of nonviolence to the larger community rather than those who are engaged in the demonstrations.

CLARK. Well, how do you maintain this type of discipline, control, and dignity in your followers who do participate in the demonstrations? You don't have police force, you have no uniform, you're not an authoritarian organization, you're a group of people who are voluntarily associated. How do you account for this, I would say, beautiful dignity and discipline?

KING. Well, we do a great deal in terms of teaching both the theoretical aspects of nonviolence as well as the practical application. We even have courses where we go through the experience of being roughed up and this kind of socio-drama has proved very helpful in preparing those who are engaged in demonstrations. The other thing is—

CLARK. Does this even include the children?

KING. Yes, it includes the children. In Birmingham where we had several young—we had some as young as seven years old to participate in the demonstrations, and they were in the workshops. In fact, none of them went out for a march, none of them engaged in any of the demonstrations before going through this kind of teaching session. So that through this method we are able to get the meaning of nonviolence over, and I think there is a contagious quality in a movement like this when everybody talks about nonviolence and being faithful to it and being dignified in your resistance. It tends to get over to the larger group because this becomes a part of the vocabulary of the movement.

CLARK. What is the relationship between your movement and such organizations as the NAACP, CORE, and the Student Nonviolent Coordinating Committee? They're separate organizations, but do you work together?

KING. Yes, we do. As you say, each of these organizations is autonomous, but we work together in many, many ways. Last year we started a voter-registration drive, an intensified voter-registration drive. And all of the organizations are working together, sometimes two or three are working together in the same community. The same thing is true with our direct-action programs. In Birmingham we had the support of Snick and CORE and the NAACP. CORE sent some of its staff members in to assist us and Snick sent some of its staff members. Roy Wilkins came down to speak in one of the mass meetings and to make it clear that even though the NAACP cannot operate in Alabama, we had the support of the NAACP. So that we are all working together in a very significant way, and we are doing even more in the days ahead to coordinate our efforts.

CLARK. Is there any machinery—does machinery for coordination actually exist now?

KING. Well, we have had a sort of coordinating council where we get together as often as possible. Of course, we get involved in many of our programs in the various areas and can't make as many of these meetings as we would like but we often come together (I mean, the heads of all these organizations) to try to coordinate our various efforts.

CLARK. What about the federal government? Have you made any direct appeal either in your own right or as part of this leadership group to have a more active involvement in the federal government in the rights of Negroes?

KING. Yes, I have. I've made appeals and other members of the Southern Christian Leadership Conference have appealed to the president and the new administration generally to do more in dealing with the problem of racial injustice. I think Mr. Kennedy has done some significant things in civil rights, but I do not feel that he has yet given the leadership that the enormity of the problem demands.

CLARK. By Mr. Kennedy, now, do you mean the president?

KING. Yes, I'm speaking now of the president, mainly. And I would include the attorney general. I think both of these men are men of genuine goodwill, but I think they must understand more about the depths and dimensions of the problem and I think there is a necessity now to see the urgency of the moment. There isn't a lot of time; time is running out, and the Negro is making it palpably clear that he wants all of his rights, that he wants them here, and that he wants them now.

CLARK. Is this not considered by some people an extremist position, that is, not really practical?

KING. Yes, I'm sure many people feel this, but I think they must see the truth of the situation. The shape of the world today does not afford us the luxury of slow movement and the Negro's quest for dignity and self-respect doesn't afford the nation this kind of slow movement.

CLARK. Dr. King, what do you think will be the outcome of

the present confrontation, the present insistence of the Negroes for their rights as American citizens without equivocation and without qualification? Do you think this will be obtained?

KING. I do. Realism impels me to admit that there will be difficult days ahead. In some of the hard-core states in the South we will confront resistance. There will still be resistance and there will still be very real problems in the North as a result of the twin evils of employment and housing discrimination, but I think there are forces at work now that will somehow ward off all of these ominous possibilities. The rolling tide of world opinion will play a great part in this. I think the aroused conscience of many, many white people all over the country, the growing awareness of religious institutions that they have not done their job, and the determination of the Negro himself, and the growing industrialization in the South—all of these things, I believe—will conjoin to make it possible for us to move on toward the goal of integration.

CLARK. So you are hopeful?

KING. Yes, I am.

CLARK. And I thank you for your hope and I thank you for your actions.

KING. Thank you.

RALPH NADER

——— ★ ———

Pollution: Environmental Violence

From *Ecotactics: The Sierra Club Handbook for
Environment Activists,* 1970

---

*One of the outgrowths of the student protest movement against
the Vietnam War was the adoption by many young Americans
of the concept of a new era of peace, brotherhood, and concern
for the natural environment. The 1970s witnessed a growing
public awareness of ecological issues and the passage of legislation against air, water, and chemical-waste pollution—and, of
course, the establishment, in 1970, of an annual Earth Day celebration. Ralph Nader (1934–   ) has been America's most
prominent advocate of consumer rights and protection since his
groundbreaking 1965 book on auto safety,* Unsafe at Any Speed.
*Since the late 1960s, Nader has fostered numerous groups com-
mitted to the improvement of the public welfare and protection
of the environment, including the hundreds of young Nader's
Raiders, Congress Watch, the Center for Responsive Law, Public
Citizen, the Center for Auto Safety, and the Health Research
Group. Nader's introduction to* Ecotactics, *the Sierra Club's
1970 collection of essays on environmental activism, strongly
espouses the ecological cause: "Pollution is violence and environmental pollution is environmental violence. . . . In the size of
the population exposed and the seriousness of the harm done,
environmental violence far exceeds that of street crime."*

F or centuries, man's efforts to control nature brought increasing security from trauma and disease. Cultures grew
rapidly by harnessing the forces of nature to work and produce
for proliferating populations. But in recent decades, the im-
balanced application of man's energies to the land, water, and
air has abused these resources to a point where nature is turning
on its abusers. The natural conditions of human health and

safety are being subjected to complex and savage assaults. Yet these assaults are no longer primarily aesthetic and economic deprivations. They are now threatening the physiological integrity of our citizens. They are exacting their insidious toll daily. During the past decade, this country has begun to show that it can destroy itself inadvertently from within. Surely, this capability must be something new in the history of man.

In taking the initiative against those whose myopia, venality and indifference produce pollution, the first step is to equate the phenomena to our basic value system. Pollution is violence and environmental pollution is environmental violence. It is a violence that has different impacts, styles, and time factors than the more primitive kind of violence such as crime in the streets. Yet in the size of the population exposed and the seriousness of the harm done, environmental violence far exceeds that of street crime.

Why then is there so much more official and citizen concern over crime in the streets? Some of the reasons are obvious. Primitive crime provokes sensory perceptions of a raw, instinctual nature; environmental crime generates a silent form of violence most often unfelt, unseen, and unheard. Environmental crime is often accompanied by the production of economic and governmental benefits: consequently the costs are played down, especially since people other than the polluters are bearing them. The slogan "That's the price of progress" is more than superficially ingrained in people continually confronted by industry arguments that any pollution crackdown will mean loss of jobs. Another reason is that power and polluters have always been closely associated. The corporate drive to reduce corporate costs and invest only in machinery and systems that enhance sales and profits is calculated to inflict as social costs on the public the contaminants of corporate activities. The same is true for the lack of attention by producers to the postproduction fallout of their products as they interact, run off, and become waste. Pesticides, nitrogen fertilizer, and disposable containers are examples of such fallout.

Governmental activity in sewage and solid waste disposal and in defense research has also burgeoned environmental violence. Deep-well disposal of chemical wastes by the U.S. Army near Denver led to earth tremors and small earthquakes as well as to contamination of the subsoil. The navy dumps tons of raw sewage into offshore waters, and its facilities, such as the notorious Fire Fighting School in San Diego, throw off pollutants into the air. Vessels carrying herbicides to Vietnam and other areas of the world could possibly provoke one of history's greatest catastrophes: Should one ship sink and should the drums containing the chemicals be ruptured, marine organisms for miles around would be destroyed, thus reducing the oxygen supply available to mankind. The transfer of these herbicides through food to humans is another specter, given the fantastic geometric progression of the concentration of these chemicals from plankton on up the food-chain to man himself. Municipal waste disposal practices are, for many towns and cities, primitive; and where waste is treated, effluents still upset the ecology of lakes, streams, and bays.

To deal with a system of oppression and suppression, which characterizes the environmental violence in this country, the first priority is to deprive the polluters of their unfounded legitimacy. Too often they assume a conservative, patriotic posture when in reality they are radical destroyers of a nation's resources and the most fundamental rights of people. Their power to block or manipulate existing laws permits them, as perpetrators, to keep the burden of proof on the victims. In a country whose people have always valued the "open book," corporate and government polluters crave secrecy and deny citizens access to the records of that which is harming their health and safety.

State and federal agencies keep undisclosed data on how much different companies pollute. Thus has industrial lethality been made a trade secret by a government that presumes to be democratic. Corporate executives—as in the auto companies—speak out against violence in the streets and are not brought to account for their responsibility in producing a scale of violence that utterly dwarfs street crime. Motor vehicles contribute at least 60 percent of the nation's air pollution by tonnage, with one company—General Motors—contributing 35 percent of the pollution tonnage. Many companies respond to critics by saying that they conform with legal pollution control standards. While this claim is often untrue—again as in the case of the domestic auto companies that are in widespread violation of vehicle pollution standards—the point must be made continually in rebuttal that the industries wrote much of the laws, stripped them of effective sanctions, starved their projected budgets, and daily surrounded their administrators with well-funded lobbyists. The same industry spokesmen who assert the value of freedom of choice by consumers fail to recognize the massive, forced consumption inflicted on consumers and their progeny by industrial contaminants.

Until citizens begin to focus on this curious relationship between our most traditional values and their destruction by the polluters, moral indignation and pressures for change at the grass roots will not be effective. Effective action demands that full responsibility be imposed on polluters in the most durable, least costly, and administratively feasible manner. The social costs of pollution must be cycled back to the polluter so that they are prevented at the earliest stage of the production or processing sequence. Achievement of this objective—whether dealing with automobiles, chemical plants, or municipal waste-disposal systems—requires communicating to the public and to pertinent authorities the known or knowable technological remedies. Moral imperatives to act become much more insistent with greater technical capability to do the job. Too many of our citizens have little or no understanding of the relative ease with which industry has or can obtain the technical solutions. As a result, too often the popular impression—encouraged by industry advertisements—is that industry is working at the limits of technology in controlling its pollution. This, of course, is nonsense. Furthermore, an action strategy must embrace the most meticulous understanding of the corporate structure—its points of access, its points of maximum responsiveness, its specific motivational sources, and its constituencies.

General Motors is considered a producer of automobiles. It is time to view that company (and others like it) not only in the light of its impact on the economy but of its impact on urban and rural land use through its infernal internal combustion engines, on our solid-waste-disposal problem through its lack of attention to the problem of junked cars, on a huge diversion of public resources through the inefficiency of vehicle operation and designed-in repair and replacement costs, on water through its polluting plants, on safety of passengers through unsafe design, and on a more rational, clean transportation system through its historic opposition to the development of mass transit. As a corporate state with annual revenues exceeding that of any foreign government except the Soviet Union, GM's average hourly gross around the clock of $2.4 million makes it a force of considerable substance.

Very little scholarly or action-oriented attention has been paid to such corporations, two hundred of which control over two-thirds of the manufacturing assets of the country. This state of affairs is due to the curtain of secrecy surrounding corporate behavior and the great faith placed by citizens on the efficacy of governmental regulations. Corporations represent the most generic power system in the country. As such, layering their transgressions with governmental controls without treating the underlying system of corporate power simply leads, as it has done since the establishment of the Interstate Commerce Commission in 1887, to the takeover of the regulators by the regulatees. This is not to say that government agencies offer little potential for disciplining corporate polluters. It is only to emphasize that the restrictive hands of industry power must be lifted before these regulatory agencies can be returned to the people. But now there are indications that a business-oriented administration will further develop a system of subsidizing the control of corporate pollution through liberal tax provisions, permissive attitudes toward unjustified price increases, and more direct payments. Such techniques have proved to be highly wasteful and inefficient and require the closest scrutiny both as policy and in operation.

Citizens' strategies for effecting corporate responsibility are concededly primitive. This is an area for great pioneering, imagination, and insight on the part of citizens willing to view the corporation not as a monolith but as a composition of different groups inside and attached to it. A partial list of these groups illustrates the broad opportunities for finding access and bringing pressure for change. The list includes unions, employees, institutional and individual shareholders, creditors, pensioners, suppliers, customers, dealers, law firms, trade associations, professional societies, state and federal regulatory agencies, and state attorney generals. To be sure, many of these groups or individuals are presently unencouraging prospects for helping one tame the corporate tiger. But recent years have shown how rapidly matters can change when committed youth are at large with unyielding stamina.

Youth must develop an investigative approach to the problems of pollution. It is one of the most basic prerequisites. Not only must there be a close analysis of corporate statements, and periodicals, annual reports, patents, correspondence, court records, regulations, technical papers, congressional hearings, and agency reports and transcripts, but there must be a search for the dissenting company engineer, the conscience-stricken house lawyer, the concerned retiree or ex-employee, the knowledgeable worker and the fact-laden supplier of the industry or company under study. They are there somewhere. They must be located.

Top corporate executives crave anonymity and almost uniformly decline to appear at universities and colleges to speak or exchange thoughts with students. This reticence is a functional one from their point of view. It perpetuates the secrecy, the detachment, and the tight-knit circle that is corporate America. It hides the quantity and quality of the decisions which pollute the environment. To widen the arena of discourse and to expose these top, often insulated, executives to the urgencies of the times, a consistent effort to bring them on campus should be undertaken.

This quest should fit in with the formal educational curricula. The problems of environmental pollution and their origins are challenges to almost every discipline of the university, from physical science to the humanities. The curricula must be made to respond to our need for knowledge about the ecosystem. Formal course work, independent and summer work can involve empirical research, even the development of new environmental strategies. Formal education—to have a lasting legacy for the student—should thus strive to combine the development in tandem of technical skills and a humane value system. Action for ecological integrity has to be viewed as a process of endless discovery. To map the terrain, one must cover the terrain. There is no manual ready to guide, only a world to discover.

DANIEL ELLSBERG

—— ★ ——

A Vital Interest in Getting Out of Southeast Asia

Testimony Before the U.S. Senate Committee on Foreign Relations, May 13, 1970

Prior to his 1970 testimony before the Senate Foreign Relations Committee, Daniel Ellsberg (1931–   ) had been senior liaison officer with the American Embassy in South Vietnam (1965–1966), assistant to the deputy U.S. ambassador to South Vietnam (1967), and consultant to the special assistant for national security affairs on Vietnam options (1968–1969). He also was a member of the group, under Secretary of Defense Robert MacNamara, that produced a major study of U.S. policy in Vietnam from 1945. Ellsberg was thus able to provide this top-secret document—the famous Pentagon Papers—to the Senate Foreign Relations Committee in 1969. By the time of his Senate testimony—the transcript of the complete hearings was published as Impact of the War in Southeast Asia on the U.S. Economy—*Ellsberg was committed to seeing an end to the Vietnam War. In 1971 he released the Pentagon Papers to the* New York Times, *for which he was charged with conspiracy, theft, and violation of the Espionage Act. The charges were dismissed in 1973.*

THE CHAIRMAN [SENATOR WILLIAM FULBRIGHT]. The committee will come to order. The committee is meeting today to hear testimony concerning the historical, political, and economic impact of U.S. policy on Vietnam and Southeast Asia. Mr. Ellsberg, will you proceed, please.

MR. ELLSBERG. Senator Fulbright, I heard you ask the first witness if we have a vital interest in Southeast Asia. I would like to begin by giving you the thought that came to my mind.

I found that my answer after the events of the last ten days or so is that the United States of America has a vital interest in getting out of Southeast Asia, getting out of Indochina.

I have participated, in the government and outside the government, in a lot of discussions over the last ten years as to what constitutes our "vital interests" and what that phrase might mean. I believe that this morning it has come to me with greater clarity than ever in my life what it means for us to have a vital interest—which is an interest that concerns the survival of this nation—in circumstances other than invasion or nuclear war.

Personally, I have thought during the last couple of years of protest in this country that it was still possible to exaggerate the threat to our society that this conflict posed for us. I feared that we might come to a pass in which there would be a major threat to our society but that we were not there yet. I am assured now that we do still survive as an American nation by the protest to the recent presidential decisions on Cambodia. But I am afraid that we cannot go on like this—as it seems likely we will, unless Congress soon commits us to total withdrawal—and survive as Americans. There would still be a country here and it might have the same name, but it would not be the same country.

I think that what might be at stake if this involvement goes on is a change in our society as radical and ominous as could be brought about by our occupation by a foreign power. I would hate to see that, and I hope very much that deliberations such as the Senate is undertaking right now will prevent that.

THE CHAIRMAN. If I understand your reply to the question I asked Mr. Cooper, it is that our vital interest is in disengaging. There is no vital interest in remaining and controlling Vietnam.

MR. ELLSBERG. Absolutely. I am saying that earlier I felt we had no vital interest one way or the other, although a considerable interest in getting out. I now think it is vital that we get out, and fast.

THE CHAIRMAN. Yes.

MR. ELLSBERG. The subject I was asked to speak about some months ago was the impact of our policy upon politics in South

Vietnam. This might seem undramatic and less relevant than some other topics as of this week. But I think that is not true. I think, in fact, that the question of politics in South Vietnam and the question of self-determination in Vietnam are crucial to the question of our ability to withdraw from South Vietnam even sooner than the year, or eighteen months, or whatever, that people are discussing right now. Specifically, I believe that moves toward self-determination in South Vietnam would mean allowing a greater voice and greater role of leadership to those Vietnamese who speak for the mass, I believe, of Vietnamese, who want this war over and who believe that American involvement is prolonging the war. That development may be the key to achieving a ceasefire and the prompt, orderly American disengagement that the health of this nation demands. (It can also greatly improve the political prospects of non-Communist elements after our departure.)

I will proceed with a brief statement; it is the first time in my life, I think, that I have obeyed orders to write a brief statement, so I will elaborate on it a little and I will be glad to have questions.

It concerns mainly what I take to be a central untruth at the heart of American explanations of our involvement in this war, and that applies over a generation of presidents, five presidents, going back to 1950.

This administration, like previous ones, has stated repeatedly that the primary purpose of U.S. involvement in Vietnam is to support and promote self-determination by the Vietnamese people, their right and ability to "choose freely their own form of government, without outside interference." That statement has never been true in the past. It is not true today.

Obviously, "self-determination" has never been the *effect* of our involvement. Not one of the regimes we have supported, from the Bao Dai regime controlled by the French, through Ngo Dinh Diem, to the military junta that rules today behind a constitutional facade, could have resulted from a process of public choice that was truly free, or free of our own outside influence.

Not one of them has "represented" even a majority of the non-Communist Vietnamese it ruled, either in terms of composition, of political origins, or of responsiveness to values with respect to social justice or the issues of war and peace. Nor has our government in its private estimates ever imagined otherwise for any of the regimes it has supported with money, advice, and, increasingly, with our armed forces.

This last is the perspective which I would like to add to the comments of Mr. Schoenbrun, which I thought were very accurate, extremely pertinent, and regrettably unknown to almost all officials in the government. I think I can add some knowledge of how these matters were seen in the government at various times from my own participation in it and from studying these matters with official access.

One of the startling things, I think, to someone coming from the outside and studying the official estimates and documents, is to realize how clearly one particular fact has been seen at virtually every phase of our involvement; namely, that the Saigon government we were supporting at that time was one that did not command the loyalty or support of the majority of its own citizens, even of its non-Communist citizens, and that it almost surely could not survive even against non-Communist challenges without our strong support in a variety of forms.

Few American officials, I think, have asked themselves whether we had a right to support such governments and thus to impose them on the majority of their citizens. They felt we had a necessity to do so, and hence the question of our "right" did not arise. Yet, as I say, I have increasingly felt that necessity to point in the other direction.

But the evident lack of self-determination in South Vietnam has not meant the failure of our policy. "Freedom of choice" has not been the effect of that policy, but neither has it ever been our intent. On the contrary, in certain specific senses, it has always been our determined purpose, on which we have acted effectively, to prevent certain forms or outcomes of self-determination by important segments of Vietnamese society. I do not speak here only of the Communists.

Our actual intent has been expressed both in our actions and inaction, words and silences, and in our internal policy statements. It is expressed most clearly in the internal statement of U.S. objectives in South Vietnam adopted as official presidential policy in March 1964. That statement said: The United States "seeks an independent, non-Communist South Vietnam." A further provision is that the South Vietnamese government, while it need not be formally allied to the United States, must be "free to accept outside assistance."

SENATOR GORE. What was the date of this?

MR. ELLSBERG. March 17, 1964, sir. It could as well have been written in 1954. It was our policy in 1954, it was our policy in 1950, '58, '60, and I believe it is our policy today. (Although the formal wording in the internal documents has been changed by the present administration to omit the requirement "non-Communist," many aspects of administration behavior convince me that it is still there in spirit.) I would like to make clear that this was by no means a policy that was first adopted in 1964. On the contrary, that statement merely put into words American objectives that had often been reflected in our policies before but not always explicitly in internal documents.

SENATOR GORE. Whenever stated it is in contravention of the Geneva Accords.

MR. ELLSBERG. That is correct, sir, and that is one reason that it has involved, as I mentioned, one of the central untruths of our policy. The policy has, in fact, been far more knowing, and one would have to say cynical, to insiders, in its contravention of the Accords and of our announced goals of self-determination, than an outsider would easily imagine. Again I would have to say this of the administrations of five presidents, three Democratic and two Republican. At each time they have been aware we were undertaking actions in contradiction to past policies of the United States, in this case our anticolonial policy, but more importantly in contradiction to treaty commitments and public declarations of various kinds.

This is one of the moral burdens which our leaders feel they are called upon to accept from time to time: the responsibility for such choices and deceptions. . . .

THE CHAIRMAN. I would like to make this observation. . . . If my memory serves me correctly, it was quite clear . . . in the early days of the hearings before this committee, particularly with Secretary Rusk . . . that the decisive question was not the balance of power other than the ideological obsession we then had. Much of it grew out of our domestic situation. That is the influence that Senator McCarthy had developed here. It had great domestic political implications, which, as you have al- ready described, caused Secretary Dulles to decline to even par- ticipate personally in the Geneva Accords.

In the many questions at that time, I think we reduced it to the point of asking if Ho Chi Minh had not been a Communist, do you think we would ever have intervened? I think it is quite clear we would not have. It was the ideological aspect that triggered our intervention, and this was true of situations not only in Southeast Asia, especially, but in Europe. I mean, in the fear of Stalin and his effect.

I always thought our departure from our traditional role, in supporting the French colonial power, was because of our fear of French weakness in Europe. . . .

MR. ELLSBERG. Mr. Chairman, having studied the docu- ments of a number of administrations and found the internal rationales in terms of strategic interests palpably inadequate, I have more and more come to look at the domestic political contexts in which those decisions were made year after year. This is something that rarely gets into the internal documenta- tion, and if it is even talked about in the executive branch, it is done very privately, one or two people at a time. I am speaking of the relation of these strategic moves to domestic politics.

THE CHAIRMAN. By strategic you mean in the interest of the security of our country?

MR. ELLSBERG. That is right. As a friend of mine, Morton Halperin, said recently, people other than the president, bureaucrats in fact, make their decisions on the basis of bureaucratic and agency considerations, and presidents typically make their own choices in terms of domestic political considerations, far more than the public realizes; but in describing their motives and reasoning to each other and to the public, both talk a language of national security and strategy, which creates certain confusions.

In this particular case, I would say that since 1949 no American president has been willing to see the fall of Indochina added to the fall of China during his administration. And that, I think, has warped very much his perception and weighing of priorities with respect to short-run and long-run interests of this country.

I believe that each president really has been willing to invest major resources to take considerable risks in order simply to postpone the fall of Saigon. He has not wanted to be in office, in effect, when the red flag went up over Saigon.

THE CHAIRMAN. That is, for political reasons here at home and not strategic reasons?

MR. ELLSBERG. Essentially political reasons. And this has led us to take strategies that were risky and costly but did promise that they would postpone this event, even if they offered little hope of averting it indefinitely, that is, of "winning" at acceptable cost.

SENATOR CASE. Can I throw out a suggestion? This unwillingness to be in office at a time when Saigon fell might be based upon a consideration that the people of the country don't believe it is a wise thing to let happen—

MR. ELLSBERG. That is right.

SENATOR CASE. And not for unworthy reasons, but from some deep instinctive feeling about what is in the national interest. Presidents, in following this feeling, haven't therefore been unworthy of the move. That is not the least worthy, I suppose, of motives: To an important degree to follow what I think is our basic guide here, and that is the instinctive movement of the people of this country in one direction or another. And that doesn't mean that everybody hasn't got the obligation to do his own thinking. But the people of this country, when they have been sufficiently informed—and they have an amazing way of getting information, including, I think, osmosis as well as watching television or listening to people on the radio and reading newspapers or listening to political speeches or what-not—the people, I think, probably are our best reliance when it comes to great policy.

MR. ELLSBERG. I agree completely. I think that is one of the premises that goes into the president's mind, and I am talking now, as I keep repeating, of five presidents. I should say I know of the premises of the most recent, Nixon, only from newspapers; the others from considerable documentation.

But I think the problem, as the president sees it, is a little more complex than that in this area. He sees, in the first instance, as you say, that the people may well punish him politically if he lets Indochina fall, and, to that extent, acting to prevent that is doing the people's will, which is his democratic responsibility. But at the same time he reads his intelligence analyses and his operational estimates, which tell him what will be required to prevent that from happening, and he compares those calculated requirements with what he thinks the public and the Congress will let him do. And there always has been a great gap between these sets of considerations.

Each president has seen, I think, that although he will lose prestige and power—that is, lose votes—if Indochina falls, he probably cannot get Congress or the people to let him do what his advisers tell him is needed to keep it from falling, reliably and indefinitely. That has meant various things. First, it meant backing a colonial regime, which we did with some distaste. We accepted that. Later it meant backing an authoritarian police state, which we did, though we didn't want to publicize it.

Third, when that began to fail in 1963 and 1964 (I came into the Department of Defense in August 1964), the president's military and civilian advisers believed strongly that unless we were prepared to bring direct military pressure on North Vietnam, the situation was irretrievable. Finally, ground troops appeared necessary.

Now during that whole period bombing and ground troops looked perhaps ultimately necessary but were ruled out. Thus, up to 1965, each president was led to take steps short of those measures, steps which he believed to be probably inadequate to the situation. He hoped these lesser steps might work and believed they would at least postpone the dilemma of using troops or bombing or of losing.

This put one further pressure on him to mislead the public as to how these lesser measures were working. We were under great pressure to imply, since advisors were all we could afford to put over there, that advisors were doing the job; or Diem was doing the job; or earlier the French were doing the job. And this meant consciously distorting what our reports were conveying to the president.

SENATOR CASE. We have had direct experience with this again and again, for what, fifteen, twenty years.

MR. ELLSBERG. Yes. When the President starts lying he begins to need evidence to back up his lies because in this democracy he is questioned on his statements. It then percolates down through the bureaucracy that you are helping the Boss if you come up with evidence that is supportive of our public position and you are distinctly unhelpful if you commit to paper statements that might leak to the wrong people.

The effect of that is to poison the flow of information to the president himself and to create a situation where a president can be almost, to use a metaphor, psychotically divorced from the realities in which he is acting. . . .

The recent U.S. adventure in Cambodia, with the U.S. administration imitating in presidential style Thieu's "loose construction" of his own constitution, warns clearly that this administration is no more ready to contemplate the "loss" of Indochina to communism, during its term of office, than any of its predecessors.

It is in the full tradition of earlier administrations, hopeful of victory in the long run but obsessed with avoiding defeat in the short run. They have their eye on the ball, and avoiding short-run defeat is an objective that is worthy of a great many American and Vietnamese lives in their opinion, I am sorry to say.

This administration is no less ready than earlier ones to incur escalating risks and domestic dissent to avoid or postpone such "humiliation." The rhetoric has changed, and I refer here to the fact that we talk more about self-determination than we did in some recent years, but the policy has not. It is one that condemns Vietnam to endless war and Americans to endless participation in it in support of a corrupt and unpopular military dictatorship.

THE CHAIRMAN. Thank you very much, Mr. Ellsberg. That is a very dismal conclusion, but I have no quarrel with it. I think if the policy persists and if the Congress is unable or unwilling to change it, I would predict that it will go on as you say.

BETTY FRIEDAN

——— ★ ———

An End to Obsolete Sex Roles

From *McCall's*, June 1971

In 1963 Betty Friedan (1921–   ) unveiled The Feminine Mystique. *The book, which questions the assumed fulfillment found in women's traditional roles as mothers and housewives, became a national bestseller and marked the beginning of the modern feminist movement, which coalesced in 1966 with the founding of the National Organization for Women (NOW). Serving as NOW's first president, until 1969, Friedan championed the causes of abortion rights and the Equal Rights Amendment. The Women's Liberation movement was clearly mainstream by the early 1970s, and Friedan became a regular columnist for* McCall's, *the popular woman's magazine. Her first column, subtitled "Some Days in the Life of One of the Most Influential Women of Our Time," contains this statement: "Until we free ourselves and men from the obsolete sex roles that imprison us both, the hostility between the sexes will continue to inflame the violence we're perpetrating in the world."*

For women in their thirties and forties, women who have patterned their entire lives on the idea that fulfillment can only come as wives and mothers, it has been painful, sometimes too painful, to change all that now. It's easier for the young to take a chance. But it's also easier for the young to fall into traps of pseudoradical rhetoric, because they haven't experienced enough of the realities of life as a woman. This revolution will be carried by the spirit of the young, but if left to the young alone, it might never be more than just rhetoric.

There are no blueprints for our particular revolution, for the relationship of woman to man is not the same as that of worker to boss, of oppressed to oppressor, of black to white. We can only find our blueprint from our own experience.

I used to think I could keep my personal life and my ideas in separate compartments. Now I realize that everything I know has grown out of my own experience. And if my words are going to affect other women, then I should share the experience on which these words are based.

In a nation as big as this, change happens through the mass media. Women have to use it, not just be used by it. The bra-burning image which enables people to dismiss us as a silly joke can and must be replaced.

That is why I have finally decided to do this column for *McCall's*. I have no intention of giving up my revolutionary credentials; I have, in fact, warned them that I will be saying things they won't agree with.

But I feel the need to deal with the new questions women must confront today, and to deal with them in the context of my own life. It was only a few years ago that women felt freakish, guilty, and alone because of feelings that we now know are shared by millions of us.

I don't think we can fully work out these problems in our own lives until we have made some basic changes in society. And if we don't seize the opportunity to make these changes now, I'm even more afraid of a feminine backlash than a masculine backlash.

To begin with, I *am* a revolutionary. This revolution is not what anyone else ever meant by revolution, but it will transform society in ways more radical and more life-enhancing than any other. I also happen to be an American pragmatist, "middle-American," if you will, since I did grow up in Peoria, Illinois. And I think we have the power to make this revolution happen now, the power of 55 percent of us who are women, along with the growing number of men who support us.

But I would be bored to write only about Women's Liberation. Women are as involved with the life-and-death questions of war and peace, the crisis of the planet and our cities, the unknowns of theology and art and space, as they are with food and children and the home. I believe the Women's Liberation movement cannot remain isolated from everything else that's happening in America today; the liberation of women is germane to the agony of our whole nation: until we free ourselves and men from the obsolete sex roles that imprison us both, the hostility between the sexes will continue to inflame the violence we're perpetrating in the world.

But I think it's time to face honestly the problems in our own movement. All these rap sessions about trapped housewives and male chauvinist pigs, comparisons of orgasms, even talking about how worthless we feel—in the end it's just wallowing in soap opera. Deliver us from self-pity so that we can deliver ourselves from wasting time on nonproblems. The pseudoradicals talk about getting rid of men and not wanting to look pretty. Others worry that we'll lose our femininity.

Femininity is being a woman and feeling good about it, so the better you feel about yourself as a person, the better you feel about being a woman. And, it seems to me, the better you are able to love men.

Men are here to stay. I happen to like many, love some, and think a one-sex world would be very boring. This is a *two*-sex revolution, or it isn't anything. Even a male chauvinist like Norman Mailer is beginning to try to understand us.

The other night, reading D. H. Lawrence's *Women in Love*, I came across words that expressed exactly what I want to do in this column. Written in the foreword to his work fifty years ago, only the word *man* has to be changed to *woman* to convey my meaning: "We are now in a period of crisis. Every *woman* who is acutely alive is wrestling with *her* own soul. The people that can bring forth the new passion, the new idea, *this* people will endure. Those others, that fix themselves in the old idea, will perish with the new life strangled unborn within them. *Women* must speak out to one another."

I am asked to speak on November 11 at a meeting sponsored by the Graymoor Friars on "The Meaning of Women's Liberation for the Church." The only subject that made my audience uneasy was abortion. The Roman Catholic bishops of New York State had just been ordered to preach a sermon threatening excommunication to any woman who gets an abortion or anybody who helps her get one. This was a direct order to the state legislators to take back the law women fought for and won last spring. I am tired of organizing marches, but we have to do something to demonstrate the power of women.

My fourteen-year-old daughter Emily and I go to visit my younger son Jonathan in his room at Columbia. He's asked for a few items—knives, forks and spoons, a rug and a table—which we bring him. Then Emily and I go shopping. I buy two long paisley dresses, very cheap, colorful, and Emily buys minis of the same material. It's the first time we've shopped together on equal terms, and it was fun for both of us.

I must say I like the freedom these long skirts give. You don't have to worry about your underwear showing, or suffer the indignity of feeling you're trying to look the same age as your daughter. I think women are going to have more and more fun with fashion, as they get more liberated. I think the way a woman dresses, treats her body, is a very basic reflection of the way she feels about herself. I'm in too much of a hurry to waste time on false eyelashes, and I'm damned if I'll torture myself with a tight girdle.

Walking home with Emily, I realize how lonesome it is with both boys gone. My divorce didn't end family life as much as the boys leaving. I won't be away so much now that I'm doing the column, but there's still not enough life with just the two of us. I suppose that's really why I got the idea of the Commune last spring, all of us sharing that great big house.

On November 23, I meet with the steering committee of the Women's Strike Coalition and NOW members about a march to dramatize the abortion crisis. I have been trying to think of some way to translate our tremendous energy and power into action, and this meeting was intended to continue the coalition that had finally come together in the August 26 Strike for Equality. There had been a big attendance, but so much silly hairsplitting.

Some women didn't want to use the word "liberation"; it meant bra-burning, they said. Others objected to the word "equality"; we don't want to be equal to men, they said, we just want to be liberated. There was something about the largeness of the action last summer that brought us over these difficulties; this one is not the same. Maybe it's my fault. I haven't had time to stay on top of it. But I do have a feeling that just another march doesn't really lead anywhere.

The weekend at the Commune is hilarious. Dick's three children come in from San Francisco, and there are Martha's two, and Emily, and Arthur's Matthew, who's three years old now. I have dreaded holidays lately. They have to be family things and if you don't have a big enough family, there can't be much gaiety any more. But this, all of us in our various states of nonmarriage, with our progeny of various ages, is almost magic. We are all strong individualists, yet we like each other better six months after sharing a house weekends and vacations than we did in the beginning. The generation gap seems not to exist. The kids develop such different relationships with various adults besides their parents. Emily blossoms in a way I haven't noticed before, with Arthur's nice gallantry toward her. As usual, halfway through the weekend I am given a lecture about not having carried my weight with the household chores. Feeling very guilty, I offer to finish cleaning up after lunch, and I do all the pots and pans while the others go for walks.

Barclay, age ten, worried that my feelings are hurt, tells me it doesn't matter if I'm not very good at cleaning up, because I "contribute morale."

We are not a real commune. We don't pool our incomes or have group sex, and we shut our private bedroom doors. But the ties that are being created here, this extended intimacy or new life-style, are real.

We have the abortion march on December 12. The weather is cold and wet, but several hundred people come. Nothing, compared to the thousands last summer, but considering the weather even that many makes a point. Kate Millett is the first speaker; I'm to be the last. But instead of talking about abortion and child-care centers, which is what the march was supposed to be about, she talks about lesbianism. Women I don't know are handing out lavender armbands and leaflets saying that since Kate has been called a lesbian (*Time* magazine had recently reported her own statement to the effect that she is bisexual), all women must show their solidarity by becoming, in effect, "political lesbians." Nobody had told me anything about this. Obviously, some of the women there knew about it, but many looked very bewildered and uneasy.

I don't agree with much in Kate's *Sexual Politics*. I just don't agree that this is a bedroom war, that men are the enemy, that sex is all that revolting and demeaning to women, that having children is something to do away with. But I had refused to review her book because I didn't want to attack her. Her private life is her own business, or should be. But if she is bisexual and willing to announce it to the press, why should the whole movement be divided by it? I have always been uneasy about the pseudoradical talk that includes the elimination of men, sex, and children among the aims of Women's Liberation. This makes for kickier headlines than child-care centers or abortion reform, but it's just a way of dismissing the whole movement as a dirty joke.

I don't believe homosexuals should be oppressed; people's sex lives are their own concern if they don't hurt anyone else. I don't know if homosexuality is any sicker than the *Playboy* type of heterosexuality, but it isn't the point of *this* movement. A lot of faces in this freezing rain look as uncomfortable as I feel, but

I have to speak up. I climb up on the sound truck, without the purple armband, and talk about the danger to the abortion law and the child-care centers. I also warn that to let this movement be diverted by a sexual red herring or degenerate into sexual McCarthyism would destroy us. I think this is more than political expedience. I have experienced the good moments of really knowing a man, as well as a bad marriage, and good moments with my own children and others; if liberation, equality, personhood for women is worth fighting for, it can't be at the price of these other goods. Maybe sexual politics are even more anti-women than they are antimen. Or are they antilife?

I wake up on New Year's Eve with a feeling of well-being. It's the kind of feeling I can't remember having had for years, maybe ever. I don't know what's going to happen, but I don't feel helpless, in a fog. I'm not about to leave the movement, but for the first time in years I want to write again. What we need are serious politics, not sexual politics.

When I realize what has to be done next, it seems impossibly big. Still, it's a lot of fun, making a revolution happen. How many months are there till the '72 elections . . . ?

HARRY A. BLACKMUN AND
WILLIAM H. REHNQUIST

——— ★ ———

The Supreme Court on
Abortion Rights: Two Opinions

U.S. Supreme Court, *Roe v. Wade*, 1973

In the 1960s, the issue of antiabortion laws began to be taken up by the new feminist movement. In the midst of worldwide discussions of overpopulation and the antiwar and civil rights protests, abortion became not only a public health issue but a question of a woman's right to control her own reproductive processes. But as the medical profession reversed itself to favor liberalized laws and some states changed their antiabortion laws, many people, led by a number of religious groups, began to question the morality of abortion, some equating it with murder. In 1973, the U.S. Supreme Court effectively legalized abortion with the landmark Roe v. Wade *decision. The opinion of the Court, as written by Justice Harry A. Blackmun (1908–   ), allowed abortions on the basis of a woman's constitutional right to privacy. Justice William Rehnquist (1924–   ), in his dissenting opinion, saw nothing strictly private in the decision to abort and saw little to support a "right" to an abortion. Rather than being settled with* Roe v. Wade, *the legality of abortion has continued to be a nationally divisive issue in the years following the decision.*

JUSTICE BLACKMUN: OPINION OF THE COURT

We forthwith acknowledge our awareness of the sensitive and emotional nature of the abortion controversy, of the vigorous opposing views, even among physicians, and of the deep and seemingly absolute convictions that the subject inspires. One's philosophy, one's experiences, one's exposure to the raw edges of human existence, one's religious training, one's attitudes toward life and family and their values, and the moral standards one establishes and seeks to observe, are all likely to influence and to color one's thinking and conclusions about abortion.

In addition, population growth, pollution, poverty, and racial overtones tend to complicate and not to simplify the problem.

Our task, of course, is to resolve the issue by constitutional measurement, free of emotion and of predilection. . . .

Jane Roe, a single woman who was residing in Dallas County, Texas, instituted this federal action in March 1970 against the district attorney of the county. She sought a declaratory judgment that the Texas criminal abortion statutes were unconstitutional on their face, and an injunction restraining the defendant from enforcing the statutes.

Roe alleged that she was unmarried and pregnant; that she wished to terminate her pregnancy by an abortion "performed by a competent, licensed physician, under safe, clinical conditions"; that she was unable to get a "legal" abortion in Texas because her life did not appear to be threatened by the continuation of her pregnancy; and that she could not afford to travel to another jurisdiction in order to secure a legal abortion under safe conditions. She claimed that the Texas statutes were unconstitutionally vague and that they abridged her right of personal privacy, protected by the First, Fourth, Fifth, Ninth, and Fourteenth amendments. By an amendment to her complaint, Roe purported to sue "on behalf of herself and all other women" similarly situated.

James Hubert Hallford, a licensed physician, sought and was granted leave to intervene in Roe's action. In his complaint he alleged that he had been arrested previously for violations of the Texas abortion statutes and that two such prosecutions were pending against him. He described conditions of patients who came to him seeking abortions, and he claimed that for many cases he, as a physician, was unable to determine whether they fell within or outside the exception recognized by Article 1196 [of the Texas Penal Code]. He alleged that, as a consequence, the statutes were vague and uncertain, in violation of the Fourteenth Amendment, and that they violated his own and his patients' rights to privacy in the doctor-patient relationship and his own right to practice medicine, rights he claimed were guaranteed by the First, Fourth, Fifth, Ninth, and Fourteenth Amendments. . . .

On the merits, the District Court held that the "fundamental right of single women and married persons to choose whether to have children is protected by the Ninth Amendment, through the Fourteenth Amendment," and that the Texas criminal abortion statutes were void on their face because they were both unconstitutionally vague and constituted an overbroad infringement of the plaintiffs' Ninth Amendment rights. . . .

The principal thrust of appellant's attack on the Texas statutes is that they improperly invade a right, said to be possessed by the pregnant woman, to choose to terminate her pregnancy. Appellant would discover this right in the concept of personal "liberty" embodied in the Fourteenth Amendment's Due Process Clause; or in personal, marital, familial, and sexual privacy said to be protected by the Bill of Rights; or among those rights reserved to the people by the Ninth Amendment. . . . Before addressing this claim, we feel it desirable briefly to survey, in several aspects, the history of abortion, for such insight as that history may afford us, and then to examine the state purposes and interests behind the criminal abortion laws.

It perhaps is not generally appreciated that the restrictive criminal abortion laws in effect in a majority of states today are of relatively recent vintage. Those laws, generally proscribing abortion or its attempt at any time during pregnancy except when necessary to preserve the pregnant woman's life, are not of ancient or even of common-law origin. Instead, they derive from statutory changes effected, for the most part, in the latter half of the nineteenth century. . . .

Three reasons have been advanced to explain historically the enactment of criminal abortion laws in the nineteenth century and to justify their continued existence.

It has been argued occasionally that these laws were the product of a Victorian social concern to discourage illicit sexual conduct. Texas, however, does not advance this justification in the present case, and it appears that no court or commentator has taken the argument seriously. The appellants and *amici* contend, moreover, that this is not a proper state purpose at all and suggest that, if it were, the Texas statutes are overboard in protecting it since the law fails to distinguish between married and unwed mothers.

A second reason is concerned with abortion as a medical procedure. When most criminal abortion laws were first enacted, the procedure was a hazardous one for the woman. This was particularly true prior to the development of antisepsis. Antiseptic techniques, of course, were based on discoveries by Lister, Pasteur, and others first announced in 1867, but were not generally accepted and employed until about the turn of the century. Abortion mortality was high. Even after 1900, and perhaps until as late as the development of antibiotics in the 1940s, standard modern techniques such as dilation and curettage were not nearly so safe as they are today. Thus, it has been argued that a state's real concern in enacting a criminal abortion law was to protect the pregnant woman, that is, to restrain her from submitting to a procedure that placed her life in serious jeopardy.

Modern medical techniques have altered this situation. Appellants and various *amici* refer to medical data indicating that abortion in early pregnancy, that is, prior to the end of the first trimester, although not without its risk, is now relatively safe. Mortality rates for women undergoing early abortions, where the procedure is legal, appear to be as low as or lower than the rates for normal childbirth. Consequently, any interest of the state in protecting the woman from an inherently hazardous procedure, except when it would be equally dangerous for her to forgo it, has largely disappeared. Of course, important state interests in the areas of health and medical standards do remain. The state has a legitimate interest in seeing to it that abortion, like any other medical procedure, is performed under circumstances that insure maximum safety for the patient. This interest obviously extends at least to the performing physician and his staff, to the facilities involved, to the availability of aftercare, and to adequate provision for any complication or emergency that might arise. The prevalence of high mortality rates at illegal "abortion mills" strengthens, rather than weakens, the state's interest in regulating the conditions under which abortions are performed. Moreover, the risk to the woman increases as her pregnancy continues. Thus, the state retains a definite interest in protecting the woman's own health and safety when an abortion is proposed at a late stage of pregnancy.

The third reason is the state's interest—some phrase it in terms of duty—in protecting prenatal life. Some of the argument for this justification rests on the theory that a new human life is present from the moment of conception. The state's interest and general obligation to protect life then extends, it is argued, to prenatal life. Only when the life of the pregnant mother herself is at stake, balanced against the life she carries within her, should the interest of the embryo or fetus not prevail. Logically, of course, a legitimate state interest in this area need not stand or fall on acceptance of the belief that life begins at conception or at some other point prior to live birth. In assessing the state's interest, recognition may be given to the less rigid claim that as long as at least *potential* life is involved, the state may assert interests beyond the protection of the pregnant woman alone.

Parties challenging state abortion laws have sharply disputed in some courts the contention that a purpose of these laws, when enacted, was to protect prenatal life. Pointing to the absence of legislative history to support the contention, they claim that most state laws were designed solely to protect the woman. Because medical advances have lessened this concern, at least with respect to abortion in early pregnancy, they argue that with respect to such abortions the laws can no longer be justified by any state interest. There is some scholarly support for this view of original purpose. The few state courts called upon to interpret their laws in the late nineteenth and early twentieth centuries did focus on the state's interest in protecting the woman's health rather than in preserving the embryo and fetus. Proponents of this view point out that in many states, including Texas, by statute or judicial interpretation, the pregnant woman herself could not be prosecuted for self-abortion or for cooperating in an abortion performed upon her by another. They claim that adoption of the "quickening" distinction through received common law and state statutes tacitly recognizes the greater health hazards inherent in late abortion and impliedly repudiates the theory that life begins at conception.

It is with these interests, and the weight to be attached to them, that this case is concerned.

The Constitution does not explicitly mention any right of privacy. In a line of decisions, however, the Court has recognized that a right of personal privacy, or a guarantee of certain areas or zones of privacy, does exist under the Constitution. . . .

This right of privacy, whether it be founded in the Fourteenth Amendment's concept of personal liberty and restrictions upon state action, as we feel it is, or, as the District Court determined, in the Ninth Amendment's reservation of rights to the people, is broad enough to encompass a woman's decision whether or not to terminate her pregnancy. The detriment that the state would impose upon the pregnant woman by denying this choice altogether is apparent. Specific and direct harm medically diagnosable even in early pregnancy may be involved. Maternity, or additional offspring, may force upon the woman a distressful life and future. Psychological harm may be imminent. Mental and physical health may be taxed by child care.

There is also the distress, for all concerned, associated with the unwanted child, and there is the problem of bringing a child into a family already unable, psychologically and otherwise, to care for it. In other cases, as in this one, the additional difficulties and continuing stigma of unwed motherhood may be involved. All these are factors the woman and her responsible physician necessarily will consider in consultation.

On the basis of elements such as these, appellant and some *amici* argue that the woman's right is absolute and that she is entitled to terminate her pregnancy at whatever time, in whatever way, and for whatever reason she alone chooses. With this we do not agree. Appellant's arguments that Texas either has no valid interest at all in regulating the abortion decision, or no interest strong enough to support any limitation upon the woman's sole determination, are unpersuasive. The Court's decisions recognizing a right of privacy also acknowledge that some state regulation in areas protected by that right is appropriate. As noted above, a state may properly assert important interests in safe-guarding health, in maintaining medical standards, and in protecting potential life. At some point in pregnancy, these respective interests become sufficiently compelling to sustain regulation of the factors that govern the abortion decision. The privacy right involved, therefore, cannot be said to be absolute. In fact, it is not clear to us that the claim asserted by some *amici* that one has an unlimited right to do with one's body as one pleases bears a close relationship to the right of privacy previously articulated in the Court's decisions.

We, therefore, conclude that the right of personal privacy includes the abortion decision, but that this right is not unqualified and must be considered against important state interests in regulation. . . .

The District Court held that the appellee failed to meet his burden of demonstrating that the Texas statute's infringement upon Roe's rights was necessary to support a compelling state interest, and that, although the appellee presented "several compelling justifications for state presence in the area of abortions," the statutes outstripped these justifications and swept "far beyond any areas of compelling state interest." . . . Appellant and appellee both contest that holding. Appellant, as has been indicated, claims an absolute right that bars any state imposition of criminal penalties in the area. Appellee argues that the state's determination to recognize and protect prenatal life from and after conception constitutes a compelling state interest. As noted above, we do not agree fully with either formulation.

A. The appellee and certain *amici* argue that the fetus is a "person" within the language and meaning of the Fourteenth Amendment. In support of this, they outline at length and in detail the well-known facts of fetal development. If this suggestion of personhood is established, the appellant's case, of course, collapses, for the fetus's right to life would then be guaranteed specifically by the amendment. The appellant conceded as much on reargument. On the other hand, the appellee conceded on reargument that no case could be cited that holds that a fetus is a person within the meaning of the Fourteenth Amendment.

The Constitution does not define *person* in so many words. Section 1 of the Fourteenth Amendment contains three references to *person*. The first, in defining *citizens*, speaks of "persons born or naturalized in the United States." The word also appears both in the Due Process Clause and in the Equal Protection Clause. *Person* is used in other places in the Constitution: in the listing of qualifications for representatives and senators, . . . in the Electors provisions; . . . in the provision outlining qualifications for the office of president; . . . in the Extradition provisions; . . . and in the Fifth, Twelfth, and Twenty-second amendments, as well as in . . . the Fourteenth Amendment. But in nearly all these instances, the use of the word is such that it has application only postnatally. None indicates, with any assurance, that it has any possible prenatal application.

All this, together with our observation . . . that throughout the major portion of the nineteenth century prevailing legal abortion practices were far freer than they are today, persuades us that the word *person,* as used in the Fourteenth Amendment, does not include the unborn. . . .

This conclusion, however, does not of itself fully answer the contentions raised by Texas, and we pass on to other considerations.

B. The pregnant woman cannot be isolated in her privacy. She carries an embryo and, later, a fetus, if one accepts the medical definitions of the developing young in the human uterus. . . . The situation therefore is inherently different from marital intimacy, or bedroom possession of obscene material, or marriage, or procreation, or education. . . . As we have intimated above, it is reasonable and appropriate for a state to decide that at some point in time another interest, that of health of the mother or that of potential human life, becomes significantly involved. The woman's privacy is no longer sole and any right of privacy she possesses must be measured accordingly.

Texas urges that, apart from the Fourteenth Amendment, life begins at conception and is present throughout pregnancy, and that, therefore, the state has a compelling interest in protecting that life from and after conception. We need not resolve the difficult question of when life begins. When those trained in the respective disciplines of medicine, philosophy, and theology are unable to arrive at any consensus, the judiciary, at this point in the development of man's knowledge, is not in a position to speculate as to the answer.

It should be sufficient to note briefly the wide divergence of thinking on this most sensitive and difficult question. There has always been strong support for the view that life does not begin until live birth. This was the belief of the Stoics. It appears to be the predominant, though not the unanimous, attitude of the Jewish faith. It may be taken to represent also the position of a large segment of the Protestant community, insofar as that can be ascertained; organized groups that have taken a formal position on the abortion issue have generally regarded abortion as a matter for the conscience of the individual and her family. As we have noted, the common law found greater significance in quickening. Physicians and their scientific colleagues have regarded that event with less interest and have tended to focus either upon conception, upon live birth, or upon the interim point at which the fetus becomes "viable," that is, potentially able to live outside the mother's womb, albeit with artificial aid. Viability is usually placed at about seven months (twenty-eight weeks) but may occur earlier, even at twenty-four weeks. The Aristotelian theory of "mediate animation," that held sway throughout the Middle Ages and the Renaissance in Europe, continued to be official Roman Catholic dogma until the nineteenth century, despite opposition to this "ensoulment" theory from those in the church who would recognize the existence of life from the moment of conception. The latter is now, of course, the official belief of the Catholic church. As one brief *amicus* discloses, this is a view strongly held by many non-Catholics as well, and by many physicians. Substantial problems for precise definition of this view are posed, however, by new embryological data that purport to indicate that conception is a "process" over time, rather than an event, and by new medical techniques such as menstrual extraction, the "morning-after" pill, implantation of embryos, artificial insemination, and even artificial wombs.

In areas other than criminal abortion, the law has been reluctant to endorse any theory that life, as we recognize it, begins before live birth or to accord legal rights to the unborn except in narrowly defined situations and except when the rights are contingent upon live birth. For example, the traditional rule of tort law denied recovery for prenatal injuries even though the child was born alive. That rule has been changed in almost every jurisdiction. In most states, recovery is said to be permitted only if the fetus was viable, or at least quick, when the injuries were sustained, though few courts have squarely so held. In a recent development, generally opposed by the commentators, some states permit the parents of a stillborn child to maintain an action for wrongful death because of prenatal injuries. Such an action, however, would appear to be one to vindicate the parents' interest and is thus consistent with the view that the fetus, at most, represents only the potentiality of life. Similarly, unborn children have been recognized as acquiring rights or interests by way of inheritance or other devolution of property, and have been represented by guardians *ad litem*. Perfection of the interests involved, again, has generally been contingent upon live birth. In short, the unborn have never been recognized in the law as persons in the whole sense.

In view of all this, we do not agree that, by adopting one theory of life, Texas may override the rights of the pregnant woman that are at stake. We repeat, however, that the state does have an important and legitimate interest in preserving and protecting the health of the pregnant woman, whether she be a resident of the state or a nonresident who seeks medical consultation and treatment there, and that it has still *another* important and legitimate interest in protecting the potentiality of human life. These interests are separate and distinct. Each grows in substantiality as the woman approaches term and, at a point during pregnancy, each becomes "compelling."

With respect to the state's important and legitimate interest in the health of the mother, the "compelling" point, in the light of present medical knowledge, is at approximately the end of the first trimester. This is so because of the now-established medical fact . . . that until the end of the first trimester mortality in abortion may be less than mortality in normal childbirth. It follows that, from and after this point, a state may regulate the abortion procedure to the extent that the regulation reasonably relates to the preservation and protection of maternal health. Examples of permissible state regulation in this area are requirements as to the qualifications of the person who is to perform the abortion; as to the licensure of that person; as to the facility in which the procedure is to be performed, that is, whether it must be a hospital or may be a clinic or some other place of less-than-hospital status; as to the licensing of the facility; and the like.

This means, on the other hand, that, for the period of

pregnancy prior to this "compelling" point, the attending physician, in consultation with his patient, is free to determine, without regulation by the state, that, in his medical judgment, the patient's pregnancy should be terminated. If that decision is reached, the judgment may be effectuated by an abortion free of interference by the state.

With respect to the state's important and legitimate interest in potential life, the "compelling" point is at viability. This is so because the fetus then presumably has the capability of meaningful life outside the mother's womb. State regulation protective of fetal life after viability thus has both logical and biological justifications. If the state is interested in protecting fetal life after viability, it may go so far as to proscribe abortion during that period, except when it is necessary to preserve the life or health of the mother.

Measured against these standards, Article 1196 of the Texas Penal Code, in restricting legal abortions to those "procured or attempted by medical advice for the purpose of saving the life of the mother," sweeps too broadly. The statute makes no distinction between abortions performed early in pregnancy and those performed later, and it limits to a single reason, "saving" the mother's life, the legal justification for the procedure. The statute, therefore, cannot survive the constitutional attack made upon it here.

To summarize and to repeat:

A state criminal abortion statute of the current Texas type, that excepts from criminality only a *life-saving* procedure on behalf of the mother, without regard to pregnancy stage and without recognition of the other interests involved, is violative of the Due Process Clause of the Fourteenth Amendment.

A. For the stage prior to approximately the end of the first trimester, the abortion decision and its effectuation must be left to the medical judgment of the pregnant woman's attending physician.

B. For the stage subsequent to approximately the end of the first trimester, the state, in promoting its interest in the health of the mother, may, if it chooses, regulate the abortion procedure in ways that are reasonably related to maternal health.

C. For the stage subsequent to viability, the state in promoting its interest in the potentiality of human life may, if it chooses, regulate, and even proscribe, abortion except where it is necessary, in appropriate medical judgment, for the preservation of the life or health of the mother.

JUSTICE REHNQUIST: DISSENTING OPINION

The Court's opinion brings to the decision of this troubling question both extensive historical fact and a wealth of legal scholarship. While the opinion thus commands my respect, I find myself nonetheless in fundamental disagreement with those parts of it that invalidate the Texas statute in question, and therefore dissent.

The Court's opinion decides that a state may impose virtually no restriction on the performance of abortions during the first trimester of pregnancy. Our previous decisions indicate that a necessary predicate for such an opinion is a plaintiff who was in her first trimester of pregnancy at some time during the pendency of her lawsuit. While a party may vindicate his own constitutional rights, he may not seek vindication for the rights of others. . . . The Court's statement of facts in this case makes clear, however, that the record in no way indicates the presence of such a plaintiff. We know only that plaintiff Roe at the time of filing her complaint was a pregnant woman; for aught that appears in this record, she may have been in her *last* trimester of pregnancy as of the date the complaint was filed.

Nothing in the Court's opinion indicates that Texas might not constitutionally apply its proscription of abortion as written to a woman in that stage of pregnancy. Nonetheless, the Court uses her complaint against the Texas statute as a fulcrum for deciding that states may impose virtually no restrictions on medical abortions performed during the *first* trimester of pregnancy. In deciding such a hypothetical lawsuit, the Court departs from the longstanding admonition that it should never "formulate a rule of constitutional law broader than is required by the precise facts to which it is to be applied." . . .

Even if there were a plaintiff in this case capable of litigating the issue which the Court decides, I would reach a conclusion opposite to that reached by the Court. I have difficulty in concluding, as the Court does, that the right of "privacy" is involved in this case. Texas, by the statute here challenged, bars the performance of a medical abortion by a licensed physician on a plaintiff such as Roe. A transaction resulting in an operation such as this is not "private" in the ordinary usage of that word. Nor is the "privacy" that the Court finds here even a distant relative of the freedom from searches and seizures protected by the Fourth Amendment to the Constitution, which the Court has referred to as embodying a right to privacy. . . .

If the Court means by the term *privacy* no more than that the claim of a person to be free from unwanted state regulation of consensual transactions may be a form of *liberty* protected by the Fourteenth Amendment, there is no doubt that similar claims have been upheld in our earlier decisions on the basis of that liberty. I agree with the statement of Mr. Justice Stewart in his concurring opinion that the "liberty," against deprivation of which without due process the Fourteenth Amendment protects, embraces more than the rights found in the Bill of Rights. But that liberty is not guaranteed absolutely against deprivation, only against deprivation without due process of law. The test traditionally applied in the area of social and economic legislation is whether or not a law such as that challenged has a rational relation to a valid state objective. . . .

The Due Process Clause of the Fourteenth Amendment undoubtedly does place a limit, albeit a broad one, on legislative power to enact laws such as this. If the Texas statute were to prohibit an abortion even where the mother's life is in jeopardy, I have little doubt that such a statute would lack a rational relation to a valid state objective. . . . But the Court's sweeping invalidation of any restrictions on abortion during the first trimester is impossible to justify under that standard, and the conscious weighing of competing factors that the Court's opinion apparently substitutes for the established test is far more appropriate to a legislative judgment than to a judicial one.

The Court eschews the history of the Fourteenth Amendment in its reliance on the "compelling state interest" test. . . . But the Court adds a new wrinkle to this test by transposing it from the legal considerations associated with the Equal Protection Clause of the Fourteenth Amendment to this case arising under the Due Process Clause of the Fourteenth Amendment. Unless I misapprehend the consequences of this transplanting of the "compelling state interest test," the Court's opinion will accomplish the seemingly impossible feat of leaving this area of the law more confused than it found it.

The adoption of the compelling state interest standard will inevitably require this Court to examine the legislative policies and pass on the wisdom of these policies in the very process of deciding whether a particular state interest put forward may or may not be "compelling." The decision here to break pregnancy into three distinct terms and to outline the permissible restrictions the state may impose in each one, for example, partakes more of judicial legislation than it does of a determination of the intent of the drafters of the Fourteenth Amendment.

The fact that a majority of the states reflecting, after all, the majority sentiment in those states, have had restrictions on abortions for at least a century is a strong indication, it seems to me, that the asserted right to an abortion is not "so rooted in the traditions and conscience of our people as to be ranked as fundamental." . . . Even today, when society's views on abortion are changing, the very existence of the debate is evidence that the "right" to an abortion is not so universally accepted as the appellant would have us believe.

To reach its result, the Court necessarily has had to find within the scope of the Fourteenth Amendment a right that was apparently completely unknown to the drafters of the Amendment. As early as 1821, the first state law dealing directly with abortion was enacted by the Connecticut Legislature. . . . By the time of the adoption of the Fourteenth Amendment in 1868, there were at least thirty-six laws enacted by state or territorial legislatures limiting abortion. While many states have amended or updated their laws, twenty-one of the laws on the books in 1868 remain in effect today. Indeed, the Texas statute struck down today was, as the majority notes, first enacted in 1857 and "has remained substantially unchanged to the present time." . . .

There apparently was no question concerning the validity of this provision or of any of the other state statutes when the Fourteenth Amendment was adopted. The only conclusion possible from this history is that the drafters did not intend to have the Fourteenth Amendment withdraw from the states the power to legislate with respect to this matter.

Even if one were to agree that the case that the Court decides were here, and that the enunciation of the substantive constitutional law in the Court's opinion were proper, the actual disposition of the case by the Court is still difficult to justify. The Texas statute is struck down in toto, even though the Court apparently concedes that at later periods of pregnancy Texas might impose these selfsame statutory limitations on abortion. My understanding of past practice is that a statute found to be invalid as applied to a particular plaintiff, but not unconstitutional as a whole, is not simply "struck down" but is, instead, declared unconstitutional as applied to the fact situation before the Court. . . .

For all of the foregoing reasons, I respectfully dissent.